Early Chinese Mysticism

Early Chinese Mysticism

PHILOSOPHY AND SOTERIOLOGY
IN THE TAOIST TRADITION

Livia Kohn

PRINCETON UNIVERSITY PRESS

PRINCETON, NEW JERSEY

Library of Congress Cataloging-in-Publication Data

Kohn, Livia, 1956–
    Early Chinese mysticism : philosophy and soteriology
in the Taoist tradition / Livia Kohn.
        p. cm.
    Includes bibliographical references and index.
    ISBN 0-691-07381-3 — ISBN 0-691-02065-5 (pbk.)
    1. Mysticism—Taoism.   2. Philosophy, Taoist.
3. China—Religion.   I. Title.
    BL 1923.K64   1991
    299'.514422'09—dc20   91-10648

Contents

Preface and Acknowledgments

THIS BOOK grew over many years in connection with a study of the fifth-century Taoist *Scripture of Western Ascension*, one of the classics of early Chinese mysticism, now translated in my *Taoist Mystical Philosophy* (Albany: SUNY Press, 1991). My interest in mysticism as a Chinese religious phenomenon arose when I wrote my dissertation on the life and legend of the Song-dynasty saint Chen Tuan. To my surprise, I found that the hagiographies did not depict him as a classical immortal who led a relaxed life, dabbled in alchemy, and eventually ascended to heaven in broad daylight.

Rather, Chen Tuan's religious biographers—above all Zhao Daoyi, the thirteenth-century author of the collection *Lishi zhenxian tidao tongjian*—described his achievements as a sense of oneness with life and death, union with the Tao, freedom from the limitations of ordinary existence, and, nevertheless, usefulness and importance to the people and the society of his time. Chen Tuan was not stylized as avoiding death or longing for the paradisiacal shores of the otherworld; rather, to him, all the living and dying on the planet were transformations of the Tao, which he willingly consented to follow.

Beyond the strongly mystical dimensions of Chen Tuan's biography, two other factors struck me as unusual at the time. First, he was obviously an intellectual, whose discussions of *Yijing* philosophy and ancient magical charts like the *Hetu* (River Chart) supposedly influenced Neo-Confucian thinking. He lived secluded in some kind of monastic setting, yet maintained amiable relations with local officials and visited the court on several occasions. He never tired of insisting that the emperor should pay attention to the quality of his government instead of concerning himself with alchemy or the pursuit of immortality. "Diligently practicing all sorts of techniques, cultivating and refining oneself do not contribute [to the harmony of the empire]," he allegedly said to Taizong in 984 C.E (*Lishi zhenxian* 47.4b).

Also, his hagiography was written largely in the terminology of the *Zhuangzi* and made frequent use of its metaphors and images. This appeared to be an interesting and fruitful starting point for an inquiry into the mystical and intellectual dimensions of the Taoist tradition. As is so often the case, the conclusion of one work raised enough questions to write several others. Where did Chen Tuan fit into the framework of the various Taoist sects and schools? Were there people like him earlier? What exactly was the tradition that produced a philosopher and mystic like him? How did the tradition develop? And was it unified? Was there such a tradition at all? In other words, was there one kind of mysticism in ancient China or were there several? If there were several, how did they interact?

Questions like these lie at the root of this study. After completing my dissertation I went to Kyoto, Japan, and began my inquiry by studying the *Zhuangzi* and its various developments. Gradually I also gained a foothold in the field of Taoist studies. In understanding the *Zhuangzi* and its tradition, I received enormous support and unfailing guidance from Fukunaga Mitsuji, my teacher and sponsor in Japan. His work on the *Zhuangzi* is justly famous and his numerous articles on the developments of the Lao-Zhuang tradition in later philosophy, ecstatic poetry, and Chinese Buddhism sketched the initial direction of my pursuit.

Many were the times when Professor Fukunaga had to dig deep in old and dusty boxes to find for me yet another offprint of an article no longer available otherwise. Numerous were the occasions when he freely shared with me his insights and enormous knowledge of the Chinese tradition over noodles and sake at his house in Kitashira-kawa. My first and deepest debt of gratitude is to him. I can never value his support and influence too highly.

In the realm of Taoist studies, my continued participation in the research seminar at Kyoto University under Fukunaga Mitsuji, Kawakatsu Yoshio, and Yoshikawa Tadao was invaluable. In addition to the disciplined reading of texts and the increasing familiarity with Japanese materials won at the seminars, I profited tremendously from a close cooperation with Anna Seidel, one of the leading Taoist scholars of the world. I could not have managed without her help, especially in the areas of bibliography and the correct understanding of the history of Taoism. I am very much indebted to her for sharing her own research methodology and her gradually growing manuscripts with me, as well as for her painstaking corrections of my fledgling attempts at scholarly research.

In the U.S., I owe a great debt of gratitude to the Center for Chinese Studies of the University of Michigan, whose generous fellowship enabled me to continue my work in an extraordinarily stimulating atmosphere. Special among my teachers there were Kenneth De-Woskin, Luis Gomez, and Donald Munro. They were extremely helpful with criticisms and suggestions for my enterprise, and I learned much about ongoing theoretical concerns in Chinese and Buddhist studies from them.

At Boston University, where I taught while the manuscript took final shape, I wish to thank my friends, colleagues, and superiors for their flexibility in accommodating my writing needs and for the support they offered me through the years. At the same time, suggestions and discussion from my highly spirited and well-read students during our seminar on Chinese mysticism in the spring of 1989 were stimulating and encouraging.

I owe a long-standing and ever-renewed debt of gratitude to Isabelle Robinet. She has always been extremely helpful and reliable in her comments on my work. In this case, she went over the translations with great care and supplied insightful suggestions on modes of interpretation. I received further help from Fujiwara Takao, who generously let me have offprints of his extensive work on *Daode jing* commentaries and interpretations, and Maxime Kaltenmark, who first pointed the *Scripture of Western Ascension* out to me as a Taoist mystical text of central importance.

In addition, I wish to express my deep indebtedness to Stephen Bokenkamp, Montgomery Link, John Berthrong, Robert Sharf, Margaret Case, Lauren Oppenheim, and the readers of Princeton University Press for their careful reading and serious comments on the manuscript. They contributed substantially to the final shape the work has now taken.

As always, deep and heartfelt thanks go to my husband, Detlef Kohn, for his patient, ever-present support of my work.

Medford on the Mystic, September 1990

Early Chinese Mysticism

Mysticism: The Chinese Case

CHINESE MYSTICISM has not received much attention in scholarly circles. It is included in anthologies of mysticism (Huxley 1946; Happold 1970) but the materials quoted there are largely the *Daode jing* and the *Zhuangzi*, as well as certain texts of Chan (Zen) Buddhism. The implicit assumption is that Chinese mysticism emerges in ancient Taoist philosophy and then again, a thousand years later, in the Chinese adaptation of Buddhism, an originally foreign religion.

Several questions arise: What were the developments between the Taoist philosophers and the later Buddhists? Is there possibly an indigenous Chinese mystical tradition that continued throughout the ages and was influenced by but ultimately independent of Buddhism? Could there even be forms of Chinese mysticism other than the quietistic withdrawal of the *Daode jing* and the sudden enlightenment of the Chan Buddhists? Should we not try to analyze the Chinese mystical tradition in a coherent historical and phenomenological study?

The answer to all these questions is undoubtedly yes. There is an indigenous Chinese mystical tradition, there are alternative forms of mysticism in China, and the history of this intriguing phenomenon can and should be explored.

This book is a first step in that direction. It concentrates on the early development of the indigenous Chinese mystical tradition, tracing it from its beginnings in the philosophical Taoism during the Warring States period to the Buddho-Taoist synthesis in the Tang. It presents its historical development as the continuation of the early philosophy and language of the *Daode jing* and the *Zhuangzi* in the Lao-Zhuang tradition. Three major mystical forms and traditions emerge—that associated with commentaries to the *Daode jing* and the *Zhuangzi*, that associated with the belief in immortality, and that associated with Buddhist doctrine and practices. The early history of Chinese mysticism is shown to evolve in two phases: the establishment and gradual integration of the three forms, reaching a synthesis in the fifth century; and the further elaboration and refinement of this synthesis in the late Six Dynasties and Tang. As a whole, however, the entire history of early Chinese mysticism is deeply related to the Lao-Zhuang tradition.

MYSTICISM AND THE LAO-ZHUANG TRADITION

The fifth-century Taoist scripture *Xisheng jing* (Scripture of Western Ascension) is a turning point in the history of early Chinese mysticism. For the first time, this text successfully integrates the three basic traditions in its presentation of the path to perfection.

First, the bulk of the text consists of Laozi's oral instructions to Yin Xi, the Guardian of the Pass and first recipient of the *Daode jing*, regarding the attainment of perfection and oneness with the Tao. This relies heavily—in both phrasing and concepts—on the *Daode jing* and the *Zhuangzi*, also using the major commentaries to these texts available in the fifth century.

Second, the text frames its teachings in the mythology of Taoist immortality and strongly emphasizes the motif of the journey, a key element of this tradition. It begins with a description of Laozi's ascent to the West and his meeting with Yin Xi in the Zhongnan mountains and ends with the sage's ascension into heaven as an immortal.

Third, the *Xisheng jing* integrates a number of Buddhist concepts. It interprets fate in the light of karma, identifies the mystical dissolution of ego-identity with the doctrine of no-self, and mixes traditional visualization techniques with the methods of Buddhist insight meditation. With this combination, the *Xisheng jing* integrates three distinct forms of early Chinese mysticism.

These three forms, in turn, are represented in three different kinds of texts.

There are first the philosophical works associated with Laozi and Zhuangzi and their younger siblings, the *Huainanzi* and the *Liezi*. Added to these ancient works are Dark Learning and later commentaries, as well as interpretations by essayists of the third and fourth centuries. These texts are philosophical documents; they are, for the most part, written in prose and consist largely of abstract discussions and illustrative stories.

Next, there are the ecstatic visions of the immortality-seekers, contained in shamanic songs, escapist poetry, and the meditation scriptures of the original Shangqing group of southern aristocrats. These documents are highly lyrical in nature; some presume to tell of personal flights, others use the visions for aesthetic purposes. The Shangqing texts, moreover, written in excellent prose, provide detailed meditation instructions for active practitioners.

Third, there are the sutras of Buddhism in their Chinese translations as well as the writings of Chinese Buddhists. Again, these are primarily doctrinal and theoretical, and written in a rather formal prose. But they also include texts that give immediate instructions and outlines of the path in a more poetic language.

These three kinds of literary sources are at the root of the *Xisheng jing*. They correspond to the three main forms, lineages, and methods of early Chinese mysticism: first, the quietistic, naturalistic tradition that developed in the direct tradition of the philosophers Laozi and Zhuangzi; second, the ecstatic, shamanic visions of immortality that were most clearly expressed in poetic songs, from the *Chuci* (Songs of the South) to Han rhapsodies and later poetry, and formed the backbone of Shangqing practice; and third, the meditational concepts and techniques of Buddhism, with their emphasis on gaining insight into the workings of one's own body and mind.

With the *Xisheng jing*, a long and varied history of interaction among these different forms finds its first culmination. The text thus marks the watershed between the first and second phase of early Chinese mysticism.

During the first phase, the philosophy and interpretation of the *Daode jing* and the *Zhuangzi*, and the belief in immortality and its expression in ecstatic flight, merge. They come together comparatively early: even before the Han, the *Chuci* show how closely the ecstatic tradition relies on expressions and metaphors of the philosophers. Similarly, Buddhism is first introduced to the Chinese elite through the terminology and concepts of the *Daode jing* and the *Zhuangzi*, borrowing expressions and concepts according to the practice of "matching the meanings," particularly popular in the fourth century.

However, while the *Xisheng jing* marks the beginning of the mystical synthesis and large-scale integration of Buddhist ideas and practices into indigenous Chinese mysticism, its full development is not felt until the late Six Dynasties and Tang—the second phase of early Chinese mysticism.

Texts of that period, then, represent the continuation of early Chinese mysticism after the first synthesis, perfecting and developing it further. Documents here include more commentaries to the *Daode jing* and the *Zhuangzi*, but now also to the *Xisheng jing*. Especially the thinkers of the fashion of Twofold Mystery formulate and develop the mystical worldview through an integration of Buddhist Mādhyamika. In addition, new Taoist scriptures are written at the time, treatises and discourses by Taoist masters give instruction and explain the process of perfection. The *Xisheng jing* continues to be cited in these philosophical works, sacred scriptures, and works of practical instruction.

What, now, do all these varied documents have in common—other than that they either influence or cite the *Xisheng jing*? Why should they be grouped together to stand representative of a development of something called "early Chinese mysticism"?

The answer to this is twofold. First, all these texts belong to the Lao-Zhuang tradition—that is to say, they all continue and develop the language and concepts contained in the works associated with the ancient philosophers Laozi and Zhuangzi. Second, they are all mystical—that is, they share a common conceptual framework and purpose. They all deal, in their own specific ways, with the pursuit of perfection, with the realization of the individual through union with the absolute.

The Lao-Zhuang Tradition

The Lao-Zhuang tradition stands between philosophical and religious Taoism. It is related to both, yet identical with neither.

The Lao-Zhuang tradition is above all a textual phenomenon, identified mainly by the use of phrases from the ancient philosophers. At the same time, whenever an ancient expression or metaphor is used, the meaning of the original term is developed—continuing yet transforming the thought of the ancients. This primarily philological delimitation allows the inclusion of such radically different textual sources as philosophical commentaries and discourses, poetry, and meditational manuals into one tradition. All these texts share the same language; moreover, they take their clues from one another. After being associated with immortality, the Tao was never the same. Once linked with nirvāna, non-action gained heretofore unplumbed dimensions— to give only a few obvious examples.

Concepts and visions of the world develop through the living situations and surroundings of thinkers, poets, and religious practitioners. They express them in a language familiar to all, yet in this process they also change the inherent implications of this very language. The tradition grows, nourished on the language and concepts of the ancients, yet increasingly different from them.

Lao-Zhuang is the living continuation of philosophical Taoism, the *daojia* of the *Shiji*. Philosophical Taoism is at the root of the Lao-Zhuang tradition, but it ends in the early Han. It is primarily one of the six major schools of the Warring States and has been amply studied as such.[1] Lao-Zhuang begins where philosophical Taoism ends—it comments on the ancient philosophers and makes use of them in other contexts, relating their ideas to concerns current at various times and using their images, metaphors, and philosophical terminology for purposes of its own.

Related to yet different from philosophical Taoism, the Lao-Zhuang tradition is also quite distinct yet not entirely separate from the Taoist religion. Taoism as an organized religion developed first in the second century C.E. with the movements of Great Peace and the Celestial Masters.[2] It then spread throughout China and into the cultural and political elite. By the middle of the fourth century, religious Taoism was a force to be reckoned with, not merely among the peasantry, but in all levels and classes of society. In 364, new revelations took place: the aristocratic elite of Jiangnan learned about the heavens of Shang-qing (Highest Clarity) with their splendid buildings, courts, and numerous deities involved in the celestial administration of the universe (see Strickmann 1978, 1981; Robinet 1979, 1984).

Shortly thereafter, in the last decade of the fourth century, Ge Chaofu compiled the Lingbao (Numinous Treasure) scriptures. His synthesis, sparked by the desire to elevate the position of his ancestor Ge Xuan in the heavenly hierarchy of Highest Clarity, not only included the Shangqing texts themselves but also drew heavily on the library of his relative Ge Hong, on Han dynasty correlative thought, and on Buddhist sutras (Bokenkamp 1983).

The fifth century, then, saw the full-fledged establishment of Taoism as a communal and popular religion throughout China. Taoist institutions developed, and the first steps were taken to establish a canon, drawing on the rapidly growing body of scriptures. Taoists served at court and, with talismans and rituals, helped legitimize rulers (Seidel 1983). Taoist practitioners, versed in all kinds of arts and techniques, swarmed through the land and set up religious communities. Before long, through the efforts of Tao Hongjing (456–536), the once-lost Shangqing scriptures were integrated into the growing religion (see Strickmann 1978). Shangqing Taoism became the leading school of the religion, a position it maintained throughout the Tang.

In opposition to Taoism as an organized and communal religion, the Lao-Zhuang tradition remained independent and oriented toward the individual. It was primarily intellectual, not devotional, and was carried by the literati and aristocratic elite. Those were people well trained in the classics, philosophy, and poetry, with time on their hands, often disappointed by the unstable political situation of their time, people greatly interested in the solution of their personal predicaments and only secondarily concerned with the salvation of all humankind.

Yet, in the increasingly religious climate after the Han, many of these thinkers and poets came under the influence of current religious doctrines and beliefs. For inspiration they turned to Buddhist disciline and the pursuit of immortality, they studied the teachings of the deified Laozi as well as the highly intricate system of the Mādhyamika. Being native Chinese and trained in the ancient philosophers, they then formulated their ideas and visions with the help of terms of Laozi and Zhuangzi, thus contributing actively to the Lao-Zhuang tradition.

To summarize, the Lao-Zhuang tradition is, in relation to philosophical Taoism, its descendant, its offspring, its continuation in other contexts. In relation to Taoism as an organized communal religion, it is its intellectual and individual offshoot, its religious philosophy, its mysticism. The Lao-Zhuang tradition is therefore a third dimension of Taoism, dependent on the other two, yet essential to neither.

The Pursuit of Perfection

Linked by language and the common tradition of Lao-Zhuang, the texts discussed in this study also share a conceptual framework. They all deal with the pursuit of perfection, with the union of an individual human being with the Tao, with the transformation of an ego-centered person into a cosmic being equally at home in the heavens and on earth. It is this quality that makes the texts mystical.

Mysticism is defined, for the purpose of this study, as the world-view that seeks the perfection of the individual through union with an agent or force conceived as absolute. In the Chinese case, the absolute is the Tao, which creates and encompasses all that exists. It is the "mother of the world" (*Daode jing* 25) and the "root to which all returns" (*Daode jing* 16). The Tao is ineffable and defies all sensual definition; it cannot be seen, heard, or felt. Yet it can be reached. Chinese mystics strive to "become one with the Great Thoroughfare" (*Zhuangzi* 6) and to live in spontaneous oneness with the Tao.

The main obstacle to this end are the senses and the intellect, which continuouly boost a separate notion of ego through emotions and desires, classifications and conscious knowledge. Mystics thus apply various techniques—fasting, purification, and meditations—to empty themselves of these and at the same time reach to the Tao deeply hidden within. The Tao, though mother of the world and its origin, is present in everyone; it appears in human beings in the form of spirit, true inner nature, or virtue. "The body is the carriage of the spirit, the habitation of the spirit, the host of the spirit," the *Xisheng jing* says (sect. 17). The Tao is the birthright and true home of everyone. When everyone recovers the true Tao, Great Peace reigns on earth.

These are the fundamental concepts of early Chinese mysticism, shared in their basic intent by all the documents discussed below. Their fundamental commonality makes it possible to discuss texts together that are widely different in genre and time. The point of this study is to show the development of these fundamental concepts through different periods and in different kinds of documents. It outlines the way in which Chinese mystical thought first developed, the different forms it took and its different interpretations, to concentrate then on the merging of the basic forms in an integrated synthesis of growing complexity. Taken separately, each text interprets the Tao and human nature differently, shows its own unique vision of the pursuit of perfection. Taken together, the texts group themselves according to the three major forms noted previously, thus constituting the history of early Chinese mysticism.

Later Chinese Mysticism

A note on the later development is in order. The synthesis reached by the Tang dynasty can be described as the indigenous Chinese mystical system at its fullest. It was simultaneous with the first development of Chan Buddhism, which shared two of its three sources, Lao-Zhuang philosophy and Buddhism, and represented one of the major forms of mysticism in the years to come. In the centuries after the rebellion of An Lushan in 755 C.E., the native mystical synthesis collapsed together with the Shangqing universe that supported it. The mysticism emerging from the rubble of destruction continued the earlier tradition in many ways, yet brought it to new conclusions, integrated new metaphors, and developed other forms of practice. Chinese mysticism since the Song is different from the earlier tradition and deserves a study of its own.

Speaking tentatively, one may venture that later Chinese mysticism might also be divided into three major traditions, which borrowed from and leaned on one another in an effort to "harmonize the three teachings." They are inner alchemy, Chan Buddhism, and Neo-Confucianism. These traditions were fairly clearly defined in the Northern Song but had already in the twelfth century begun to influence each other and merge into a new synthesis. Even the great Zhu Xi was intrigued by Taoist respiration techniques (Miura 1983); many inner alchemical practices were enthusiastically taken up by Ming Confucians (Liu 1970, 1970a); Taoist masters resorted to Chan techniques in selecting and educating their students (Hawkes 1981) and described the accomplishment of the golden elixir as a form of enlightenment (Fukui 1987, Azuma 1988). Moreover, Wang Yangming's concern with the mind was based on Chan influence (Ching 1976); the Confucian concept of sagehood became increasingly an accumulation of so-called enlightenment experiences (Taylor 1978); Chinese Buddhist thinkers often resorted to Taoist concepts and systematizations (Berling 1980; Hsu 1979)—to name only a few exemplary instances of integration and influence already known and studied.

Of course, not all practitioners of these traditions were mystics, not all their techniques were aimed at complete oneness with the Tao, virtue, or Buddhahood, and not all of them had the same aims or encouraged the same kind of worldview. A detailed account of what their distinctive characteristics and who their major representatives were has yet to be written. It goes beyond the scope of this book, which is limited to the early tradition. However, the book intends to lay some groundwork for such a future study of later developments. Certain typical features of Chinese mysticism remain constant, not only in the understanding of the universe but also in the concrete setting of the tradition.

OUTLINE OF THE BOOK

While the bulk of this study is addressed to readers unfamiliar with the Taoist tradition, and concentrates on illuminating its conceptual and textual differences and developments, the first chapter presents a discussion of the religious phenomenon of mysticism, summarizing its interpretations in psychology and religious studies under the consideration of the Chinese tradition. In other words, the chapter reverses the direction of the study and asks what, given the information available today, the religious phenomenon of mysticism looks like from the Chinese perspective. The concept that emerges differs in important ways from the classical Western model.

The single most important difference is the centrality of the mystical experience. In Underhill's description and in much of the scholarly discussion of mysticism, the mystical experience is at the pivot of it all. It is overwhelming and ineffable, timeless and yet full of knowing certainty. Christian mystics have described its wonders time and again as they have their agonies when it eluded them for a period in the so-called dark night of the soul.

There is no such emphasis in China. There are experiences, yes—the complete oblivion of all, for example, described often as "the body like a withered tree, the mind like dead ashes," and the ecstatic visions of the gods and palaces of the otherworld, to name the most fundamental. But there are no personal reports on the overwhelming and powerful nature of certain specific experiences that could be compared in impact and importance to their Christian counterpart. Having searched through the literature without finding such reports, I attributed this lack for a long time to the nature of Chinese culture. Religious autobiography just was not a genre in medieval China, and indeed the earliest first-hand accounts of the troubles and delights of the quest for perfection date from the Ming dynasty.

Then I wondered: if there had been such overwhelming mystical experiences of central importance to the process, if people had gone through the equivalent of the "dark night of the soul," then instructional manuals and biographies should refer to them, if only as warnings. They certainly do so for visions of demons and deities, clearly telling adepts how to deal with them. To quote an example, the *Dingguan jing* (Scripture on Concentration and Observation), a Tang-dynasty text, says quite explicitly:

> If there are thoughts and fantasies during
>   concentration,
> Manifold delusions and countless evils,
> Also specters and wicked sprites
> Will appear accordingly.

> But when you see
> Realized Ones or the Lord Lao,
> Divine wonders and amazing sights,
> This is an auspicious sign.
>
>   (lines 27–28; Kohn 1987, 138)

Similarly, the *Zuowang lun* (Discourse on Sitting in Oblivion) is very explicit about the difficulties that adepts can expect to face, and outlines the radiance of spirit and boundless joy they may eventually attain. Yet neither has quite the same importance, the same centrality as the mystical experience in the Western interpretation of mysticism. While Christian mystics fixate on the experience, it seems, the Chinese concentrate on the transformation of body and mind. The key to being a mystic, then, is not whether one has had a certain experience, but to what degree one's self has already been transformed into cosmic dimensions, how sagely and non-acting one has become.

The underlying reason for this difference in emphasis regarding experience is the nature of the worldview at the foundation of the two religions. The Christian tradition poses a transcendent divine agent, a God totally other; it therefore concentrates on rare visions of the deity, granted through his mercy, that are overwhelming, ineffable, and entirely out of this world.

The Chinese tradition, on the other hand, sees its ultimate in the Tao, a divine force so immanent that it is even in the soil and tiles, so much a part of the world that it cannot be separated from it. Oneness or union with the Tao is the birthright of every being, not a rare instance of divine grace. It is natural to begin with, and becomes more natural as it is realized through practice.

The Chinese mystical experience of oneness with the Tao, quite logically, is astounding only in the beginning. It represents a way of being in the world completely different from ordinary perception, sensually and intellectually determined. The longer the Taoist lives with the experience, the more he integrates it into his life and being, the less relevant it is. Thus, neither is the experience itself the central feature of the tradition, nor is there a pronounced "dark night of the soul," a desperate search for a glimpse of the transcendent divine. The Tao is here and now, residing right within oneself. The main difficulty Chinese mystics face in realizing the Tao is consequently the scatterbrained and pleasure-seeking nature of their ego-centered self. This, in turn, is amply discussed in the texts, together with varied techniques to overcome it.

Related to this feature of early Chinese mysticism is the importance it places on interpretation. No experience, however mystical, ever stands quite alone; it is always related to ways of thinking and feeling and being in the world (see Proudfoot 1985, 137). The various Chinese experiences of oblivion or ecstasy are consequently valuable only inasmuch as they lead to the right kind of nondualistic perception, to a sagely way of life, to the ascension into the heavens as an immortal. The discussion of the theory of mysticism in the first chapter mirrors these Chinese contentions. Mystical experiences grow out of human existence; following the work of Abraham Maslow, they might be described as intense peak-experiences. Only when such peak-experiences are religiously defined do they become mystical. Only then may they trigger a mystical quest.

The mystical quest, then, proceeds in several distinct stages. There is, first of all, an emptying of the ordinary ego-centered mind, a cleansing of sensually based classifications. Second, there is the filling of the newly created vacuum with the doctrines and concepts of the tradition in question. This gives the mystic a proper framework to understand what is happening to him or her (Proudfoot 1985, 147). Third, the mystic reaches enlightenment, union, or oneness, and the reorganization of consciousness is complete. Social life resumes again, on a new and higher level.

Comparable stages are known from the Christian tradition as the purgative, the illuminative, and the unitive forms of the mystical life. The purgative phase is a period of purification, of emptying and cleaning out all the learned values of ordinary life. The illuminative phase opens the self to the absolute, teaching the mystic what to expect. His expectations, finally, are fully realized in the unitive stage when union with the absolute is attained.

The worldview that the mystic acquires in the second stage is described in the works of mystical philosophy; it closely accords with the ideas of the tradition chosen. Such a worldview is not static and, although it contains certain basic concepts and is based on specific documents, it is shaped by the understanding and reinterpretation of the individual as he or she proceeds toward the higher stages. An advanced practitioner may eventually write down his or her particular understanding of the world, won through the synthesis of traditional ideas and immediate experience, and thereby contribute to the ongoing development of the mystical tradition.

The Chinese Tradition

After the theoretical discussion of mysticism, the book proceeds to outline the early Chinese tradition. It begins in chapter 2 with the major texts of philosophical Taoism—the *Daode jing* and the *Zhuangzi*. Both texts elucidate the basic concept of the Tao, describe a fundamental understanding of the human situation in the world, advise the practice of quietude and oblivion leading to the attainment of oneness with the Tao, and outline the role of the sage or true person as the mediator between heaven and earth.

Neither the *Daode jing* nor the *Zhuangzi* contains much in the way of practical instructions for aspiring mystics, but, as described in chapter 3, later commentaries have not failed to interpret these texts in various imaginative ways to include even such information. Among the commentaries to the *Daode jing*, Heshang gong in particular merged its concepts with the ideas and practices of traditional Chinese medicine, integrating for the first time a physical dimension into the mystical tradition.

The *Zhuangzi* has come down to us in the edition and with the commentary by Guo Xiang, whose integrated cosmology and soteriology has continued to serve as the basic conceptual framework of later mystical thinkers. Guo Xiang was the first to include the social hierarchy and the political organization of the country in the organic order of the Tao. For him the world as it was meant to be, as it would be if we let it go naturally, is entirely perfect and spontaneously attains a state of Great Peace. In order to get there every individual has to forget his or her artificial and culturally defined self and thus return to a state of oblivion. This in turn will make perfect accordance with the Tao possible, a harmonious going-along with all-that-is. Ideally the perfection of the Tao should be found not only by an individual mystic but by humanity at large.

In a different line, as discussed in chapter 4, the metaphors and concepts of the *Daode jing* and the *Zhuangzi* are used to express the ecstatic vision of shamanic flight and the ideal of ascension to immortality. The vision of this form of early Chinese mysticism concentrates most strongly on the motif of the journey to far-off places and into the heavens. Textually, this form is expressed first in the *Chuci*, while the earliest descriptions of mystical journeys are found in the *Zhuangzi*, the *Huainanzi*, and the *Liezi*. This line of the tradition also contains a strong shamanistic element, inheriting the ideas and visions of shamans' songs documented in the *Chuci*.

In the following centuries, the flight to immortality is expressed in poetry and Shangqing visions. Chapter 5 describes first the poetic tradition, which begins in the early Han with Sima Xiangru's rhapsody on the ecstatic excursions of the Great Man, and is continued by the Seven Sages of the Bamboo Grove in the third century. Imperial travels over the earth and into the heavens were then integrated into the Shangqing practice of immortality. The Tao in Shangqing, no longer vague, obscure, and undefinable, was clearly described in terms of yin and yang, the four seasons, and the five agents. It is most purely present in the heavens, the stars, and the immortals of the otherworld. The Shangqing practitioner attains oneness with the Tao as a form of control over everything by establishing himself or herself in the center of the cosmos after having traversed the entire universe in ecstatic excursions.

Simultaneous with the development of Shangqing Taoism, Chinese Buddhism took its first halting steps. Its impact on Chinese mysticism is the subject of chapter 6. Strongly interpreted in the beginning along the lines of philosophical Taoism, the earliest aristocratic Buddhist of some import, Zhi Dun of the fourth century, is a telling example of the merging of concepts and practices. Himself a monk and in his ideas strongly influenced by the doctrines of karma and dependent origination, he was yet very much at home with the thought of Laozi and Zhuangzi. To this he added the idea that one should take active steps in favor of enlightenment or oneness and not merely unlearn, escape, or forget the ordinary world around oneself. The concept of monastic discipline, of a positive religious morality and lifestyle to replace the ways of the world, thus finds its way into the Chinese religious tradition.

Buddhism and Taoism continued to interact on various levels. The salvational movement of Lingbao absorbed Buddhist terms and concepts in enormous numbers, the imperial court staged various Buddho-Taoist debates in order to establish the predominance of one or the other political faction. At the same time, mystical thinkers began

·ized system that integrated the ancient concepts
Xiang's vision of the *Zhuangzi*, the ecstatic as-
mmortality, and the moral discipline and medi-
ɔuddhism.
. containing the mystical synthesis is the *Xisheng jing*
.ury. Here certain Buddhist notions of body, mind, and
ʌked with countless references to the *Daode jing*, with Guo
vision of a society at one with the Tao, and with the ultimate
ʌ of ecstatic ascent into the heavens of the immortals. Commentaries to the text, particularly Wei Jie's of the sixth century, continued the
trend.

In the Tang dynasty, as described in chapter 7, the mystical synthesis came into its own. The seventh century saw the emergence of the
Chongxuan (Twofold Mystery) trend of Taoist philosophy as a fashion
of interpreting the *Daode jing*. An adaptation of Buddhist Mādhyamika into the indigenous Chinese tradition, Chongxuan remains committed to the *Daode jing* and the ideal of oblivion. Among its various
philosophers is especially Li Rong, another commentator of the *Xisheng jing*, who clearly integrates physical practices into the more theoretically oriented discussion.

From the eighth century we have a number of practical manuals and
hands-on descriptions of the mystical process. These materials serve
to complete our understanding of the tradition and its idiosyncrasies.
Famous Taoist masters, such as Sun Simiao, Sima Chengzhen, and
Wu Yun, have left behind detailed instructions on how to become an
immortal in one of the higher reaches of the galaxy. They describe
initial purgation through physical practices and meditation exercises;
illumination as adepts begin to reorganize their worldview along the
lines of the *Daode jing*, Guo Xiang, Buddhist doctrine, and Twofold
Mystery; and an ultimate union with the Tao that causes adepts to
become ever subtler and eventually vanish from this plane to take up
a seat next to the Jade Emperor of the Great Tao.

The book concludes with an evaluation of certain typical characteristics of early Chinese mysticism and their varied interpretations
through the ages. There is, first of all, the Tao—the underlying
ground of all existence and ultimate goal of all mystical endeavors.
Then there is the dualistic understanding of the world in terms of yin
and yang, inner and outer. Chinese mystical thinking works in concentric circles of the within and the without, distinguishing ever-
higher levels of purity and oneness from gross ordinary perception.

Another recurring feature of Chinese mysticism is, third, the importance given to the body and the distinction made between the cosmic
body or shape and the personal body or conscious identity of the indi-

vidual. Related to this is, fourth, the dynamic integration of mystical practices. Mystics proceed from the body to the mind and on to the Tao. They employ a large number of varied techniques in attaining purity and oneness.

A last characteristic of Chinese mysticism that becomes increasingly obvious in the discussion is the political relevance of physical and mental oneness. The sage of the *Daode jing*, the Great Man of the poets, and the true person of later writers are all important political figures. They are responsible for the harmonious functioning of the world at large, they are the harbingers of Great Peace for human society. Early Chinese mysticism, although it encourages its practitioners to move away from the world of ordinary consciousness seen as impure and defiled, yet also places a strong emphasis on their eventual return as perfected beings to an active participation in life and society.

Mysticism: Experience, Practice, and Philosophy

RELIGION IN HUMAN EXPERIENCE

Whenever a group of human beings lives together in an organization of some sort or another, they begin to build a world that explains the validity of the status quo. "Every human society is engaged in the never completed enterprise of building a humanly meaningful world" (Berger 1969, 27; see also Proudfoot 1985, 146). The theoretical and imaginary world is used as a frame of reference for the proper understanding of why things are what they are and none other. Since things are the way they are, the interpretative model has to contain the truth about them; for this reason, it must in itself be a true depiction and description of what the world, concrete and theoretical, is like. The world-building process, within a social context, mirrors the fact that human life itself is an ongoing exercise in sense making.

Both society and the individual must, in their efforts to justify and interpret existence, by necessity resort to means that lie beyond the basic fact of existence as such. They therefore "transcend" reality while searching for an explanation of reality. As Peter Berger has shown, the explanations themselves turn around in due course and become realities of their own. The interpretative framework begins to demand certain actions, adaptations of concrete reality and human psychology, in order to remain valid (Berger 1969, 17). At the same time, it is of course subject to change and transformation, variations and revisions. The concrete experiences of human beings and the interpretations attached to them never coincide one hundred percent. There is always a gap between feeling and consciousness, between experience and reflection, between subjectivity and objectivity—a gap that is as much temporal as it is categorical.[1]

Nevertheless, one can define certain basic rules or structures that apply to them both. There are certain human characteristics and tendencies that pervade the pure experience of life as much as its conscious interpretation. Again, Peter Berger took first steps in this direction. In his discussion of a possible "anthropological starting point for theology, . . . of what might be called *signals of transcendence* within the empirically given human situation" (Berger 1969a, 65), he suggests five lines of argument connecting the human experience with the interpretative framework supplied by religion.

"Signals of Transcendence"

First of all, there is the propensity for order. To establish a meaningful world, people must organize random data into a systematic whole and, in the case of religion, into a sacred cosmos. Underlying this process is a fundamental human faith in order as such, a need of the human being to feel integrated and properly positioned. This is evident already in the behavior of children who demand the reassurance that everything is in order, that parents and teachers and friends are there and do exactly what they should do. The same faith in order appears in the establishment of proper family and business relationships, of clearly defined areas for each individual as much as in the application of social etiquette. People and things can be proper and improper in a simple everyday fashion, and also in a religious and sacred way. Yet, the basic assumption that there needs to be order is already a step beyond concrete reality, it implies the existence of a transcendent principle (Berger 1969a, 68).

Next, there is the ubiquity of play. Playful elements are present in practically all sectors of human culture; thus the human experience can hardly be considered without them. Play is a way of establishing a new and independent cosmos within existing reality. Play suspends ordinary time, as Berger has it: "In the 'serious' world it may be 11 A.M., on such and such a day, month, and year. But in the universe in which one is playing it may be the third round, the fourth act, the *allegro* movement, or the second kiss" (Berger 1969a, 72). Play also allows people to step into a new and different identity, a way of being that is at all times more enthusiastic and joyful than its ordinary counterpart. The joy achieved in play suspends time further; it opens up a glimpse of eternity, of transcendent timelessness. A similar suspension from ordinary time is achieved in the act of ritual, and in the recreation of religious truth in worship and prayer. Just as in play, the world entered in religious practice gives liberation and peace.

Third, there is the universal fact of hope. Human life cannot grow and continue without the hope that things will go on, will be better, will turn out worthwhile. The human mind plans and thinks of the future; it cannot and will not stay in the present only. One of the motors that propels it ahead is hope—hope beyond the present crisis, the sickness, the poverty, the oppression, and, ultimately, hope beyond death. Death remains unimaginable for human beings; its reality is denied in an act of hope (Berger 1969a, 78). All hope implies the denial of the present reality as final. Religious hope, in the same vein, denies that this entire life is final, and offers some image of how it can and will continue—and be better and happier and truer.

Next again, there is the basic human sense of wrong, or "the argument from damnation," as Berger calls it (1969a, 81). What is meant here is that there are certain acts and certain attitudes that are universally felt to be wrong. Brutality, cruelty, torture, especially when aimed at the helpless and innocent, are "deeds that cry out to heaven" (Berger 1969a, 82). The grounds for damnation of such deeds are found not so much in the lawbooks and codes of justice as in the inner feeling of every individual. This does not mean that they are not being committed, but that there is a fundamental human sense of wrong that condemns them. On a higher plane, the same sense leads to the conception of a transcendental agency of justice, a divine judge, a law of fate that will see that everyone eventually gets his or her due. The feeling that evil is basically wrong, that certain deeds must not be done, is the root of the belief that divine justice will be done.

Fifth, one finds an inherent human sense of humor, the feeling that discrepancies or incongruities are comic. Situations, and especially human situations, are funny when they belong to two different series of events, to two different planes of being. One cannot jump levels; one cannot escape from the logic of a particular situation—and when one imagines the situation resulting from such a jump or escape, it turns out funny or ridiculous. The ability to imagine such a jump and then to look back and laugh at the impossibility or incongruence of the resulting situation is at the root of human humor. The mental faculty to look at oneself from the outside and to see one's limitations, yet not to despair over them is essential to being human. On a religious plane, "the comic reflects the imprisonment of the human spirit in the world" (Berger 1969a, 87); it reveals a sense for the narrowness of one's existence while at the same time implying a feeling for the reality of other possible levels of being.

These five characteristics of humanity—the sense of order, playfulness, hope, justice, and humor—are all present quite obviously in everyday life. They are a representative and illustrative list of human traits that can possibly be interpreted as roots of a religious conceptualization of the experience of being in the world. As Berger points out, the five constitute "by no means an exhaustive or exclusive list," and "to provide one would entail constructing a philosophical anthropology and, on top of it, a theological system to go with it" (Berger 1969a, 90). He does not go that far, nor is it necessary for the clarity of his argument.

Religion as a whole, and in its specific manifestations, can be understood as being deeply rooted in the basic experience of being human— individually and socially. It continues fundamental patterns of world building, undertaken by all human societies, into more transcendent and higher levels. Yet even the movement away from common facts, and into the realm of the transcendent, is already entailed in the characteristics of humanity. At the same time, it is impossible for anyone to experience life and the universe in a religious manner without accepting and submitting to the theoretical framework of belief offered by any given religion. While it may be basically human to develop an ordered understanding of oneself, suspend time and reality in acts of play, have hopes for the future, feel that certain things "are just not done," and laugh about oneself once in while, none of these things per se constitute a religious worldview or experience.

Order only becomes religious when it is considered sacred and necessary; the suspension of normal time in play is only turned transcendent when activated in acts of worship; hope in religion means the conviction that this life (and death) is not the end; justice becomes divine justice, and humor turns into the cheerfulness of the spirit in the light of mundane limitations. The theoretical framework, the established social norm must always accompany the inherent capabilities of human beings if an integrated and identifiable whole, religious or social, is to be established.

Dimensions of Mysticism

The argument regarding mysticism will proceed along the lines indicated by Peter Berger. Certain basic human faculties and tendencies converge with certain established conceptualizations and a mystical worldview results. In the case of mysticism, I disagree with Peter Berger's view that it "is not accessible to everyone" (1969a, 90). Rather, following the Chinese model and the recent works by Wayne Proudfoot (1985) and Steven Katz (1978, 1983), I think that mysticism rests, like any religious belief or experience, on the very foundations that Berger pointed out so adroitly: inherent human characteristics and a conceptual framework of reference. There has to be a foundation within the fundamental makeup of humanity that allows for the experience of something higher and purer and greater.

At the same time, even though human beings have such experiences, only in cases in which there is a deep concern with religion are they interpreted in the light of a force or an agent conceived as absolute. Only then can they possibly trigger a mystical quest. In other words, no experience is mystical per se, but is only made so by the conceptual interpretation that is attached to it.[2] This, however, does not mean that one cannot pinpoint certain characteristics of the experience or identify its psychological root. Abraham Maslow's concept of the peak-experience offers such a psychological root of the mystical experience—claiming neither that all such experiences are the same nor that all peak-experiences are mystical (see Maslow 1964, 1970). Rather, peak-experiences only become mystical when they are consciously related to a given religious worldview.

A mystic is therefore someone who, already concerned with religious questions, has a strong peak-experience. This experience can be described as a "primitive experience in which there is a radical transformation of the experiential self sense and radical axiological and existential grounding" (King 1988, 275). It may very well have all the characteristics traditionally associated with mystical experiences: ineffability, noetic quality, transiency, and passivity.[3] Based on his or her religious preconceptions, the mystic then interprets this as an experience of a force or an agent conceived as absolute rather than as the result of some ordinary cause such as food, drink, sleep, a joyful occasion, or the like.

The experience turns into a conversion only when it triggers a mystical quest. The mystic wishes the state glimpsed so briefly to become accessible at will and eventually be the permanent reality of his or her mind. With the help of a variety of practices—such as fasting, austerities, meditations, and trances—old feelings and emotions, ideas and conceptions are cleared away, and the new state is attained. First only induced once in a rare while, it ultimately becomes permanent. The personality of the individual, disrupted by the experience of something interpreted as higher and greater, is reintegrated on a higher and greater level (see Deikman 1982).

In the end, the individual loses all sense of personal consciousness; he or she feels at one with the absolute agent or force, believed to be first glimpsed in the intense peak-experience. The old self is gone; a cosmic self is found. The mystic who has maintained seclusion from other human beings for the time of transformation returns to society, a cosmic and universal spirit in human guise. Unlike the mystical experience proper, mystical practices have been described in great detail. Historians of religion, physicians, and psychologists have studied their effects. Mysticism on the practical plane is therefore accessible and well known.

Beyond these two facets of mysticism, there is its theoretical, conceptual manifestation. Formulated by necessity in the language, and according to the philosophical views common at the time and place, of the individual mystic, mystical philosophy in general deals with cer-

..i definable issues. The first of these is the nature and manifestation of the absolute as glimpsed in the experience. Often the assumed absolute agent or force is seen as the foundation that underlies all existence, of which the phenomenal world is only a part.

Another issue common to mystical philosophy is the nature of human beings. Since the mystic believes to have personally experienced the absolute, he or she claims that people in general have the ability to do so. He thus proposes that human beings, besides various ordinary psychological faculties, such as the senses and reason, also possess spiritual intuition. This intuition is hidden by the senses and critical reasoning. These forces therefore have to be quieted and emptied to make spiritual cultivation possible. The more one develops this intuition, the easier an experience of the absolute becomes.

A third issue common to texts of mystical philosophy is the methods used to overcome egoistic tendencies and liberate people from their baser instincts. This usually includes not only certain set practices but also a conscious reorganization of the individual's worldview. Mystics give prescriptions for other mystics on how to think correctly. Just as their lives, experiences, and training were determined by the tradition in which they grew up, so will the paths of their successors be influenced by their works and thought.

Most mystical literature that has come down to us throughout the ages is concerned with these theoretical issues. A mystical document therefore expresses the rational and conceptional interpretation of an individual's visions and experiences. The experiences are seen apart from ordinary life and therefore placed in the semantic position of being ineffable. This term is used to deny its referent any representational role in the commonly accepted framework of reference (Proudfoot 1985, 129). To support this position and yet render it accessible, mystical writers frequently resort to paradoxes and contradictions. They often apply a level of language and discourse consciously intended to go beyond ordinary thinking. Nevertheless, texts are texts. They are written in human language and apply human ideas and systems. They can be studied as philosophical documents representing a religious way of making sense of the world.

The study of mysticism, therefore, divides into the three distinct areas of mystical experience, practice, and philosophy. The first is best left to psychologists and physicians, who are properly equipped to make statements about people's experiences, based on laboratory experiments and inquiries through questionnaires and personal interviews. Mystical practice, while still best studied in its actual activity, is also accessible to historians of religion. Mystics have frequently left instructions for future generations; there are numerous practical manuals on forms of purification and methods of meditation.

In mystical philosophy, finally, the student of religion comes into his own. Subtle differences between texts, the development of terminologies, changes in emphasis and interpretation—those are the issues that make a philologist's heart beat faster. Conclusions involve structures of worldview, patterns of understanding. The texts tell us little about concrete practices and nothing about actual experiences. The study of mysticism in a historical setting, based on texts, is and remains an abstraction. It can only acknowledge practical measures indicated in the literature and remains limited to dealing with conceptualizations of experiences.

MYSTICAL EXPERIENCES AND THEIR EFFECTS

Mystical experiences, however described as ineffable and placed outside ordinary frames of reference, are part of being human. They occur in the body and are accompanied by physiological changes (see Deikman 1982). According to recent psychological studies, there are two major bodily characteristics of intense religious experiences: changes in the balance between ergotropic and trophotropic activation; and the dominance of the right over the left hemisphere of the brain (Davidson 1984).

The terms ergotropic and trophotropic denote states of overall excitement and quietude of the living organism, including levels of intestinal, muscular, respiratory, and mental activity.

> To characterize the coordinated complex of sympathetic-visceral, cerebral, behavioral, and skeletal muscle reactions (which are adaptive for emergency situations), Hess coined the term "ergotropic activation." Rage induced by hypothalamic stimulation represents an extreme point on the ergotropic continuum.
>
> In contrast, stimuli which increase parasympathetic activation are associated with effects (presumed to be adaptive for cellular restitution) which include sleep-like EEG-activity, decreased muscle tone, and behavioral quiescence. This complex of events, the mirror image of ergotropic activation, was termed "trophotropic."
>
> (Davidson 1984, 384; see also Fisher 1980)

In other words, people normally maintain a balance between the two extremes of excitement and quietude. A person with an imbalance toward the ergotropic side will be overly stimulated on all levels of being, while someone in a state of prevailing trophotropic activation will appear to be in suspended animation or deep trance.

Mystical experiences, then, appear to occur at a point where the ergotropic-trophotropic balance is broken down. They happen most likely at the extreme point of either excitement or quietude, when the state rebounds into its respective opposite. Deep meditation, for example, involves an imbalance toward the quiet or trophotropic side. On the other hand, mystical experiences of enlightenment attained through deep meditations—especially in the Hindu and Buddhist traditions—are characterized by great excitement and physical heat. The opposite is also true. Activities like the excited dances of the Sufi Whirling Dervishes or the practice of Ishiguro Zen, which involves prolonged shouting and violent abdominal contractions, induce an imbalance on the excited or ergotropic side of the nervous system. The resulting mystical experience is accordingly described as a deep trance, during which the body is entirely without movement. To summarize these findings, Davidson says,

> The suggested progression from trophotropic meditation to ergotropic ecstasy quite possibly involves . . . either "imbalance" resulting from intense prolonged trophotropic activation, or the postulated "rebound" of the ergotropic system. . . .
>
> [On the other hand,] when people undergo extreme excitation, induced either by psychologic or intense sensory stimuli, a state is reached when the subject collapses, and extreme changes of mental and physical states supervene involving altered states of consciousness and greatly heightened suggestibility.

(Davidson 1984, 386)

Similar mechanisms of excitement and quietude apply also in sexual activity, in the forgetful exhaustion of an artist immersed in his or her work, and in other situations of human life that allow experiences of high value and personal meaning.[4]

Another physiological characteristic of the mystical experience is the predominance of the right hemisphere of the brain. This is especially true for the cognition experienced during and in the wake of the experience proper, for its ineffability, passivity, sense of unity, and so on. Each hemisphere of the brain is specialized for a different form of cognition.[5] In general, the left side deals with verbal and mathematical skills. It supports sequential, conceptual, and analytic thinking. Also, the left controls the motor functions of the body. The right hemisphere, on the other hand, deals with artistic and geometric skills. It favors nonverbal and holistic thinking and is based on direct perceptual or intuitive cognition (see Davidson 1984, 390).

Under normal circumstances and in healthy individuals, the two sides of the brain work together harmoniously, either in rapid alternation or by functioning simultaneously. Yet, in most individuals one hemisphere is dominant vis-a-vis the other. In a mode of thinking that is organized sequentially through language, the left side usually prevails over the right. Mystical experiences in this context may be interpreted as the strong emergence, for a time, of the right hemisphere of the brain. Such experiences indeed have all the characteristics of right-hemisphere cognition. They are ineffable and defy linear description and verbalized expression; they involve a sense of wholeness and unity and afford direct participation in the object of vision. There is a sense of wholeness and intuition, often enforced by a loss of personal identity and individual limitations.

Mystical experiences, so far as physiology can tell us, therefore occur at the breaking point of the balance between ergotropic and trophotropic activation, and involve a predominance of right-hemisphere cognition. Mystical practice consequently consists in the gradual strengthening of the right side together with an increase in either ergotropic or trophotropic activation. The texts of mystical doctrine, furthermore, are written after the experiences of such extreme states of activation have rebounded into their opposite. They are an attempt to express the world, as seen from the right hemisphere of the brain, through language—the tool of the left.

Interpreting the Experience

The mystical experience is never isolated but depends in its mystical quality on the cognitive context in which it appears. A sudden experience of oneness without proper preparation may be dismissed as unimportant or explained away as due to outside influences. On the other hand, when the experience happens in an already existing cognitive framework, it may become a turning-point in someone's life and assume the quality of a conversion. Again, the experience may be the result of a definite quest and prolonged mystical practice. Then it signals the successful end of a long journey. Though vastly different and difficult to access, there are yet certain typical phases that people undergo. The experience has an inherent structure.

First, there is the trigger. This refers to the situational setup in which the experience takes place, and the outside or psychological stimulus that sets it off (Ellwood 1980, 68). Far from being a random moment, this trigger is already an indicator for the later interpretation of the experience and its cognitive integration into the individual's life. Someone who has a strong feeling of wholeness and beauty due to an exposure to nature will interpret it in just these terms. A person who is surrounded by religious symbols and is overcome by the experience during prayer will find in it a vision of the sacred.[6] The trigger, while in itself only responsible for the exact setting of the experience in time and space, is yet part of a larger background influence working in the individual's life. It is thus responsible for the way the experience is integrated in the life later on.

Second, there is the moment of the experience proper. It is "a sudden, seemingly spontaneous flash of absolute power or ecstasy" (Ellwood 1980, 69). It is short yet powerful and includes typical characteristics, such as ineffability, a noetic quality of true knowledge, transiency and timelessness, passivity and the sense of being grasped by something greater, a consciousness of oneness with everything, and the transcendence of the phenomenal ego.

Third, there is the afterglow. Here the intensity of the experience recedes, but a sense of heightened consciousness remains (Ellwood 1980, 70). It is not yet back to normality, not yet a purely rational state of left-hemisphere cognition. Nevertheless, there are already the earliest efforts of relating the experience to other experiences, of integrating it meaningfully into the prevalent cognitive system. The experience is embedded in a framework of associations, taken from the background influence that gave rise to the trigger, from the immediate surroundings, sights, and symbols, and from the rebounding rational activity.

As a rule, the experience is then interpreted meaningfully—again a process that can be divided into several stages (Ellwood 1980, 71). First, the aforementioned afterglow associations take place. Next, relevant supporting information is collected outside the experience, from friends and co-seekers, from books and records. Still, the individual is creating a meaningful cognitive framework only for himself or herself. Only in a third step is the more universal relevance of the experience asserted. It is actively related to established theories and mystical practices and gradually shaped into an organized mystical doctrine that also includes the symbols and sights associated immediately with the experience itself. Teaching the experienced truth to others, the mystic develops a highly personal synthesis of traditional beliefs and individual impressions.

While the experience obviously loses intensity with distance in time and through conscious interpretation, it gains importance for actual life. From a merely personal and fundamentally ineffable feeling it is transformed into the foundation of a meaningful life and serves as the basis of an integrated worldview. Beyond that, it may lead to the writing of sacred scriptures and religious philosophies and may thus become meaningful for a larger group of religious practitioners.

Peak-Experiences and Being-Cognition

Beyond the mystical experience and its immediate interpretation, there is the practice of mysticism, which deals with the transformation of the individual from an ego-centered being into a cosmic human being. In contemporary psychology, Abraham Maslow has described the analogous process in terms of the transformation from a deficiency-oriented motivation or Deficiency-cognition to growth-oriented motivation or Being-cognition. To think in terms of deficiency means to concentrate primarily on outside objectives. It leads subjectively to such emotions as anxiety, fear, worry, anger, and the like. Being-cognition, on the contrary, is self-justifying, cheerful, and compassionate.[7] People moving in that direction often experience special moments of complete happiness called peak-experiences. Mystical experiences in miniature, peak-experiences are full of joy and meaning; they transcend the ego and give people a sense of unity with all-that-is.

Peak-experiences may come about through love, parenting, or being in nature. They may develop through aesthetic perception, in a creative moment, as therapeutic or intellectual insights. Any of these qualifies as a peak when it is subjectively felt as a highlight of life, a moment of highest happiness and fulfillment (Maslow 1964, 73). Not only the happiest and most thrilling moments, peak-experiences are also times of greatest maturity, individuation, and selflessness. Psychologically speaking, they are the moments of perfect health and, as they are accepted and integrated into life, make human beings more human (Maslow 1964, 97).

All people have peak-experiences, but they react to them differently. Some simply ignore them, others attribute them to outside causes such as food or music, and yet others find in them an encounter with the sacred. As a general rule, the stronger the experience, the greater is the likelihood of a religious interpretation. Also, the more an individual accepts peak-experiences positively and acknowledges them as a meaningful part of life, the more frequently they recur. The higher the frequency of peak-experiences, the more positively they are felt and the more Being-cognition becomes part of the individual's consciousness.

Being-cognition is the psychological equivalent of the selfless cosmic consciousness of the accomplished mystic. It is characterized by a sense of wholeness and perfection, a feeling of life's richness coupled with an awareness of its simplicity and beauty. There is also a strong moral sense of goodness, justice, and honesty. People are vibrant with energy and feel that life flows smoothly and without effort; they are playful, cheerful, and self-sufficient (Maslow 1964, 83). In Being-cognition as in mystical oneness, an individual experiences life, the world, everything as whole and free from purpose and strife.

The mind is powerful and highly concentrated. An individual in a state of Being-cognition gives full attention to any object and does not evaluate it in some external or separate context. He or she does not subtract from reality's integrity by "rubricizing" it. There are no conscious categories, comparisons, or judgments in his or her mind. In Deficiency-cognition, repeated perception of the same object leads to habituation and boredom. In Being-cognition the observer retains the freshness of the present moment. In a similar vein, mystics have a sense of intense immediacy; they do not evaluate things in terms of polarities and conflicts, but transcend dichotomies to take in the whole. Rather than thinking in linear structures, people in Being-cognition envision the world in patterns of circles or spirals, fusing all polar extremes into an integrated unity (Maslow 1964, 91). Even in the most generalized system of abstraction, even in language, they refuse to classify the unique, and repeatedly insist on the ultimate ineffability of their truth.

THE QUEST: STAGES AND PRACTICES

A mystical quest is the conscious, active attempt to make an initial mystical experience more accessible. It is the pursuit of perfection within a traditional religious context. As a general rule, the quest proceeds through two distinct levels, including two fundamentally different kinds of practices. It moves first to empty and free the individual from the thought and feeling patterns of past habituation. Then it proceeds to fill the resulting void with new modes of cognition and intuitive knowledge (see Proudfoot 1985, 147). Both stages employ physical as well as meditational practices. Much happens simultaneously, and individual practitioners often work differently. Yet there are certain basic structures, certain typical modes of practices.

According to the traditional Western scheme, the mystical quest begins with the Purgative Life, during which the practitioner empties and purifies the old self with the help of predominantly physical practices. Moving on to the Illuminative Life, he or she learns new modes of thinking and feeling in meditative and spiritual practices. The quest is over and the desired state achieved when he or she reaches the Unitive Life, at which all opposites are integrated on a new level.[8]

To begin with, during the stage of emptying, mystics feel that old feelings and conceptions hinder the development of the desired state, and drive them out relentlessly through a variety of means. The unified divine state can only be reached when all traditional conceptions are abandoned. Yet, at the same time, there must be a clear concept of the desired state if the individual is not simply to go out of his or her mind completely. While at first merely a memory of things seen and felt during the conversion, the new dimension of life finally breaks through during the stage of filling. The empty space created before is now replenished with a new understanding of the world in accu_ ance with mystical doctrine. This is the stage at which delightful visions and ecstatic feelings occur. Without getting entangled in this "pseudo-nirvāna," the mystic strives ultimately to be "chronically enlightened" (Davidson 1984, 389), to attain a permanent and self-supported state of integrated cognition.

In the final state, a mystic represents a wholly integrated spiritual person, a self more human than the one left behind. Free from petty desires and emotions, fully at one with a larger reality beyond the ordinary, he or she can then proceed to return to the common world, to enter the Life of Action as "a center of creative energy and power in the world" (Happold 1970, 101). The quality of the mystic is judged accordingly by the final success. Only whose personality is permanently cosmicized truly deserves this name. Otherwise, he or she may be an ecstatic or a visionary, may be proficient at intentionally inducing altered states of consciousness (see Tart 1969), but ultimately unable to maintain the mystical state for long. The return to an ordinary existence, the despair of a limited self in the face of the knowledge of greater dimensions signals the as-yet unsuccessful mystic, the seeker on his way.

Purgation of Body and Mind

After the conversion, beginning mystics set about to reorganize their lives along the lines first glimpsed during the experience. The major obstacle is soon identified: involvement with and dependence on the senses. This includes most ordinary forms of cognition, the value systems used in human society, as well as the relevance attached to physical sensations and feelings.

More concretely, what stands in the way of a new cosmic vision is first of all the habit of depending on one's senses to judge reality. Something felt as a pleasant sensation is thought of as valuable and positive; all things experienced as unpleasant sensually are judged negatively and thought of as bad. The mind has become strongly habituated to maximize the pleasant and avert—or at least minimize— the unpleasant. Mystics discover that life, instead of being characterized by harmony and oneness as it should be according to the experience, is a series of ups and downs, a rat race of pleasure hunting and running away from the ugly.

Next, mystics find themselves caught in a network of established values. Originally based on sensual experiences, these values in turn reinforce the dependence on the senses. Since these values are, furthermore, shared by most other members of society, mystics see themselves entangled in a net of strife. They begin to perceive ordinary life as only geared to the short-lived satisfaction of ever-greater sensual desires and social demands. The mystic vision of a divine reality takes all this out of perspective. The value system topples; working toward oneness and a more cosmic level of cognition becomes more important than the participation in sensual delights and material progress. Things so dear before now are hindrances to realization.

Third, mystics recognize that their consciousness is deficiency-oriented. It consists of a series of positives and negatives, and is determined by a dichotomy of good and bad, right and wrong. Rooted in the pleasant/unpleasant evaluation given by the senses, perpetuated by the social values of the environment, the mystic's own mind works according to judgments and classifications. Unable to give a balanced evaluation, it rubricizes things at once. Painfully, mystics feel that their world consists largely of pigeonholing, and lacks the creative harmony felt to be possible during the mystical experience.

Standing in the way to divine oneness, all these things need to be eliminated as soon and as thoroughly as possible. One obvious step is the separation from society, the refuge in seclusion or a religious community. Then sensual control is tackled as the deautomatization of learned reactions and behavior patterns (Deikman 1980, 247). Physically, poverty and the simplicity of life cleanse the sensual apparatus. A strict diet or a limited period of fasting help to reconstitute the body. Ascetic practices and physical exercises take the edge off the senses' pestering for the warmer, softer, sweeter. Austerities and mortifications of the flesh belong to this stage of the quest as much as seclusion, poverty, vegetarianism and celibacy.[9] Often, developing mystics have an inherent sense for the most helpful physical practices. In organized tradition, advanced masters give advice on the best steps to take, when to relax or exert effort.

On the mental level, control of the senses comes through meditation techniques, usually involving high levels of concentration. By focusing the attention on a single object, the mind is stilled and thoughts are eliminated. Mystics gain a feeling of detachment; the mind reasserts itself vis-à-vis the powers of the senses. A meditation at this stage may be the counting of the respiration as in Buddhism, the focusing of the attention on the lower abdomen or basic visualizations as in Taoism, or prayer in the form of recollection as in Christianity—all forms psychologists have called "concentrative."

Contemporary meditation research distinguishes between concentrative, receptive, and combined types of meditation, based originally on Buddhist systems (Shapiro and Walsh 1984, 6). These roughly correspond to the two basic stages of mystical development. Concentrative meditation means that awareness is fixated on one single object. In receptive or mindfulness meditation, there is an open awareness of all stimuli in a nondiscriminative manner. Combined meditation, then, means that the meditator lets his or her awareness alternate between open and fixed states (Walsh 1984, 28).

Psychologists, in various experiments involving mainly practitioners of Zen and Transcendental Meditation, have found concentrative meditation conducive to a state of tranquility and psychological well-being. They conclude that the experience of a concentrated mind is similar to the state induced in relaxation therapies, such as self-hypnosis, progressive relaxation, autogenic therapy, and biofeedback (Davidson 1984, 377). These techniques are so similar, in fact, that it is not always possible to relate a particular effect on a person's subjective well-being to a specific relaxation method employed. Nor is there any effect of concentrative meditation significantly different from that of other comparable practices (Bono 1984, 209). The only thing quite clear from psychological research on concentrative meditation is "the hardly surprising conclusion that meditators are in a state of relaxation" (Davidson 1983, 301).

For aspiring mystics this means that together with withdrawal from the world of activity and physical austerities, a training in concentration of mind will bring the senses to a state of rest. They find a feeling of well-being, harmony, and relaxation, reducing the hectic involvement and passionate hankering of the earlier life. The structure of the ordinary personality is shaken, there is a first openness for a new perception, cosmic or divine. An empty space has been created in which illumination can take root.

Illumination and Insight

This stage of the mystical quest is primarily concerned with cognitive contents. It sees the active learning of a new worldview in the terms of the tradition chosen, but also based on personal experience. Physically, much is still happening. There are sensations of ecstatic freedom, lightness of the body, a reduced intensity of hunger and thirst, and less need for sleep. Yet now these phenomena are merely part of the process and neither promoted nor prohibited. As a rule, though, practitioners are warned not to get too involved with any exaggerated states or visions. The body, always participating actively in everything that goes on, has ceased to be of central concern, the senses have become secondary to the development of a new unitive mind.

The new mind necessarily has a certain structure. It requires the affirmation of a clearly defined worldview. For this reason, the differences between mystical traditions of the world increase on the level of illumination. Practitioners know clearly what to expect from their newly changed concepts and how to interpret their developing mystical experiences. It may be God's grace one sees in the clear radiance around oneself, it may be the Tao, or it may also be Buddha-nature or Brahman. But, depending on what one is (sub)consciously expecting, one's vision will change. Experience, even mystical experience, is selective. However much one cleans the doors of perception, so long as one is human and therefore subject to the necessity of making sense of one's life and world, one will prefer the parts of any experience that confirm one's views to those that do not. This is neither unfortunate nor unintended. As Chinese texts emphasize, a mind left to itself will run wild; if one continues to deconstruct and empty oneself of conceptions without giving the mind any positive direction for reorganization and renewed integration, one will be lost and turn mad.

At the same time, once sense making has begun, the traditional teachings develop into personal interpretations. There is always a portion of a mystic's worldview that remains largely personal, while other sections depend on the established doctrines of the chosen teaching. Within this framework, mystics have much freedom to create their worldview. This freedom is the reason for the fascinating variety of mystical doctrines, which often disregard the boundaries of established traditions in favor of new syntheses.

The new worldview does not develop in a day, but grows gradually, reinforced by personal experiences and organized teachings. Eventually the aspiring mystic identifies with it to such a degree that all life, including sensual experiences, is unified under its shield. This stage is a habituation to a new way of life, the emergence of a new form of consciousness. A new person is shaped, but again a person characterized by set ideas and set habits, clear values and clear patterns of behavior. The sage emerges with a cosmic mind. He or she feels love and compassion toward all beings, is receptive toward the world, hesitates to pass judgment, and never frets over material possessions (see Deikman 1982). The sage is fully himself or herself as part of all; he or she feels perfectly secure in the certain knowledge of cosmic truth.

Meditation practice in this stage of development tends to be receptive and observant. This includes Buddhist mindfulness practice, Taoist ecstatic encounters of the divine, as well as Christian contemplation and the Prayer of Quiet (see Happold 1970, 75). The senses calm; the mind can dispassionately and with nondiscriminating awareness turn to the various things that happen within and without. It forms new impressions and develops new ways of seeing and interpreting reality. Mindfully observing physical and mental forces, ecstatically exploring the palaces and treasures of the gods, or quietly waiting for the deity to appear, the power of the concentrated and purified mind is turned toward a newly found reality and applied to create a new way of thinking and feeling.

Recently two psychologists have undertaken a Rorschach study of practitioners of a mindfulness practice called Insight Meditation. This is a Theravadin Buddhist technique in the lineage of the Burmese master Mahasi Sayadaw. The Rorschach test reveals a person's perception of reality and inner conflict structure in the way he or she associates patterns on the basis of inkblots. The study ranked the subjects according to the five levels of beginners, concentration practitioners, insight meditators, advanced insight meditators, and one enlightened master.

There was no significant difference among beginners, concentration practitioners, and nonmeditators. Insight practitioners characteristically tended to see reality as being in constant motion. They perceived "inkblots as an interaction of form and energy or form and space" (Brown and Engler 1984, 245) and were predominantly concerned with the dynamics of energies as they changed and continued to create new forms. Moreover, they often perceived the energies as part of their bodies. As the study has it, "the number of references to bodily parts and internal organs and the psychic energy centers within the body is very high. . . . One possible interpretation of this contiguity between body and energy responses is that insight into bodily (and mental) processes becomes a vehicle through which to observe the fundamental energy transformations of body/mind/universe" (1984, 248). Advanced practitioners also tended to stress their belief in the oneness of all, the fundamental aliveness of the universe, and the importance of love and goodwill. Their "intrapsychic structure had undergone a radical enduring reorganization" that resulted in "a whole unified person whose internal psychic differentiation and organization would simply represent his diversified interests and abilities" (Brown and Engler 1984, 260).

The most interesting results emerged from the enlightened master. First, the master saw the inkblots themselves as a projection of the mind; second, he integrated all ten blots into a systematic description of the Buddhist teaching, thus revealing a level of oneness with his beliefs that is extremely rare. A similar result has only been found in the test results of an Apache shaman who also "used the ten cards as an occasion to teach the examiner about his lived worldview" (Brown and Engler 1980, 260).

Mystical practice as a whole can thus be defined as the active search for a new level of being. It begins with cleansing the ordinary mind and controlling the senses. The process empties the mystic of the old self; it deautomatizes his or her reaction and affords relaxation and calm. Then the quest develops to the careful renewal of personality

and worldview along the lines of a given teaching. It integrates the
wisdom of the tradition with personal experience until consciousness
is unified on a new and higher level. The new personality is characterized by calm and inner peace, benevolence and sympathy. Deeply
embedded in the truth of the traditional teaching, it is yet full of creative energy. The mystic has found realization. A sage, he or she goes
back to an active life in society, sometimes spelling out the newly
found vision in works of mystical doctrine.

MYSTICAL PHILOSOPHY

Mystical philosophy is the theoretical, conceptual description of the
mystical worldview. For the practicing mystic, it contains guidelines
to the attainment of absolute truth. Mystical philosophy is the
worldview that adepts learn during the second phase of the mystical
quest; it is the intellectual framework that provides an explanation
and systematic interpretation of increasingly sophisticated spiritual
experiences. Once a mystic has attained the ultimate state, he or she
may develop a more personal vision of the world and teach it to followers. A new form of mystical philosophy thus develops, although it
never leaves the conceptual framework of the mystic's culture and
chosen tradition.

The history of mystical philosophy depends on the complex relation
between personal experience and cultural interpretation. Continuously unfolding, it depends on the individual's involvement with the
tradition and the intensity of the experience. As William James puts it,

> Even in soliloquizing with ourselves, we construe our feelings intellectu-
> ally. Both our personal ideals and our religious and mystical experiences
> must be interpreted congruously with the kind of scenery which our think-
> ing mind inhabits. The philosophic climate of our time inevitably forces its
> own clothing on us. Moreover, we must exchange our feelings with one
> another, and in doing so we have to speak, and to use general and abstract
> verbal formulations. Conceptions and constructions are thus a necessary
> part of our religion.

(James 1936, 423)

Similarly, Ninian Smart says,

> The distinction between experience and interpretation is not clear-cut. The
> reason for this is that the concepts used in describing and explaining an
> experience vary in their degree of ramification. That is to say, where a con-
> cept occurs as part of a doctrinal scheme it gains its meaning in part from a
> range of doctrinal statements taken to be true.

(Smart 1980, 82)

Such ramifications or influences from current systems of worldview enter into the experience both a priori and a posteriori. In other words, an experience happens in a specific way due to the expectations and psychological mind frame of the individual. After its occurrence, the experience is interpreted using the same or similar concepts. Yet there are wide differences in degree. As a rule, one might say that "the higher the degree of ramification, the less is the description guaranteed by the experience itself" (Smart 1980, 83). In other words, the more intellectual presuppositions there are, the less attention is paid to new perspectives emerging in the experience. Mystical experiences, with their strong impact on the established worldview of the individual, are therefore (1) prone to occur at times of doubt and a wavering in one's personal concepts; and (2) so intense in their nature that they do not allow a straightforward continuance of ordinary life.

Intense experiences disrupt the discursive thought habits of the individual. Such experiences, though always related to cognition, therefore take some priority over discursive thought. The sense of oneness, of liberation from ordinary perception, made increasingly a permanent part of the mystic's self through continued practice, lends itself to description and discursive analysis only with great difficulty (Hocking 1980, 225). The state is duly taken out of ordinary discourse by being placed thus in a position of ineffability (Proudfoot 1985, 129).

At the same time, its description may take on a number of different forms (Moore 1978, 103). There are reports of inner uproar and turbulence describing the state immediately before or after the experience; there are confessions of the anguish during the quest, so familiar from the Christian tradition; there are also speculative systems describing the structure and purpose of the universe; there are lucid and theoretically sound interpretations of human nature and life; there are messages of joy and hope telling everyone that there is a way of becoming truly human; and there are the clear practical instructions for how to go about attaining the cosmic state.

Central Issues of Mystical Philosophy

Mystical documents, in whatever form, describe the theory and concepts of the mystical worldview. By necessity they use human language and resort to the philosophical views common at the time and place of their writing. They are multiple and culturally mediated. Nevertheless they tend to concentrate on certain central issues.

The first of these is the nature and manifestation of the absolute in relation to the ordinary world. Since the absolute is described as entirely different and placed in the position of ineffability, it has to be completely separate from the world perceived by the senses and the intellect. This entails an inherent dualism in all mystical thought, a structure that opposes something higher and greater, whether immanent or transcendent, to the world of everyday life and ordinary perception.

A second issue common to mystical philosophy is closely related to the first. Given the dualistic nature of reality, the question of why and how this came to be so arises. Mystical thought therefore contains a metaphysical explanation of the state of the world, an ontological analysis of human beings. Or, failing this, it has a cosmology and an anthropology (see Robinet 1988, 66). In all cases, it provides a theoretical model for the functioning of the world and explains why the absolute is no longer actively and visibly part of it. Frequently it poses a development of decline and a process of disintegration.

A third issue central to mystical thought is the nature of human beings. Since mystics believe to have personally experienced the absolute, they maintain that all people have the necessary faculty to do so. They often describe this faculty as a spiritual intuition beyond the senses and the intellect. Only by leaving ordinary thought and feeling behind can one develop this intuition. Explanations of exactly how different forces of the mind interact and develop thus make up a large portion of mystical documents.

Related to these three fundamental issues are the claims mystics make regarding the attainment of mystical union. First, the ultimate state of complete oneness with the absolute is described as the recovery of a unified state of nondualism from the reigning dualism of the world. Next, the paths that lead to this unified state immediately mirror the mystics' metaphysical or cosmological doctrines in that they all claim to reverse the process of decline. Third, the methods and practices mystics prescribe for the adepts of the path correspond directly to their theory of human nature.

Seen from this angle, it is obvious that mystical philosophy varies as widely as religions in general. It is also evident that particular practices prescribed in specific traditions—such as, for example, meditation—are not the same as mysticism in general (see Gimello 1983). Mystical philosophy depends entirely on the worldview and language of a given culture, and so does the state of mystical union aimed for and—presumably—attained.

Most mystical documents that have come down to us through the ages are culturally specific, however much they share their basic concern with certain definable theoretical issues. A mystical document therefore expresses the rational and conceptional interpretation of an individual's visions and experiences. The experiences are seen apart from ordinary life and are therefore placed in the semantic position of being ineffable. This term is used to deny its referent any representational role in the commonly accepted framework of reference (Proudfoot 1985, 129). To support this position and yet render it accessible, mystical writers frequently resort to paradoxes and contradictions. They often apply a level of language and discourse intended to go beyond ordinary thinking. Nevertheless, texts are texts. They are written in human language and apply human ideas and systems. They can be studied as philosophical documents representing a religious way of making sense of the world.

The Perennial Philosophy

First coined by Gottfried Wilhelm von Leibniz and developed by Aldous Huxley (1946), the perennial philosophy presents a general idealized abstract of the conceptualizations presented by the various mystical traditions of the world. Its worldview can be summarized in four statements.

1. The phenomenal world of matter is only a partial reality. It is actually the manifestation of an underlying, more real Ground.
2. Human beings by nature cannot only know the underlying Ground by reasoning but also by direct intuition. This intuition serves in some way to unite the knower and the known.
3. The nature of human beings is structured dualistically. Human beings consist of a phenomenal ego of which they are conscious in everyday reality, on the one hand, and of a non-phenomenal, eternal self by which they partake in the underlying Ground, on the other. More than that, it is possible for human beings to overcome duality, to identify with the underlying Ground and to become fully one with it, i.e., to develop a cosmic sense of self.
4. It is the chief end of human existence in the world to discover and become the cosmic truth of the self. The ultimate aim of human life is to realize the underlying Ground intuitively and become fully one with it. Thereby humanity can realize the truth of the individual as well as that of the entire world.

(Happold 1970, 20)[10]

Despite the vast cultural differences, the perennial philosophy claims that all mystical systems of the world have these beliefs in common. More than that, since these beliefs are virtually ubiquitous, perennialists claim that they have a common referent. In other words, the mystical experience is one throughout the world and so is the force or agent glimpsed therein.

Recent scholarship has raised the question of whether this is possible (Katz 1978, 1983). If human experience in general is culturally determined, how can there be an identical mystical experience throughout the world? And if there is no one mystical experience, how can there be identical beliefs? The answer is that there cannot. There are vast differences in the beliefs of even two mystics living in the same century and coming from the same cultural background (see Gimello 1983). How much wider must the gap be when they are farther apart in time and space?

Nevertheless, mysticism as the worldview that describes the attainment of an absolute through overcoming the limitations of human sensual and intellectual faculties is certainly present in all high civilizations of the world. Mystics from however disparate times and cultural backgrounds recognize in one another the search for more purity, for a more harmonious life, for being more human (see King 1988, 261). From a certain point onward, belief systems become irrelevant in the face of pure human qualities, of sageliness and a holy life. That is where mystics understand one another, where they can relate to poets, artists and other people—however unreligious—who have developed higher forms of cognition.

The perennial philosophy as a system of beliefs is a theology in the guise of religious studies. It does not prove the identity of mystical experience, nor does it substantiate the existence of a universal holy Ground. Mystical traditions, however similar structurally, are fundamentally different. Their absolutes are not one: there is God, Allah, Buddha, Brahman, the Tao, or even "cosmic consciousness." Their metaphysical systems differ accordingly, and so do their ideals and practices. No two experiences, even of drinking coffee, are ever the same. How could mystics the world over see and feel the same thing if their beliefs and methods differ so widely?

On the other hand, the work done by followers of the perennial philosophy need not be discarded. It might still be used as a pointer, as a sign of where to look for mystical philosophy, not to pinpoint similarities, but to clarify differences. Unlike psychologists, historians of religion study systems of worldview; they read texts and interpret terminologies. Presupposing that the authors of those texts either had or believed in some experience or the other, historians can put the mystical experience aside. The identity or difference of the authors' experiences is irrelevant to the study of their philosophies. What counts is the identity or difference of their writing. And to elucidate difference, identity must first be established; a *tertium comparationis*, a basis for comparison, must be found, a set of central issues common to all mystical texts. Here the perennial philosophy with its four statements might still find a place.

This Study of Mysticism

In the event, mysticism as mystical philosophy, as a system of worldview, can and should be studied on three different levels. There is first the most general level, in which the mysticism of one tradition is compared to that of another. Then there is the intracultural level, in which mystical trends and traditions are identified and their developments delineated. Third, there is the detailed study of individual texts, which consists of careful study and detailed analysis of a single work.

Using the central issues of mystical philosophy as its basic framework of reference, this study belongs to the second level. It does not compare early Chinese mysticism to that of other religions, nor does it provide an in-depth analysis of any of the documents cited. To place Chinese mysticism in a wider framework, further work needs to be done, and these introductory pages only indicate the direction such comparison might eventually take. Also, many of the texts discussed below have been studied elsewhere, as is indicated in the references. This book summarizes their findings in order to develop an overall picture of early Chinese mysticism. The aim is to show its different forms and traditions, how they developed and interacted, and what their distinctive characteristics are. It is intended to locate the phenomenon of mysticism in the context of Chinese indigenous thought and religion, to contribute to a better understanding of this tradition and its specific forms.

CHAPTER TWO

The Foundations of Chinese Mysticism

LAOZI AND THE DAODE JING

The oldest text of the Chinese mystical tradition is the *Daode jing,*
translated as the "Scripture of the Tao and the Virtue" or of the "Way
and Its Power" (Waley 1934). Known also as the *Laozi* after its alleged
author, a philosopher of the sixth century B.C.E., this is a short text of
about five thousand characters. Because of this feature it has also been
named the "Scripture in Five Thousand Words." The text divides into
eighty-one chapters and two major sections. The first section deals with
the Tao (chaps. 1–37); the second with *de* or Virtue (chaps. 38–81).[1]

The ideas and concepts contained in *Daode jing* are quite ancient,
although the document is, textually speaking, not quite as old as tradition has it. Rather, the consensus nowadays is that it was put together
on the basis of aphorisms from various sources in the Warring States
period, around 250 B.C.E.[2] It definitely existed in the beginning of the
Han dynasty, as the discovery of two copies of the text in the tomb at
Mawangdui show. Commentaries to the *Daode jing* are exceedingly
numerous and include many obscure and highly scholastic works.
Only very few, like the one by Wang Bi, have seriously influenced
traditional interpretation of the text.

In terms of contents, the *Daode jing* gives expression to the fundamental concepts of early Chinese mysticism. It focuses strongly on
cosmology and the political role of the sage. At the same time, the text
conspicuously lacks concrete descriptions of mystical methods, physical or otherwise. Nor does it show the emphasis on the mind and on
the development of the individual known from later mystical literature. In other words, the *Daode jing,* as it stands, is not obviously a
mystical document. It could equally likely be read as a work on ideal
government or on the moral and cultural decline of humanity. On the
face of it, the text is written on the background of a magico-religious
world, where the ruler is the apex of humanity and the hub of the universe. It deeply deplores the disintegration of this world and advises
the return to simplicity in life and mind as the way to its restoration.

On the other hand, by claims of the later tradition, the *Daode jing* is
a mystical text of the first importance. Together with the *Zhuangzi* it

has shaped and influenced Chinese mysticism like no other text. Later commentators and interpreters have duly undertaken tremendous efforts to fill the parts left open in the text by understanding its terms and passages allegorically and symbolically. Obscure in its origins as much as in its language, the *Daode jing* has been surrounded by ambiguity, mystery, and the sense of a higher sphere throughout its long history.

Laozi in History

Laozi, the "Old Master," is the alleged author of the *Daode jing*. First information regarding his life and work is found in chapter 63 of the *Shiji* (Record of the Historian) by Sima Qian (154–80 B.C.E.).

According to this source, Laozi was a native of a small village in the south of China, a state then known as Chu. Often known by its Shang dynasty name, Bozhou, the place is now located near the city of Luyi in eastern Henan.[3] Laozi's surname was Li, his personal name Er, and he was styled Dan. He served as a historian in the archives of the Zhou.

At one time, the text reports next, Laozi met Confucius, who asked him for instruction in the rites. Laozi, however, criticized him for his arrogant behavior and worldly concerns. It is much better, he said, to abandon all desires and ambitions, and live a simple life beneficial to health, longevity, and society at large. Scolded thus, Confucius was allegedly full of admiration and compared Laozi to a dragon whose "ascent into heaven on the wind and the clouds is something which is beyond my knowledge."

The *Shiji* completes Laozi's basic biography by reporting on his emigration to the West. This episode, famous throughout the literature, has given rise to much mythological speculation in religious as well as mystical Taoism.[4] It runs:

> Laozi cultivated the Tao and the Virtue. His essential teaching was how to withdraw from society and be without worldly fame. For a long time he lived under the Zhou. When he saw that the Zhou was declining, he decided to leave. He reached the pass [on the western frontier]. There Yin Xi, Guardian of the Pass, told him: "You are about to withdraw completely. Would you please write a work for me?" Thereupon Laozi wrote a work in two sections to explain the Tao and the Virtue. It had more than five thousand words. Then he left. Nobody knows what became of him.[5]

While the biography of Laozi proper ends with this emigration, Sima Qian goes on to relate the life stories of various other people. First, he speaks about Laolaizi, another native of south China, who allegedly wrote a book on the Tao in fifteen sections. Like Laozi, he was a contemporary of Confucius. Next, the *Shiji* provides more details about a certain Dan, historian of the Zhou, who lived in the fourth century. Some people, it states, claim that this Dan was in fact Laozi. Even Sima Qian is confused at this point and finds it hard to tell fact from fiction.

The biography concludes with a short survey of Laozi's descendants of the Li clan. It deplores the squabbles between the philosophical schools, which make history so difficult to write. All this being said, Sima Qian finds that Laozi was an ancient recluse of some renown who had some interesting ideas.

All in all, the *Shiji* biography thus includes information on four people: a person called Li from the south of China; a historian serving in the Zhou archives; a ritual master who met and taught Confucius; and a saint Laolaizi who wrote a Taoist book in fifteen sections (Waley 1934, 106). Any one of these people might have been the philosopher Laozi, yet none of them is a truly historical figure. Only the genealogy of the Li clan is historical fact. The philosopher Laozi, however, was associated with the Li family only during the Han dynasty. The Li clan decided to adopt him as their illustrious ancestor, as many noble families thus related themselves to heroes of old (see Seidel 1969, 1–11).

D. C. Lau has shown that the story of Confucius as a disciple of Laozi in matters of ritual propriety, found also in the *Zhuangzi* and the *Liji* (Book of Rites), was not common knowledge before the third century B.C.E. Rather than historical fact, he concludes, it is therefore part of the folklore—frequently polemical—that surrounded ancient philosophers (Lau 1982, 122). Nothing specific is known about Laolaizi. As regards the Zhou historian Dan, even the *Shiji* expresses doubts about his identity. The ancient thinker Laozi, known only as the "Old Master," thus remains in obscurity.

A. C. Graham approaches the problems of Laozi's original identity differently (1990). According to his reading of the sources, the tale that features Confucius inquiring about the rites was already current in the fourth century B.C.E. It might indicate that Laozi was in fact a minor official under the Zhou, well versed in matters of ritual and thus a hero of the Confucians. As such, he was then mentioned in the "Inner Chapters" of the *Zhuangzi*, a text that frequently used Confucian figures in its stories. Only later, with the appearance of the *Daode jing*, was Laozi claimed as a Taoist thinker.

In a second step, Laozi was further identified with the Grand Historiographer of Zhou, who in 374 B.C.E. predicted the rise of the state of Qin. This identification greatly ingratiated the Taoist school to the rulers of the strong state of Qin as well as to the first emperor of China. In addition, it established a claim of extended longevity for their founder, particularly useful in view of the First Emperor's immortality aspirations. The story about Laozi's departure for the West would then explain why the Old Master was no longer available to advise the emperor in person. Under the Han, of course, the close connection to Qin became a liability. Laozi was duly resettled, his birthplace now the Han rulers' place of origin (Graham 1990).

In all cases, the philosopher Laozi as a thinker of the sixth century B.C.E. eludes the light of history. Nonetheless, Sima Qian's biography is an important starting point for the understanding of this figure and the work associated with him. For one, it exhibits a strong association of Taoist thought with the south of China, a feature that played an important role in the later tradition. Also, certain characteristics and events recorded in the *Shiji* developed into important motifs of Laozi's later hagiography and thus became essential to the beliefs of religious Taoism.

Laozi, the Cosmic Deity

By the end of the Han dynasty, the belief in the god Taishang Laojun, the Highest Venerable Lord, as a cosmic personification of the eternal Tao had been generally established.[6] Laozi as a universal deity and identical with the Tao itself appears first in the *Laozi ming* (Inscription for Laozi), dated 24 September, 165 C.E. The inscription was compiled as part of formal imperial ceremonies celebrating the cosmic deity in the birthplace of the historical philosopher. Bian Shao, the author of the text, was a local scholar-official. He was neither a follower of Taoist philosophy nor did he venerate the cosmic creator Laojun or believe in any of the popular cults of the time. Such cults had developed not only around Laozi but also in devotion to the Queen Mother of the West, Xiwangmu, and other heavenly deities.[7]

The *Laozi ming* divides into five parts:

1. A summary of the facts known about the philosopher Laozi. This includes the account of the *Shiji* together with a description of Laozi as the prophetic adviser of the Zhou dynasty.
2. Laozi, the cosmic deity. He resides in the center of heaven and the beginning of time; he changes and transforms in accordance with the rhythm of the universe, described in *Daode jing* terms.
3. The emperor's vision. Emperor Huan has seen Laozi in a dream; therefore he has decided to worship him. The emperor is a sincere follower of the Tao; he is like the Shang king, similarly blessed by a divine vision.

4. Views of the author. Bian Shao sees Laozi as a hermit who lived toward the end of the Zhou. His virtue and perfection caused the present veneration.

5. Praise for Laozi. Laozi has realized cosmic truth and potency; he is fully in harmony with the universe; he transforms with the world; he shares the brilliance of the sun and the moon; he joins the five planets (see Seidel 1978, 39–46).

A similar picture of Laozi emerges in the *Laozi bianhua jing* (Scripture of the Transformations of Laozi), a Dunhuang manuscript dated to the second century C.E. (S. 2295, Ofuchi 1979, 686). Its author was a certain Wang Chou. The text was revised in 612 by a monk of the Xuandu guan (Monastery of Mystery Metropolis) in Chang'an. Rather than an official court statement, the *Laozi bianhua jing* is the expression of a popular messianic cult that sprang up toward the end of the Han dynasty in the southwest of China. Dating and placement of the text depend on its contents. It ends with the description of five distinct appearances of Laozi in the Chengdu area between 132 and 155 C.E.

Laozi here is the savior of humanity. He represents the creative, ordering power of the universe, which descends again and again to change human and natural life for the better. Laozi is the Tao; the Tao has always helped rulers to achieve and maintain perfect harmony in the world. He has descended under various names and revealed numerous scriptures in the past. Since he has always done so, he will come again and save the people (see Seidel 1969a). The *Laozi bianhua jing* describes him as follows:

Laozi was at the origin of the Great Beginning,
Revolving in the Great Expanse.
Alone and without companion,
He was moving in the times of yore, before Heaven
  and Earth.

Coming out of the hidden and returning thereto,
Being and nonbeing,
He is the First One.[8]

Within this broader cosmological scheme, Laozi's birth as a philosopher of Zhou, who teaches Confucius and transmits the *Daode jing*, is only one apparition among many. Laozi the thinker is merely one transformation in the eternal chain of the Tao's everlasting change. The philosopher is no longer simply a human being; the Tao is no longer only a philosophical concept, referring to the organic, inherent order of the world. In the merging of both, philosopher and Tao, the cosmicization of humanity coincides with the humanization of the universe. This coincidence, then, forms the mythological paradigm for the individual Taoist's aspirations to mystical oneness as well as for the communal practice of the Tao.

MYSTICISM IN THE *DAODE JING*

The *Daode jing* can be read in several different ways—as a philosophical handbook on how to live prudently in the world; a discourse on the ways of politics; an esoteric treatise on military strategy; a utopian tract; or a text that advocates "a scientific naturalistic" attitude toward the cosmos (Schwartz 1985, 192). There is no question that all these dimensions are present in the text as it stands. For our purposes here, however, and for numerous intellectuals of traditional China, the *Daode jing* has been most of all a mystical text. First and foremost, it was considered a work that presented a certain cosmological interpretation of the universe and provided instruction on how to live in perfect harmony with this universe to create a world envisioned as ideal.

The Tao

The most important and basic concept of the *Daode jing* is the Tao. The Tao, best described as the organic order underlying and structuring the world, cannot be named or known, only intuited. It is unconscious and without name. It is organic in that it is not willful, but it is also order because it changes in predictable rhythms and orderly patterns. If one is to approach it, reason and the intellect have to be left behind. One can only intuit it when one has become as nameless and as free of conscious choices and evaluations as the Tao itself.

The Tao cannot be described in ordinary language, since language by its very nature is part of the realm of discrimination and knowledge. Language is a product of the world; the Tao is beyond it—however pervasive and omnipresent it may be. The Tao is transcendent and yet immanent. It creates, structures, and orders the whole universe, yet is not a mere part of it. As the *Daode jing* says,

> The Tao that can be described as Tao is not the
>   eternal Tao.
> The name that can be named is not the eternal
>   name.
> The nameless is the origin of heaven and earth;
> The named is the mother of the myriad beings . . .
>
> Mysterious and more mysterious—
> The gate of all that is wondrous.
>
> (chap. 1)[9]

All conscious attempts to reach the Tao by means of human sense faculties are bound to fail. Human eyes and ears are limited to the realities of this world; they are attuned to the objects around them, not to the inner subtleties, the underlying potency. The Tao is completely beyond human perception.

> Look at it and do not see it:
> We call it invisible.
>
> Listen to it and do not hear it:
> We call it inaudible.
> Touch it and do not feel it:
> We call it subtle . . .
>
> Infinite and boundless, it cannot be named.
> It belongs to the realm of no beings.
> It may be called the shape of no-shape,
> It may be called the form of no-form.
>
> Vague and obscure!
> Meet it, yet you cannot see its head,
> Follow it, yet you cannot see its back.

(chap. 14)

However vague and elusive, the Tao is at the root of all existence. It makes the world function, brings all beings to life, and orders the entire universe, ever transforming and changing continuously. The Tao also ordered human society at the dawn of history. In that society everyone participated fully in the cosmic order; consciousness and culture were not yet there to separate humanity from the organic order of the universe. The oneness and harmony of the Tao reigned throughout. It protected and nurtured all beings like a benevolent mother (see Chen 1974).

> There is a being, in chaos yet complete;
> It preceded even heaven and earth.
> Silent it is, and solitary.
> Standing alone, it never changes.
>
> It moves around everywhere and never ends.
> Consider it the mother of all-under-heaven.

(chap. 25)

The Development of the World

While the Tao exists continuously and is always present in all-that-is, the original development of the world proceeded in several stages.

The Tao brought forth the One.
The One brought forth the two.
The two brought forth the three.
The three brought forth the myriad beings.

The myriad beings rely on yin and embrace yang.
In them, these energies are merged in harmony.

(chap. 42)

The primordial stage sees the Tao alone and in chaos. Next, the Tao is concentrated in a potent cosmic unity. As such, it becomes pure and powerful cosmic energy (*qi*) and is called the One. The One is later associated with the Great Ultimate (*taiji*) of the *Yijing* (Book of Changes). The One, the concentrated Tao as creative power, then goes on to bring forth the two energies yin and yang. These in turn merge in harmony and bring forth the next level of existence, symbolized by the number three. This integration of the two energies is the basis for the creation of all beings. The myriad beings thus participate in the Tao and are joined in essential cosmic harmony.

A similar development takes place within human beings. The oneness of primordial creation, the purity of cosmic energy, is the original endowment that all living beings receive from the Tao. It appears in the fulfilled state of the embryo and the infant, a state of nondifferentiation and wholeness. As people grow up and engage in active life, oneness is lost. The dualism of yin and yang then dominates human consciousness and the world. As a result, everything people see happening around them is perceived as depending on the interaction of opposites. The *Daode jing* states,

Being and nonbeing bring forth each other;
Difficult and easy complete each other;
Long and short shape each other;
Up and down slant each other;
Sound and voice match each other;
Front and back follow each other.

(chap. 2)

As yin and yang change into each other at their peak, so all opposites in the world alternate. Whatever is yin can only maintain its yin-nature until it reaches its pinnacle. Then it reverts back to yang, and vice versa. For people's activities, this means that the straightforward pursuit of a goal does not always lead there. Rather, the text advises,

If you want to shorten something, you must first
    lengthen it;

> If you want to weaken something, you must first
> strengthen it;
> If you want to abolish something, you must first
> develop it;
> If you want to hold on to something, you must
> first let it go.
>
> (chap. 36)

The active presence of yin and yang in human life and consciousness leads first to varying attitudes and modes of behavior in the
world. Eventually their ever-more-sophisticated interaction brings
about an increasing cultural and psychological complexity. Gradually
the golden age of an intact, harmonious, and simple society declines.
The Tao becomes weaker and seems to be lost completely. The most
obvious manifestation of this loss is the sensual involvement of people with the things around them, their increasing dependence on outside objects.

> The five colors blind people's eyes;
> The five tones deafen their ears.
> The five flavors spoil their palate;
> Excitement and hunting madden their minds;
> Goods hard to get do harm to their ways.
>
> (chap. 12)

The multiplicity of cultural attainments cripples people's instinctive
nature: not only their eyes and ears but also their spontaneously good
moral characters. Originally people are full of propriety and compassion; they naturally know how to be truly and wholly in the world. As
these things are lost, formal moral codes and social rules, documented
especially in the so-called Confucian virtues, rise to the fore. A conscious knowledge of right and wrong replaces spontaneous intuition.
As a result, human beings impose their conceptions and wills on nature instead of following it along. All official rules and personal guidelines to correct behavior can do little to patch up the deficiency of Tao.
Instead of the organic order of the Tao, disorder and confusion prevail
in the world. As the *Daode jing* describes it,

> When the great Tao declined,
> There were benevolence and righteousness.
> Knowledge and wisdom appeared,
> There was great hypocrisy.
>
> When the six family relationships ceased to be
> harmonious,
> There first were filial piety and love.

When the country fell in disorder,
There first were ministers praised as loyal.

(chap. 18)

Simplicity and Non-Action

To remedy the disorder and decline, the *Daode jing* asserts, it is essential to return to simplicity. People should lead a simple life on the outside and develop a pure mind within. It is especially incumbent upon those in authority to recover the purity of the Tao. Only the ruler's virtue can lead the country as a whole to a full recovery of cosmic harmony.

> Give up learning and be free from fear,
> Give up sageliness and discard wisdom—
> The people will profit a hundredfold.
>
> Give up benevolence and discard righteousness—
> The people will recover filial piety and love.
> Give up skill and discard profit—
> There will be no more thieves or robbers.
>
> These four are mere ornament and not enough.
> Therefore make the people hold on to these
>   principles:
> Manifest plainness and embrace simplicity,
> Reduce selfishness and have few desires.

(chap. 19)

But how to go about attaining these inner states of plainness and simplicity? For this, the most accessible aspects of the Tao are used as bridges: the cosmic energy, present in all that lives, and the One, that state of primordial unity within.

> Maintain your soul and embrace the One—
> Can you make them stay?
> Concentrate energy and attain weakness—
> Can you be like an infant?
>
> Clean and purify your profound insight—
> Can you make it spotless?
> Love the people and govern the state—
> Can you be without action?

(chap. 10)

A change in consciousness, a regression of the mind back to purity, will bring about the desired result. But this cannot and should not be undertaken by everybody. Rather, the text addresses itself to the ruler who loves the people and governs the state. Once the ruler has attained the One and has concentrated his energy, the Tao will radiate through him. He will bring peace and purity to the people. The ruler then deals with society by acting in non-action (*wuwei*). He does not impose his individual, personal patterns on the flow of nature. He attains the perfect way of being in the world and follows the natural course of things as they come and go. Without acting willfully or driven by purpose, he recognizes the signs of the cosmos and moves along with it in intuitive harmony. Such government brings peace. On the other hand, any active management of worldly affairs leads to failure and harm.

> Desiring to take over all-under-heaven and manage
>   it,
> This, I see, will not succeed.
> All-under-heaven is a sacred vessel,
> It must not be managed.
>
> Managing only leads to harm;
> Control always brings loss.

(chap. 29)

Nonintervention is thus the key to good government, to a harmonious and peaceful world. This nonintervention also includes an attitude of nonviolence—it propagates a freely moving, open and relaxed life in the world. Non-action is the perfect way to keep the world flourishing and people happy.

The Sage

The perfected human being in Taoism can be any individual, man or woman, from any social stratum—in fact Taoist literature often presents simpleminded wood-gatherers or fishermen as true sages. In the *Daode jing*, however, the sage is ideally the ruler. He stands at the apex of human society and mediates between heaven and earth, a sacred shaman-king. The sage has realized the original Tao; in his mind he is like heaven and earth. Because of his exposed position in society, he has the power to impart purity and harmony to others. Wherever the sage goes, all around him partakes of cosmic oneness. There are no disasters or misfortunes.

> Heaven is eternal and earth everlasting.
> Heaven and earth can be eternal and everlasting,

Because they do not exist for themselves.
Thus they can exist forever.

Therefore the sage places himself in the
    background,
But finds himself in the foreground.
He puts himself outside,
And yet he always remains.

(chap. 7)

    The sage is at one with the entire world because he has become one with the Tao. The radiance of his Tao causes the people to recover their original purity and their harmony with the rhythm of the universe. Society gives up sophistication, culture, and luxury. Ritual propriety and formal moral codes are no longer needed. The ideal life of plainness and simplicity develops naturally. People once again live in small communities, take care of their simple needs, and happily refrain from venturing into the unknown.

A small country with few people,
Let there be ten times and a hundred times as many
    utensils,
They will not be used.

The people value their lives and do not migrate
    far.
Even if there are ships and carriages,
None will ride them.
Even if there are armor and weapons,
None will display them.

Let the people again knot cords for writing.
Let them relish their food, beautify their
    clothing,
Be content with their homes, and delight in their
    customs.

Although a neighboring state may be visible,
Although one may hear its cocks crow and its dogs
    bark,
Yet the people grow old and die
Without ever visiting there.

(chap. 80)

    The ideal state of a harmonious society, where people lead a life of simplicity, is later continued in the ideal of Great Peace. Similarly, other basic features of the later tradition are present to a certain degree already in the *Daode jing*. It presents the Tao as its central concept; the terms of its description establish later standards. It mentions the One and the *qi*, cosmic vital energy; later interpretations detail their exact cosmological relationship to the Tao and to humanity.

The *Daode jing* also pinpoints the human predicament, the loss of the Tao through sensual involvement and desires. Later thinkers specify and analyze their nature and development. It points out the way to recovery of the primal state of purity by advocating the return to simplicity and plainness. It does not spell out exactly what constitutes harmony with the Tao, or how to attain it. Later commentators eagerly fill in the gaps. They seek perfection in an alignment with the rhythm of yin and yang, and advocate the practice of seclusion, meditation, and fasting. Also, the *Daode jing* emphasizes the central position of the sage and the way of non-action. Later Taoists continue this while incorporating Confucian and Buddhist notions.

The Free and Easy Wandering of the *Zhuangzi*

Beyond the *Daode jing*, Chinese mysticism took its basic system from the *Zhuangzi*, whose metaphors and expressions were widely used as technical terms in the later tradition.[10]

Zhuangzi, according to his biography in the *Shiji*, was a native of the southern country of Meng, an area that is today Henan. He died around 290 B.C.E. and thus was a contemporary of Mencius and also of Qu Yuan, the author of some shamanistic songs in the *Chuci*. He held a small government post but valued his personal freedom above professional advancement, refusing the invitation of King Wei of Chu (r. 339–329 B.C.E.) by comparing the life of an official to the fate of the sacrificial ox led to slaughter. Sima Qian praises Zhuangzi's literary style and allegorical writings but finds his teachings, though based on the sayings of Laozi, too overwhelming to be of practical use (*Shiji* 63; see Fung and Bodde 1952, 2:221).

It is precisely this overwhelming nature and high literary quality of the text *Zhuangzi* that continued to inspire thinkers, mystics, and poets of later ages. However, before it made an impact on the mystical tradition, the *Zhuangzi* underwent a development. Although compiled in the early Han dynasty (Graham 1980, 1989; Roth 1990), the edition of the text we have today—in thirty-three chapters (seven inner, fifteen outer, and eleven miscellaneous)—goes back to the third century C.E. At all times, moreover, the text consisted of several layers and did not represent the homogeneous teachings of a single philosopher or a single philosophical school.

Rather, the text *Zhuangzi* was composed of documents of at least four different schools (Rand 1983, 5). A. C. Graham distinguishes the following:

1. the Primitivists, who reject all government (chaps. 8–10 and parts of chap. 11);
2. the Individualists like Yang Zhu, also known as Hedonists or Yangists, who believe that the ultimate aim of life is pleasure and that nothing is ever worth physical harm (chaps. 28, 29, and 31);
3. the Syncretists, who probably edited the book originally. Their world-view is characterized by a combination of *Yijing* philosophy, five agents and yin-yang theory with the ideas of Laozi and Zhuangzi (chaps. 12–15, as well as chap. 33);
4. the school of Zhuangzi himself, represented mainly in the "Inner Chapters" (chaps. 1–7), but also in chapters 16–27 (Graham 1980, 459).[11]

The fundamental position of Zhuangzi, as it can be discerned from the chapters most closely associated with his thought, is one of antirationalism. He contends that logical thinking as it is expressed in language does not afford any reliable knowledge of or access to the world as it really is. Instead of conscious distinctions and rational opposites, Zhuangzi then advocates the realization of true spontaneity in the Tao. He proposes, as A. C. Graham describes it, "a supremely intelligent responsiveness which would be undermined by analyzing and choosing" (1989, 186).

This spontaneity can be found in many different ways, as it will appear in the world in innumerable different facets and forms of behavior. Zhuangzi never pins down spontaneity; he refuses to prefer one form over another. He never insists on any one way to attain it, but opens up possibilities of thinking and acting. In the book, he then illustrates what he means by a variety of glittering examples. He tells stories about craftsmen perfecting their trade through utmost inner concentration of mind and total going-along with the ways of the world, and records interviews with accomplished swimmers and archers about the secret of their special knacks.

In all these cases Zhuangzi finds the attainment of spontaneity in a going-along with the ineffable Tao. True people for him are those who have merged their thoughts and actions with the ever-changing transformations of the universe. Once at one with the Tao, such people act from their innermost being; they no longer deliberate or think about their actions. Free from all choice, they reflect the situation with perfect clarity and duly respond in the only possible and perfectly appropriate way (Graham 1989, 190).

At one with the flow of life, language itself becomes a flowing stream of words, not really saying something, yet also not *not* saying something.[12] Zhuangzi's own discourse bears this out. He is unpredictable and creative, changing from rational philosophical discussion to allegorical stories and poetic dreams. He lets his mind wander freely, allows new insights to appear and vanish as they develop, and remains smilingly removed even when apparently at his most serious. The second chapter is a case in point. It consists, as A. C. Graham characterizes it, of "a scattered series of notes which conveys more than anything else in ancient China the sensation of a man thinking aloud" (1989, 178).

On equal footing with abstract philosophical discourse, Zhuangzi frequently applies metaphorical and literary modes to express his ideas. His literary format is exceedingly powerful and has never ceased to fascinate readers, ancient and modern. It has continued to inspire numerous thinkers, poets, and mystics of traditional China. At the same time, his creative mode of presentation makes it difficult to discern with clarity the specific concepts and ideas Zhuangzi held.

Integrating the multifaceted descriptions of Zhuangzi's worldview into an organized whole, the Japanese scholar Fukunaga Mitsuji has proposed an interpretation that, though influenced to a certain extent by Guo Xiang's later commentary, seems to capture the essentials as they were understood and perpetuated by the Chinese themselves.[13] According to Fukunaga, Zhuangzi begins with the conviction that human beings do not feel at home in the world—an understanding shared by many of his contemporaries.

But Zhuangzi does not look for causes in the social and political framework of the times. Rather, he claims that people are unhappy in the world because of their rationally determined minds. To him, the world is perfect as it is—nothing one could do or say would make it better. It is a reality to be accepted as such. To change being in order to influence consciousness would have sounded absurd to Zhuangzi. Although he agrees that the problem of existence lies in the discrepancy between being and consciousness, he insists that the change must take place in the mind alone.

According to Fukunaga, the first step Zhuangzi advocates to transform the mind is to understand properly what consciousness is and how it causes problems in people's lives. He claims that human beings are strangers to the world because they set up abstract categories and intellectual divisions to deal with life. They thereby destroy life's purity and simplicity. Zhuangzi agrees with the *Daode jing* in acknowledging that the reality of being is nothing but an ongoing process of change. But people place a distance between themselves and their experiences by giving names to things. They perceive them as good or bad, desirable or undesirable.

Human self-consciousness—and again Zhuangzi concurs with other ancient Chinese philosophers—is most immediately expressed in language, in "names." But he does not advocate a "rectification of names," as Confucius did, nor does he support the effort to make the conscious network more coherent and improve its accordance with reality. Rather, Zhuangzi contends that all names, all self-consciousness, have to become part of inner spontaneity. The silence of immediate experience has to be restored. Human estrangement for Zhuangzi comes when people set up mental categories and emotional values in dealing with things. Then they begin to love life and hate death; they increasingly shift between extremes, emotionally and intellectually, instead of taking things for what they are. Good and bad, joy and anger, right and wrong, liking one and disliking another—these attitudes represent the fundamental error of human existence in the world.

Zhuangzi's solution to the predicament is to "make all things equal," as the title of the second chapter suggests. The first step in this direction is the realization of one's erroneous behavior in the past. One must first understand that passing judgment and having feelings about things are harmful to oneself. One must realize that there is no need ever to feel separate from the inherent perfection of all. In fact, one always participates in the Tao, the absolute, the One. The absolute is the now; it is right here to be participated in absolutely.

With this initial realization, according to Fukunaga's reading of the text, one can begin actually to reorganize one's consciousness. This is done by first closely inspecting and examining the reasons why one remained in such error all these years, why the distorted views arose to begin with. The source of all discrimination, it is found, lies in the tendency to split one's identity into many different "I"s by comparing oneself with others and by making deliberate choices. There is an "I" that is richer than the next man, and another "I" that is not as smart as someone else. There is an "I" that thinks it will live on and on, and there is yet another "I" that knows perfectly well it will die. Any conscious ego-identity, according to Zhuangzi, will always be one-sided. It shifts continuously from one "I" to the next without any constancy. The ego is established on the basis of evaluative comparison and rational choice; it changes as fast as one continues to compare and choose.

Having understood this flaw in one's thinking, the fundamental error in one's conception of oneself and the world, one can now proceed to get rid of it. The process that leads to spontaneity is called "forgetting": first one forgets living beings without, then one forgets mental classifications within. Increasingly one merges one's mind with the Tao, the underlying flow of existence as such. The mind becomes one with chaos or Hundun. In different chapters, this process is described in various ways.

In one reading, there is no more clear distinction between dream and reality; then, the delineation between people and animals becomes vague; or again, all consciousness merges into chaos. Zhuangzi dreams he is a butterfly and later asks himself whether he is not actually a butterfly dreaming he is Zhuangzi. This is an illustration of the conscious merging between dream and reality, between the animal and the human realm; it shows how the mind sees the continuous flow of spontaneous existence. There is no more rational knowing, no more emotional clinging, no more definite identity. Another passage describes the effect of reaching complete oblivion. The body is dispensed with, the mind is gone, there is only oneness and immersion, one joins the "Great Thoroughfare," the Tao. When there is no more perception, when all classifications have been given up, when chaos is recovered, life and death cease to exist. Fully at one with the flow of existence, with the Tao, one is able to enjoy everything as it is. This is "free and easy wandering"; this is "perfect happiness." Attaining this, the true person fully realizes the spontaneity of the Tao.

At the basis of Zhuangzi's worldview therefore lies the elimination of the rational, dividing intellect. Yet the process of elimination also begins with the intellect itself. One must first become aware that not all is well with the way one thinks and feels. Rational intellectual speculation about the human predicament and the critical questioning of one's personal identity are the starting point of Zhuangzi's quest, which soon leads to the mystical immersion in chaos and the ecstatic joy of free and easy wandering. His system is monistic in that it does not allow a breach between the Tao and the individual. Everything is and always has been the Tao; the Tao is the pure flow of existence as such. Its specific power that makes things come to life and causes them to develop is then called "virtue" or "spirit," terms that play an important role in the later tradition.

Zhuangzi's ideas carry over into Chinese mysticism of later ages, among them particularly his notion that the basic flaw of human existence lies in rational thinking and his refusal to come to terms with established language, except to destroy it by its own means. Yet Zhuangzi's concepts also undergo a transformation. The critical and rather flowing evaluation of language and self-consciousness of the second chapter is later replaced by stereotyped assumptions, often influenced by Buddhist-inspired doctrines. Also, the vagueness that

Zhuangzi leaves in all his writings, the image of the Tao as something truly unfathomable—not even a single attempt is made to grasp it, to imprison it in abstract or cosmological patterns—is later lost.

Zhuangzi's Philosophy and the Daode jing

The basic outlook of the *Zhuangzi* is in many ways compatible with and derived from the *Daode jing*. Yet there are several points of difference. First of all, the "Inner Chapters" of the *Zhuangzi* emphasize the individual's development and conspicuously lack political or social concern. Words dealing with politics occur only in a negative sense. The ideal human being realizes himself as a true person, free from society and active involvement. He or she is not the sage of the *Daode jing*, who is the ideal and perfect ruler.

Also, the *Daode jing* describes the Tao as the "mother of the world," as an underlying potency responsible for the harmonious working of nature. As such, the Tao was manifest in the perfect life of the golden age, to which society should return. The *Zhuangzi* sees the Tao merely abstractly as the flow of existence as such. The Tao is the principle of the universe. To return to the Tao does not imply going back to the past, but rather the attainment of complete oneness with the rhythm of the world. Zhuangzi's ideal of "free and easy wandering" is a state of floating freely along with life.

The concept of history differs accordingly. The *Daode jing* assumes an ideal golden age in the past followed by steady decline. History brings corrupt society and degenerate culture. For Zhuangzi, on the other hand, history moves as an ongoing flow. The times are never better or worse than before; all that happens is just part of the never-ceasing changes of the Tao. One can therefore reach harmony and recover purity by accepting the present for what it is, not in the futile search for a past long gone.

Again, non-action in the *Daode jing* is a way of dealing with the things of this world—with government, material goods, and culture. In the *Zhuangzi*, it is a state of consciousness. Non-action is the quality of the true person's mind, whatever he or she does in the world. It is constituted by the complete absence of conscious evaluation, by the disappearance of all likes or dislikes. Non-action means to go along with whatever situation has developed; it is not a prescribed way of (not) acting.

All these points reflect the fundamental difference in how the *Daode jing* and the *Zhuangzi* understood rational self-consciousness. In the *Daode jing*, conscious knowledge is the result of the historical decline. To return to original harmony means to reduce knowledge in favor of simplicity of thought and perception. In the *Zhuangzi*, on the contrary, all conscious knowledge is bad, since it forestalls the unity between subject and object. The *Zhuangzi* therefore proposes the complete dissolution of the conscious mind in chaos, the utter forgetfulness of all, replacing rational choice with spontaneous accordance. While the *Daode jing* wishes to remedy an unsatisfactory situation socially and through simplicity, the *Zhuangzi*, much more radically, encourages a thorough revolution of people's very minds (see Fukunaga 1946, 42; Knaul 1985, 73).

CHAPTER THREE

Developments in Commentary Literature

EDITIONS AND EARLY COMMENTARIES OF THE *DAODE JING*

The *Daode jing* has come down to us in three major editions:

1. The standard edition of Wang Bi (226–249).
2. The so-called old text edition by Fu Yi of the Tang.
3. The recently (1973) excavated Mawangdui manuscripts.[1]

The earliest of these is, of course, the text found in the tomb at Mawangdui, followed by several Dunhuang manuscripts dated to the period of the Six Dynasties, and a number of Tang-dynasty stone inscriptions. All these editions present the same text in fundamentally the same order. The integrity of the tradition is astounding and certainly has to do with the sacred nature of the document and the divinization of its alleged author. Recited as early as the Later Han dynasty in the context of organized religious Taoism, it was even before then a major scripture known by any well-educated Chinese. And of course to know meant, in the old days, to memorize and be able to recite.

As regards early commentaries to the *Daode jing*, works with which thinkers of the Six Dynasties and Tang would be familiar, the dating becomes less obvious. Some of the most important ones have been under serious debate. The only securely dated early commentary is Wang Bi's of the third century C.E. Tradition has it, however, that there is at least one earlier work on the *Daode jing*, by Yan Zun of the first century B.C.E.

Yan Zun

Yan Zun, also known as Yan Junping, was a fortune-teller in the markets of Chengdu in Sichuan. Especially versed in the divination of the *Yijing*, he was also greatly interested in the *Daode jing*, about which he wrote the *Daode zhigui* (Pointers to the Tao and the Virtue; DZ 693, fasc. 375–77). Its first part was lost in the Six Dynasties, while its author was increasingly described as an immortal (Robinet 1977, 11).

Yan Zun's commentary seems to have been largely along the lines of philosophical Taoism, as opposed to religious Taoism, which is concerned primarily with immortality and the cultivation of long life. Yan Zun does not find references in the *Daode jing* to practical methods of nourishing life, as some later commentators did. Rather, he emphasizes its notions of tranquility and simplicity. He encourages his readers to remain aloof from positive and negative judgment and to strive for sagehood as the ideal realization of true humanity.

In addition, certain ideas contained in his work became important later. He defines the Tao as beyond being and nonbeing and claims that the sage should remain unattached to either. Yan Zun distinguishes two levels of truth, an inner truth of the Tao and an other truth of being in the world. One is truer than the other. The truth within is more powerful and eternal than the ever-changing reality of outside existence. In fact, outer reality is merely the "trace" of the inner workings of the Tao. At the same time, worldly phenomena are clearly ordered because they are supported by the Tao. Every being has its part, its share in the Tao, and thereby its destiny is determined (Robinet 1977, 22).

These ideas become relevant later. The notion that all beings share in the Tao plays a central part in Guo Xiang's philosophy; the concept of the "traces" and "that which left the traces" is an essential notion of early Chinese Buddhism; and the relationship between being and nonbeing repeatedly concerns mystical thinkers of later ages.

Wang Bi

Wang Bi, also known as Wang Fusi, lived in the first half of the third century (226–249). He was a member of the new intellectual elite who engaged in Pure Talk (*qingtan*) and thought deeply about the metaphysical principles underlying the world. As such, he became one of the foremost representatives of the Dark Learning (*xuanxue*) school of Chinese philosophy.[2]

Dark Learning signified the return to the ancient texts, to the simplicity of the classics. It was characterized by a lack of interest in the current political issues of the day; a rejection of the scholastic hair-splitting of the Later Han; and a strong tendency toward metaphysical and ontological speculation. The three "Dark" texts that gave the school its name are the *Yijing*, the *Daode jing*, and the *Zhuangzi*. Their cosmological and mystical ideas were discussed especially in combination with Confucian speculation on the ideal functioning of human society.

Wang Bi is a typical representative of that line of thought. Besides his commentary to the *Daode jing* (DZ 690, fasc. 373),[3] he wrote a commentary on the *Book of Changes*, the *Zhou yi lueli* (Exemplification of the

Principles of the Book of Changes) and a treatise called *Laozi weizhi lilue* (The Structure of the Laozi's Pointers).[4]

Wang Bi's major contribution to the development of Taoist thought is his concept of original nonbeing, *benwu*. His concern lies with the relationship of nonbeing and being, the One and the many, the ruler and the people, the hexagram's first line versus the remaining five lines. His interpretation of nonbeing, as Isabelle Robinet has pointed out, represents a step back from the concept of the Tao in the *Daode jing* (1977, 75). There the Tao was utterly infinite, ineffable, incalculable. Wang Bi established it in identity and outline; he gave it a distinct role in the world. The One in the *Daode jing* is one aspect of the Tao, the germinal state of the world as it develops from the underlying ground. For Wang Bi, the One is the Tao; or rather the Tao is the One. The depth of the ground is reduced, it is named and subjected to a clear-cut pattern.

For Wang Bi, the Tao is not only the One. He also identifies it with original nonbeing and with the Great Ultimate. As such, the Tao is the clearly understood root and origin of the world. It relates to the world of being as silence does to language, to use a fortuitous comparison by Isabelle Robinet (1977, 75). While silence is the absence of language it is yet more than that. Silence underlies language, which punctuates it only fleetingly. Similarly, nonbeing lies beneath all being. It is its absence and yet more; it is its cause and its reason. As Wang Bi says in his commentary to the *Daode jing* (DZ 690, fasc. 373),

All being originates from nonbeing. Therefore, the time before there were physical shapes and names is the beginning of the myriad beings. When shapes and names are there, [the Tao] raises them, educates them, adjusts them, and causes their end. It serves as their mother. The text means that the Tao produces and completes beings on the basis of the formless and the nameless. They are produced and completed but do not know how or why. Indeed, it is mysterious and again mysterious.

(chap. 1; 1.1a)

Wang Bi thus establishes a definition of the relation between the Tao and the world. He describes them as the underlying basis and its surface effect. To clarify his point, he speaks of nonbeing and being, the root and the branches, substance and function. His distinctions and philosophical terms became in due course an integral part of Chinese thought. Later mystical authors make use of them as well, but they often return the Tao to its original mystery. They speak of it as nonbeing and emptiness; they call it vague and obscure.

Another important concept of Wang Bi is his understanding of return. Return for him signifies the reduction of the many to the One, the recovery of unity from duality. In his commentary to the *Daode jing*, he follows the quietistic tendency expressed in the original text and accepts the attainment of complete simplicity through withdrawing from social involvement and calming the mind.

> In emptiness and tranquility, one observes the return of all beings. All being begins with emptiness, all movement, from tranquility. Therefore, although beings move together, they ultimately return to emptiness and tranquility . . .
>
> Returning to their origin means rest. It is called tranquility. Tranquility means recovering the life span. . . . This means to achieve the constancy of life. Therefore it is called eternity.

> (chap. 16; 1.10a)

Utmost reduction—complete return and utter tranquility—are at the same time the greatest integration and the most perfect recovery of life, of movement and activity (Robinet 1977, 66). The law of yin and yang is applied here. Any tendency taken to its extreme reverts automatically to its opposite. Be completely quiet, unify with the One, and the entirety of life, the whole range of multiplicity of the world, will be yours. One of the basic concepts of Chinese mysticism, the alternation between yin and yang, forms the theoretical reason why withdrawal from the world and solitary meditation ultimately mean intense involvement in the world. As Wang Bi has it, the sage, utterly merged with original nonbeing, "penetrates the perfection of natural so-being. He permeates the inner essence of the myriad beings. Therefore he goes along with them without acting; he is in harmony with them without imposing on them. He removes their errors and eliminates their delusions. Hence their minds are not confused and beings fully realize their inner natures" (chap. 29; 2.7b). Thus the sage can perfectly serve the world, join all beings, and bring about a more integrated and harmonious society.

PHYSICAL MYSTICISM: THE HESHANG GONG COMMENTARY

Similar ideals but different methods of achieving them are found in another early commentary on the *Daode jing*: the work by Heshang gong, the Master on the River. Also contained in the Taoist Canon (DZ 682, fasc. 363) and reconstituted in its entirety on the basis of citations in other works (Fujiwara 1973), the text was translated into English by Edward Erkes (1958). It has recently been studied by Alan Chan (1991). Legend has it that Heshang gong lived during the time of Emperor Wen (179–156 B.C.E.), but the earliest stories about him date from the third century C.E. (Robinet 1977, 25). Moreover, evidence that the text as we now have it goes back only to the fifth century has been strengthened considerably over recent years.

According to the original legend, nobody knew the real name of the immortal Heshang gong, the Master on the River. He lived near the Yellow River under the Han emperor Wen in the first century b.c.e. and spent his time studying the *Daode jing*. Emperor Wen was a great devotee of Laozi and his teachings. He had the text recited at court, but had difficulties understanding certain passages. Eventually he learned about Heshang gong and summoned him to give an inspired explanation of the text.

Heshang gong refused the summons. The emperor, greatly intrigued,

> strode on his horse and paid him a visit. He said, "In all-under-heaven, there is no place that does not belong to the ruler. Among all the people living in the world, there is not one who is not the ruler's vassal. There are four great halls in my palace, and I live in the greatest. You may have the Tao, but you do not have the people. You cannot make others obey your orders—why do you behave as if you could? I warn you, I can make people rich and honored or poor and despised."
>
> All of a sudden, the Master on the River clapped his hands and stood up from his seat. Imperceptibly he rose up into the air, light as a cloud, rising from the ground more than a thousand feet. He continued to ascend to the mysterious emptiness of the sky.
>
> After a long time, he looked down and said, "Above, I do not reach heaven, in the middle I do not belong to humanity, and below I do not live on the earth. Whatever people you may rule, Your Majesty would hardly be able to make me rich and honored or poor and despised."

The emperor finally understood that Heshang gong was a divine personage. He sank to the ground and apologized abjectly, begging this "Lord of the Tao" to explain the text to him. Heshang gong promptly came down from his cloudy retreat and handed the emperor a manuscript of the *Daode jing*. He explained, "If you study this with care, all your questions will be naturally solved. Since I wrote this commentary, more than seven thousand years have passed, but I have only given it to three people so far. You are the fourth. Do not show it to anyone who is not ready for it!"

The emperor kowtowed to express his gratitude. When he looked up again, Heshang gong had vanished.[5]

A typical revelation legend, this story features the eccentric immortal from heaven disguised as a common hermit, who refuses to discuss his ideas and practices with ordinary people. The emperor appears as a humble student of the Tao, who receives the sacred truth with the serious intention to change his life accordingly.[6] The fruitful interaction of both then leads to the ruler's attainment of the Tao, which in turn causes a perfect government of the world. In this the story uses the mythological theme of the Tao serving as adviser to the dynasty. Already in the *Laozi bianhua jing*, the Tao appears in various transformations and helps the government through the revelation of sacred texts and cosmic charts. A warning not to show the text to anyone is added as part of the standard procedure, just as the immortal's ascent into heaven is a typical motif of such stories.

Problems of Dating

The Heshang gong legend places the Heshang gong commentary in a Han-dynasty context. However, the text's authenticity was already doubted in the seventh century. Tang scholars considered the legend rather fanciful and could not find it corroborated in respectable historical sources, such as the *Hanshu* (History of the Han). They doubted that Heshang gong was a historical figure at all. Song literati, on the contrary, accepted the text again as a Han document. Only Qing scholars considered the possibility that the text consisted of different textual layers (see *Siku quanshu zongmu tiyao*, chap. 28). They concluded that certain passages of the text were similar to Wang Bi's commentary to the *Daode jing* (chaps. 6, 10) and went back to the third century. They dated the majority of the text later, to the Six Dynasties (see Kusuyama 1979, 18).

Until recently, contemporary scholars dated the Heshang gong commentary to the Han dynasty on the basis of citations in early materials (Seidel 1969, 32, n. 4; Robinet 1977, 27). Also, they found the text similar to the *Xiang'er* commentary (Rao 1956).[7] The *Xiang'er* seemed certainly a document of the Later Han, as it was closely associated with the early Celestial Masters around Zhang Daoling and Zhang Lu.

In recent years, however, the study of philosophical and cosmological concepts outlined in the text, as well as its relationship with other Taoist materials, has led Japanese scholars to conclude that it should be dated instead to the fifth century (Mugitani 1985; Kobayashi 1985). They believe that the finished version of the Heshang gong text did not come into existence before the fifth century—the time when the development of Taoism as a religion gained momentum throughout China (Kusuyama 1979; Kobayashi 1985a). Nevertheless, they also agree that Heshang gong's work contains some ancient ideas and that a *Daode jing* commentary was already associated with the legendary Master on the River in the third or fourth century. They assume that the sections of the text containing advice to the ruler about the practice of non-action and proper government are oldest. Those parts that interpret the *Daode jing* in terms of physical practice and meditation are dated later (Kusuyama 1979, 160).

At the same time, the recent study by Alan Chan places the text again in a Han dynasty context (Chan 1991, 107–18). In terms of its metaphysical and ontological conceptions, the text indeed does not deviate specifically from other ancient Chinese authors, such as Huainanzi, Hanfeizi, Yan Zun, and Wang Bi (Robinet 1977, 30). Moreover, in many ways its major contributions to the Taoist pursuit of perfection are in close agreement with the theories and practice of Taoist self-cultivation found in such early documents as the *Huainanzi* and the *Guanzi* (see Ishida 1989; Roth 1991a). The Heshang gong commentary establishes an intimate connection between cultivating oneself and governing the country (*zhishen zhiguo*). It also links *Daode jing* philosophy with the worldview and practices of Chinese medicine and Han-dynasty cosmology, both aspects that played an important role in the development of religious Taoism. The Heshang gong commentary thus furnishes important documentation on the phase between philosophical Taoism and the Taoist religion.

Self-Cultivation and Government of the Country

Heshang gong frequently refers to self-cultivation and the act of governing a country in a parallel manner (Kusuyama 1972). For him, the creation of political order is structurally isomorphic with the cultivation of personal longevity. Politics and philosophy, as well as magic and morality, are thus interconnected in his thought—realms that are clearly distinguished in our terms (Robinet 1977, 30). In a way that strongly reminds the reader of the "Great Learning" chapter of the *Liji*, the cultivation of oneself, of one's *shen* (personal body or identity), leads to the correct order of one's house, one's community, the land, and all-under-heaven. As the commentary says (DZ 682, fasc. 363),

> In the old days, skillful practitioners of the Tao cultivated themselves and then extended this cultivation to the government of the country. They never used the Tao to teach the people brightness and wisdom, cunning and hypocrisy. Rather, they used the Tao and the Virtue to teach the people simplicity and plainness. They were without hypocrisy and falsehood.
>
> Who is always full of wisdom will be a robber of the state. Who is entirely free of wisdom will be a blessing to the state. This is the basic model for both, the cultivation of oneself and the government of the country. Anyone following the basic model will join his virtue with Heaven.
>
> (chap. 65; 4.5ab)

Since the personal body, the selfhood of the individual, is so central to the realization of the Tao, one must not seek the Tao anywhere outside of oneself. All cultivation of the self takes place behind closed doors, within oneself.

> Skillful practice of the Tao searches it within the body and never goes outdoors. Thus it leaves neither track nor trace.
>
> (chap. 27; 2.9a)

> A sage never leaves his house to know the world. He knows other people through himself, other families through his own family. This way he can look at all-under-heaven.
>
> (chap. 47; 3.9a)

There is such a close relationship between the personal body and the country because both are structured in the same way, both participate in the Tao in equal fashion. As Heshang gong has it,

> The Tao of heaven is the same as the Tao of humanity. Heaven and humanity pervade each other, essence and energy continue each other. When the ruler of humanity is clear and tranquil, the energy of Heaven will naturally be upright. When the ruler of humanity is full of desires, the energy of Heaven will be troubled and turbid. Thus all good and bad fortune, profit and harm, issue from one's own self.
>
> (chap. 47; 3.9a)

So far, Heshang gong concurs with the *Daode jing*. The ruler's purity and oneness have an immediate impact on the world. Then Heshang gong goes one step further. The relationship between self and world becomes mystical. The country really is the same as the self; the preservation of one also means the continuity of the other. He says, "The country is the self. The Tao is its mother. When one can preserve the Tao within the self, keeping the essence and energy from being labored and the five spirits from suffering hardship, then one can live forever" (chap. 59; 3.19b).

To attain perfect stability in country and self one must reduce passions and attachments to the world. The sage—as in the *Daode jing*, the sage for Heshang gong is first of all the ruler—withdraws to solitude to free himself from all connections with the world. He concentrates on his body and ensures the continued active presence of the various spirits that keep it alive: "The sage governs the country just as he governs himself. He drives out all attachments and desires, abandons all trouble and confusion, holds on to the Tao, embraces the One, and guards the five spirits [residing in his body]" (chap. 3; 1.3ab).

Once ready for active government, the sage deals with the world exactly as he dealt with his self-cultivation. He becomes the paragon of non-action. As the text says, "Among the rulers of the world, few have been able to attain the non-action that reaches close to the Tao. A government through non-action is attained by governing the country as one would cultivate oneself" (chap. 43; 3.7a).

Medical Worldview and Breathing Exercises

The parallel between self-cultivation and world government, so characteristic for Heshang gong's thought, depends in turn on the integration of medical worldview with the philosophy of the *Daode jing*. Both self and world have a clearly understood and definable structure; they both depend on the Tao. Cultivation in all cases proceeds to purify the existing structures, which are essentially the same. To realize one consequently means to realize the other.

Heshang gong's system is not only based on the cosmological assumption that all existence is pervaded and supported by the Tao. It also subscribes to the medical theory of the human body, first documented in the environment of Han-dynasty *fangshi* and later integrated into Taoist cosmology and meditation.[8] Chinese traditional medicine defines the fundamental share all beings have in the Tao as their vital energy (*qi*). Everyone is endowed with this cosmic force at birth, but there are different kinds of *qi*: yin and yang, heaven and earth, pure and turbid, light and solid. Depending on one's endowment, one will be tall or short, dark or light, weak or strong, impulsive or complacent. Even sageliness is determined through energy. Heshang gong says, "Within heaven there is yet another heaven. The vital energy received at birth can be rich or poor in quality. One who attains harmonious and fruitful energy will become a wise man or a sage. One who attains confused and turbid energy will become greedy and licentious" (chap. 1; 1.2a).

More specifically, the vital energy within the human body appears in definite forms. Represented as spiritual forces or body divinities (*shen*), it resides in certain energy centers, most commonly described as the five "intestines" or orbs. These are located in the liver, lungs, heart, spleen, and kidneys of the human body.[9] According to Heshang gong, nourishment of the five spirits is an essential prerequisite for attainment of the Tao. This attainment in turn means not only sagehood and purity of mind, but also long life and even immortality:

Whoever is able to nourish the spirits within will not die. By spirits I refer to the spirits of the five orbs: the spirit soul in the liver, the material soul in the lungs, the spirit in the heart, the conscious intention in the spleen, and the essence together with the will in the kidneys. When these five orbs are exhausted or harmed, the five spirits will flee.

(chap. 6; 1.5a)

It is not known exactly how medical practitioners nourished their five spirits. They probably subscribed to specific diets, took drugs, practiced gymnastics, and controlled their breathing (see Kohn 1989). Heshang gong especially favors the latter. According to him, the vital energy that people receive from heaven and earth is manifest in all the orbs, but especially in the heart and the digestive system. It enters the heart in the form of breath through the nose, and the stomach in the form of food through the mouth. He interprets the *Daode jing* accordingly, especially the reference to the "mysterious female" in chapter 6.

The Tao of prolonged life lies with the Mysterious Female. Mysterious is heaven, within human beings it is the nose. Female is earth, within human beings it is the mouth.

Heaven feeds people with the five energies. They enter the body through the nose and are stored in the heart. These five energies are clear and subtle, they form essence and spirit, intelligence and clear perception, sound and voice, as well as the five kinds of inner nature.

Heaven's manifest counterpart is the spirit soul. The spirit soul is male. It enters and leaves the human body through the nose. It is aligned with the Tao of heaven. Thus the nose is the Mysterious.

Earth nourishes people with the five tastes. They enter the body through the mouth and are stored in the stomach. The five tastes are turbid and coarse, they form the physical body, bones and flesh, blood and arteries, as well as the six kinds of emotions.

Earth's manifest counterpart is the material soul. The material soul is female. It enters and leaves the human body through the mouth. It is aligned with the Tao of earth. Thus the mouth is the Female.

The nose and the mouth are the gateways by which the primordial energy that pervades Heaven and Earth comes and goes. Inhalation and exhalation through the nose and the mouth continues without interruption, subtly and miraculously. It is as if it would go on forever, yet seems not to be there at all. In one's application of breathing, remain relaxed and comfortable. Never make haste or labor the exercise.

(chap. 6; 1.5ab)

Breathing in the highest possible alignment with heaven and earth will therefore lead to perfection, a state not only manifest in mental purity and harmonious non-action, but also in long life and immortality. Followers of this method will gain an existence as everlasting as heaven and earth. With this, the mystical tradition has developed from a vague philosophy of the Tao and the world to a clearly delineated path leading directly into the heavenly spheres. Though as yet a far cry from the elaborate physical exercises developed later, the Heshang gong commentary shows in exemplary fashion how physical aims and techniques, along with their theoretical system of cosmic correspondences, are connected with the ideas of the ancient philosophers.

LATER EDITIONS OF THE ZHUANGZI

The *Zhuangzi's* in-depth analysis of the human mind and language alone explains its enormous impact on the mystical tradition. However, to understand the ways of its interpretation, one has to look at the history of the text.

Only the "Inner Chapters" go back to the philosopher himself. The text as a whole was compiled in the beginning of the Han dynasty, edited probably at the court of Liu An, Prince of Huainan, where the *Huainanzi* was also put together. Even at that time the text included materials from different schools, more-or-less associated with the name of Zhuangzi.

Unlike the *Daode jing*, the *Zhuangzi* was not valued highly during the Han dynasty. No edition remains from this period. After the end of the Han, with the rise of Dark Learning, intellectuals again turned to the *Zhuangzi* and various new editions appeared. There was first the edition by Sima Biao, dated to after 265 C.E. Then there were those by Mr. Meng and by Cui Zhuan; both date to the late third century. A more prominent version was by Xiang Xiu. Long believed to be plagiarized by Guo Xiang, this was in fact closely related to Cui's edition (see Fukunaga 1964). Cui Zhuan and Xiang Xiu interpreted the text in terms of the Individualist or Hedonist argument, an outlook clearly expressed in Xiang Xiu's refutation of Xi Kang's *Yangsheng lun* (Discourse on Nourishing Life).[10]

All early editions are lost and cited only occasionally in later sources. We know that the versions of Sima and Meng divided the text into fifty-two chapters altogether (seven inner, twenty-eight outer, fourteen miscellaneous, and three explanatory). Cui's and Xiang's editions contained only twenty-seven chapters (seven inner and twenty outer). Exactly what was in these books can only be speculated about.[11]

More information is available on Guo Xiang's version of the *Zhuangzi*, edited around the year 300. His edition soon became the standard version and has survived to the present day. Most enlightening, Guo Xiang also wrote a postscript to explain the revisions he undertook. This postscript is still extant in the Kōzanji Temple in Kyoto, Japan.[12] Here Guo Xiang says that he found Zhuangzi's work full of strange ideas, daring metaphors, and lofty expressions. To make his meaning clear to the uninitiated, he found it necessary to revise the text radically. A certain number of chapters—altogether about one-third of the old manuscript—were excluded completely. "Some of them," he states, "were similar to the *Shanhai jing* (Classic of Mountains and Seas), others resembled the manuals used by dream interpreters. Some came from the *Huainanzi*, others again belonged to works dealing with speculations about names and reality."

The text seems to have been widely varied, containing profound and shallow parts side by side. Guo Xiang says he found it hard to make sense of the work as a whole, but tried his best to include as much as possible in the coherent philosophical system he outlines in his commentary. As he has it, "I contented myself with summarizing all and refrained from inquiring into its logic. I reduced the text to thirty-three chapters, selecting its best and most complete parts, those which could reasonably be made into one whole" (Knaul 1982, 55).

Guo Xiang therefore thoroughly reorganized the *Zhuangzi*. He eliminated folkloristic parts and shortened the manuscript, as he himself admits; from later citations it is evident that he also rearranged the text and removed those sections he considered merely explanatory to his commentary. Guo Xiang did thus not hesitate to impose his personal understanding and philosophical preferences on the text. The ancient original *Zhuangzi* was lost and ever since the fourth century it has been received through Guo Xiang's eyes. His philosophical systematization had a tremendous impact on the later tradition. Once his views were found agreeable to Chinese literati, his interpretation was accepted as the correct standard and all variants gradually vanished in the mist of history.

Guo Xiang's Mystical Philosophy

Unlike the *Zhuangzi*, Guo Xiang's commentary does not leave much doubt about his ideas. He has strong convictions about the way the universe works and how people function therein, and presents them in a well-organized, thoroughly thought-out soteriology, which represents an important development of Chinese mystical worldview.[13]

The World As the Tao

For Guo Xiang, everything exists the way it is and because it is. There is no principle or agency at the origin of life. He says in his commentary (DZ 745, fasc. 507–19),

> What existed before there were beings? If I say yin and yang were first, then that means yin and yang are beings, too. What, then, was before them? I may say nature was first. But nature is only the natural way of beings. I may say perfect Tao was first. But perfect Tao is perfect nonbeing. Since it is nonbeing, how can it be before anything else? So, what existed before there were beings? There must always be another being without end. Thus I understand that beings are what they are by nature; they are not caused by anything else.
>
> (24.39b)

There is ultimately no cause to make things what they are. "Thus," Guo Xiang says, "the principle of self-transformation becomes clear" (3.46a). The universe exists by itself and of itself; it is existence just as it is. Nothing can be added to or subtracted from it; it is entirely sufficient upon itself.

The universe, though spontaneous, is not without structure. It is structured first because it is in continuous motion and changes without interruption. Second, it is structured by principle (*li*), a cosmic power that makes everything be what it is. "Each individual has principle as much as each and every affair has what is appropriate to it" (3.14b). This principle is inescapable just as the characteristic of change is in everything that is. Principle determines the particular way of being of the entire cosmos as much as of each individual being and affair.

Principle is intimately linked to share or lot (*fen*). That is to say, it corresponds closely with the fact that any concrete existence is only possible through obtaining some share in the Tao, in the universal flux of existence. This share or part that every being has in the Tao determines his, her, or its position in the cosmos, while principle is responsible for the particular way in which this position is filled.

Organized according to the cosmic laws of principle and share, human society is basically an organic whole. The political structure is a natural body. Since it is an integral part of nature, there can be only one perfect society. This society is hierarchical, closely knit, and well ordered—similar to the ideal of Great Peace, held equally by Confucians and Taoists in the end of the Han (Eichhorn 1957; Kandel 1979; Kaltenmark 1979). The ideal ruler in this system is the direct executive of the cosmos. "The ruler's virtue is like heaven's being naturally high" (1.21b), Guo Xiang states categorically. The ruler governs the world through perfect non-action. As Guo Xiang describes it,

> When the king does not make himself useful in the various offices, the various officials will manage their own affairs. Those with clear vision will see; those with sharp ears will listen; the wise will plan; and the strong will provide protection. Why take any action? Only mysterious silence, that is all!
>
> (5.52a)

Non-action is thus defined as action in true harmony and accordance with things. People realize themselves by doing exactly what they are best suited for and nothing else. Despite these rigorous limitations of people's activities, Guo Xiang's system is not deterministic. Rather, society and human life are for him the arena in which people live up to their given abilities and opportunities. The world and the Tao are there for human beings to realize themselves for what they really are.

Human Beings Defined through the Cosmos

People ultimately are the Tao in a microcosmic form. They all share in it (*fen*); they are structured by its principle (*li*). The share that everyone has in the Tao determines the individual's "inner nature" (*xing*); everybody's principle is found in his or her "fate" (*ming*).

Inner nature, says Guo Xiang, "is what people rely on spontaneously without ever being conscious of it" (2.35b). It is the way people are naturally, their inherent psychological makeup, which is entirely independent of knowledge or consciousness. It has nothing to do with people's subjective wishes or concrete hopes, but is there and cannot be changed. Obtained at birth, any enforced change of inner nature must result in suffering, as much as any development along its lines will be to the good. In a sense, inner nature is therefore very restricting, very limiting; this should be so because it represents the individual's participation in the Tao. Everyone has a natural intuitive sense of what is good and bad in a particular situation. But people have for generations distorted their inner natures, their feeling and idea of themselves. Therefore they continue to strive for things that are not appropriate for them.

Fate, on the other hand, is parallel to principle; it is the life that one is ordered or fated to have by heaven (see Kaltenmark 1965, 657). "That which one is given is one's fate" (4.11a), Guo Xiang says. Fate is there to be accepted, not to be changed. It orders human existence in exactly the same way that principle structures the universe. It determines every individual's birth, age, opportunities, chances—all the outer circumstances of his or her life. Fate means the concrete conditions of life; inner nature means the basic psychological character of the individual. Respectively representing nurture and nature, fate and inner nature are together responsible for the development of the individual's life. Again, as in the case of inner nature, fate should be fulfilled, not counteracted. The more one works along with one's destiny, the better one realizes oneself, and the more contentment, happiness, and perfection one experiences. The more one tries to avoid it, the harsher the realities of life appear.

The proper attitude toward inner nature and fate is accordance, harmony, adaptation, and even resignation to the given realities. The more spontaneously such accordance is achieved, the better. Conscious knowledge and active decision making have no part in this, since they cause a rift between subject and object and make spontaneity impossible. Unfortunately, people do not accord with the Tao—as manifest in inner nature and fate—spontaneously, but they have developed consciousness and have thereby separated themselves from the true Tao.[14]

Human Consciousness and Theory of Knowledge

In the past, human beings were fully spontaneous and had not yet developed self-consciousness. At that time, the world was well ordered, in a state of Great Peace. Gradually consciousness developed through the decline of spontaneous purity. The decline took place in four stages.

1. Chaos Complete
   This is the state of complete forgetfulness of heaven and earth, of total abandonment of the myriad beings. Outside never examining time and space, inside never conscious of one's own body. Thus people are boundless and free from all fetters, they go along with beings and are in full accordance with all.
2. Beings
   Even though forgetfulness is no longer complete now and beings are recognized as existing, yet there is still the forgetfulness of distinctions between this and that.
3. Distinctions
   At this stage, there is a distinction between this and that for the first time. However, there are no evaluations in terms of right and wrong.
4. Right and Wrong
   If [the distinction between] right and wrong were not there, the Tao

would still be complete. With the destruction of the Tao, emotions begin
to be partial and love develops. As long as one cannot forget love and
free oneself from egoism, there is no way mysteriously to become one in
oneself and with others.

(3.1b–2a)

Originally people did not discriminate anything at all; then they
began to recognize other beings. Gradually they learned to distinguish between this and that, and eventually evaluated everything according to its being good or bad, right or wrong, useful or useless.
People's definitions therefore came to determine the place of everything in the world. This place may or may not be natural to the thing
in question. As Fukunaga has it, "the road is made by people walking
along a path over and over again. Things are named because people
use them in a specific manner. Only thereby do they become what
they are" (1978, 1:78). Value judgments and feelings about things are
thus distortions of natural spontaneity and unconsciousness. The
final stage of the decline is reached when ego-centered love develops:
"Someone who opens up and loves another, the world calls an altru-
ist. Yet this person only desires to be loved in return. So in fact he is
behaving very egoistically" (15.13a).

This ego-centered love appears in social morality as institutional-
ized virtue. Benevolence and righteousness for Guo Xiang are mere
traces of love. They belong to a state of intense decline, in which the
pure Tao has all but vanished.

Reversing the Decline through Unlearning

To reverse the development of conscious knowledge one must return
to forgetfulness; in unlearning distinctions, one gradually attains unknowing. The process leading there is called "sitting in oblivion"
(*zuowang*). It is first described in the *Zhuangzi*.

> "What does 'sitting in oblivion' mean?" Confucius asked. "I smash up my
> limbs and body," Yan Hui replied, "drive out perception and intellect, get
> rid of physical shape and abandon all knowledge. Thus I merge with the
> Great Thoroughfare.
>
> (19/6/92)[15]

Guo Xiang comments,

> Practicing this forgetfulness, how can there be anything not forgotten?
> First forget the traces, such as benevolence and righteousness; then put
> that which caused the traces out of the mind. On the inside, unaware of
> one's body, on the outside never know there is a universe. Only then will

one be fully open, become one with the process of change and pervade everything.

(8.39a)

Through increasing forgetfulness, the pursuit of knowledge (*zhi*) is replaced first by opening up everything to the light (*ming*). Then neither darkness nor light nor any opposites are perceived any longer. Instead of knowledge, there is "unknowing" (*wuzhi*); instead of conscious mental activity and feeling, there is "no-mind" (*wuxin*). Once all things are forgotten, one proceeds to forget the forgetting. One "forgets and again forgets" or "decreases and again decreases," as the *Daode jing* has it (chap. 48). All beings are then the same in one's perception; there is no more good and evil, no more right and wrong. One has attained the state at which all beings are made equal. Then, whatever "I" may develop, whatever state the "I" may find itself in, forgetfulness pervades all, all is one. Guo Xiang says,

> Taking shape is "I" arising,
> Being alive is "I" at work;
> Growing old is "I" decaying,
> Being dead is "I" at rest.
>
> All these states are different,
> and yet they are the same,
> because they are all "I."
>
> Though all four are changes,
> They never are not "I."
> How could this "I" be cherished?

(7.23b)

The ultimate oneness of existence is at work within and through oneself. By becoming fully one with all, the individual dissolves in the flow of life. He or she attains perfect oneness and harmony with the Tao. At this stage, a new sense of self emerges, a self no longer limited to the ego or defined by the body. This new self is identical with universal principle. As Guo Xiang describes it,

> This life of mine, I did not bring it forth. Thus all that occurs throughout my life of perhaps a hundred years, all my sitting, getting up, walking, and staying, all my movements, all my quiet, all hurrying and resting of mine— even all the feelings, characteristics, knowledge, and abilities I have—all that I have, all that I don't have, all that I do, all that I encounter: it is never me, but principle only.

(6.16a)

In such a state, the person at one with the Tao no longer acts according to individual feelings, wishes, and intentions. Rather, the pure creative force of the universe, the radiant spirit of the world, acts through him or her. The Tao takes care that the person fulfills his or her inner nature and fate to perfection. Everyone has such access to the Tao in the realized mind within. This mind is pure spirit, the individual's inborn virtue of the Tao. It guides people perfectly and ensures their happiness. Guo Xiang says, "The ways of the human mind are such that naturally there is nothing that is not done. Going along with them and just following and complying with them, people will naturally be tranquil and fulfill their duties spontaneously" (13.10b).

Forgetfulness thus leads to a new life, a way of life in harmony with the perfect rhythm of the universe. The sage, the fully realized human being, emerges.

The Ideal Life of the Sage

The life of the sage in Guo Xiang's thought has an inner and an outer perspective. On the inside, in the mind of the sage, there is only tranquil freedom and unified perception. On the outside, in the actions of the sage, there is harmony with the natural processes, a complete accordance with the flow of life.

The mind of the sage is no longer limited to an ego or a specific identity. Rather, his mind has become one with the spontaneous current of nature. As Guo Xiang describes it, "The mind of the sage attains to the perfect union of yin and yang; he penetrates the wondrous destinies of the myriad beings. Therefore the sage can be one with the changes and in harmony with the transformations. He will find everything all right wherever he may go. He embraces the myriad beings, and none ever deviates from its perfect natural state" (1.29b).

With this quality of a pure mind, the sage occupies a position of complete calm in the midst of a world of dualistic thinking. Desires and emotions revolve around him like an ever-turning wheel: "Taking right and wrong as a circle, the sage establishes himself in its middle. Thus he gets rid of all rights and wrongs. From such a position, he is free to respond to right and wrong, and this responding will be just as endless as the ever-ongoing circle itself" (2.29a). In taking up this position in the center of things, the sage sees his aloneness. He is utterly without opposite, whole in nature and himself; he stands beside heaven and earth and is at one with all beings.

In his outside actions, the sage responds perfectly to any situation in life. His movements are like natural processes; his actions appear spontaneous, yet are in fact inevitable. Free from self, free from merit, free from fame (*Zhuangzi* 2/1/22), the sage leaves no traces. He does not change anything in the world, nor does he become an example for others. "A good traveler leaves no track or trace," as the *Daode jing* has it (chap. 27).

According to Guo Xiang, the sage appears to others as a meek and withdrawing person, who rests in perfect tranquility of mind no matter what he does. He accepts everything he encounters as yet another manifestation of universal change, and never gets excited. He keeps out of danger and remains free from harm, because he is pure in his actions, not because he possesses any magical powers. The *Zhuangzi* says, "A true person enters the water and does not get wet; he enters the fire and does not get burned" (15/6/5). Guo Xiang interprets, "A true person naturally walks on dry land without, however, purposely avoiding water. He naturally is far away from fire, but does not intentionally run away from it. He might not feel heat as heat, yet he would never run toward a fire . . . or plunge into water, or endanger his life in any other way" (7.6ab). Yet, the sage is not afraid of danger either, since fear is an ego-based emotion he has completely left behind. In real danger, Guo Xiang says, the sage will still emerge uninjured, because no harm can be inflicted on anyone without fear.

All these questions are academic, though, as the sage always encounters useful and propitious situations. "He will always step into good fortune" (19.14b–15a) and will never be hit by calamities. This is not only because the sage has given up all notion of "calamity," but also because he is one with universal principle, from which no wrong can ever come.

On a wider social level, if everyone attains the perfect forgetfulness and realizes sageliness, all contention and disorder in the world cease. Everyone fulfills his or her share in the cosmos and lives in complete harmony along with universal principle. The ideal society without strife or friction is born, the Tao is realized on earth, and Great Peace rules.

Guo Xiang's Development of the *Zhuangzi*

Guo Xiang's ideas and Zhuangzi's philosophy have certain basic assumptions in common.

1. All life is change; the world is in a state of constant flux.
2. Human beings are part of this flowing and ever-changing existence.
3. They can do nothing about it, yet they worry and establish intellectual categories to deal with it.
4. All categories are artificial and place a distance between people and their lives.

5. Human beings must free themselves from these categories and return to a natural accordance with life.
6. Freedom is won by abolishing conscious knowledge.
7. Complete freedom of mind means going beyond all categories. This is sageliness.

These ideas can be said to represent the gist of early Chinese mysticism in general. Yet even between the *Zhuangzi* and Guo Xiang, there are interpretive differences. On the whole, Guo Xiang is more rigorous and systematic. Where the *Zhuangzi* just states things in either philosophical or metaphorical discourse, Guo Xiang defines his terms and limits the ideas in a coherent system.

A case in point is the notion that people are part of natural evolution, that life and death are one whole. The *Zhuangzi* just states this fact and illustrates it with the story about the four masters facing death (chap. 6). The four masters have realized that life and death belong to the same flow of existence and face illness and death with calmness and a detached curiosity. Who knows what will become of them next? Maybe one part of the body will become a chicken and another a crossbow pellet. All this is part of the natural transformation of things. Not only is it useless to have feelings about it, but it would also be most ungrateful to demand a special kind of existence other than what one has.

Where the *Zhuangzi* remains vague about the exact relation of people to the Tao, Guo Xiang defines the ties that bind people to the universe in terms of inner nature and fate. He supports this definition by a cosmology that assumes an organization within the process of never-ceasing change. The system of "share" and "principle" is conspicuously absent from the *Zhuangzi*. It goes back to the *Xunzi* and therefore belongs to the ideal of a strictly structured society, a hierarchical organization more typical of Confucian thought than of Laozi or Zhuangzi.

Similarly the term *xing*, "inner nature," hardly occurs in the "Inner Chapters" of the *Zhuangzi*. When they refer to the essential nature of human beings, they use terms instead like *qing*, "inner essence" or "feeling." Inner nature as the "innermost characteristics of life" (30/12/39) is more typical of the Primitivist and the Syncretist outlook.

"Fate" (*ming*) in the *Zhuangzi* causes all the concrete conditions of life. Not influenced by human wishes, they cannot be changed by human interference. Thus Zhuangzi advises: "To understand what you can do nothing about and to be content with it as with fate—this is the perfection of virtue" (10/4/43). Guo Xiang raises this to a cosmological level by connecting fate with principle. He thereby supplies a profundity of meaning quite absent in the *Zhuangzi*.

Guo Xiang closely follows the *Zhuangzi* in the contention that intellectual categories are the main reason why people are not happy and at one with the Tao. Yet he does not agree that all words and ideas are ultimately separate from truth. For Guo Xiang, words and ideas are part of the cosmos just as everything else. They exist, so they have a right to be. Zhuangzi leaves the position of words and ideas open, but recommends the dissolution of self-consciousness into chaos. Guo Xiang demands that people must stop being trapped by words and ideas. They must take them for what they really are and never attach feelings to them.

Guo Xiang thus proposes a well-structured reorganization of consciousness, while the *Zhuangzi* only indicates possibilities by presenting various models. One of these models, the process of oblivion and the "fasting of the mind" (9/4/26), is described as a natural occurrence stimulated by reflection on one's personal situation. It begins with the intellectual realization that it is impossible to know whether one knows, that there is no solid, definite "I" to rely on. Saying that much, Zhuangzi becomes vaguer, using various literary devices, such as metaphorical stories, fables, and fictional dialogues, to illustrate his point. Guo Xiang, on the other hand, develops a comprehensive cosmological and psychological system, causing—one might imagine—Zhuangzi to criticize him: "He really seems to know a whole lot about the mind and the universe. How does he know that he knows? How can he claim that unknowing is better than knowing?"

The process of losing one's conscious ego-identity in favor of oneness with the Tao according to the more radical passages in the *Zhuangzi* leads to the utter erasure of all that exists from one's consciousness. In Guo Xiang, on the other hand, it leads to a freedom from specific ego-centered attitudes and feelings toward things, not to the general loss of perception. In both cases, freedom is won by abolishing conscious knowledge—of all and everything in the *Zhuangzi*, of one's personal prejudices in Guo Xiang.

This freedom, according to Guo Xiang, enables one to go along with one's inner nature and fate. One identifies with cosmic principle and loses oneself as a personal entity. This is the fulfillment of humanity, "spontaneous realization," the state of perfect accordance. In the *Zhuangzi*, realization is less distinctly defined, yet goes farther. It is total freedom, complete nondependence. The huge Peng bird and the little quail in the first chapter, for example, are each in full accordance with their natural being—Guo Xiang's state of spontaneous realization. But Zhuangzi then contrasts them with Liezi who, though already able to come and go with the wind, has not yet attained full realization. He says, "Had he only mounted the truth of heaven and earth, ridden the changes of the six energies and thus wandered through the boundless, then what would he have had to depend on?" (2/1/21).

Zhuangzi thus reaches for a mastery over the cosmos, for oneness with the creative forces behind the manifest world. Guo Xiang limits his ideal to a perfect going-along. Zhuangzi transcends, Guo Xiang prefers complete immanence. Similarly, "free and easy wandering" is, for Guo Xiang, not freedom without restraint. Rather, he identifies it with "spontaneous realization," the perfection of one's nature in the fulfillment of one's duty to society. Guo Xiang, therefore, postulates that freedom is found by doing fully what one has to do. The *Zhuangzi*, to the contrary, demands boundlessness and independence. Society is a positive structure and an integral part of the Tao for Guo Xiang; in the *Zhuangzi*, it is an ugly necessity. The sage in Guo Xiang always does his duty and "when the world has the Tao he joins in the chorus with other people" (30/12/31). The true person in the *Zhuangzi* leaves the world behind.

Already at this early stage, the two extreme poles of early Chinese mysticism thus become obvious: the escapist versus the integratist. On the one hand, there is the ideal of getting away from everything to a freedom of roaming beyond the clouds. On the other, there is the dream of contributing to a better and more highly integrated, purer, and more Tao-realizing society. This is also evident in the tension between immortality as an ecstatic existence in heaven and long life as a purified, harmonized state of body and mind while on earth. Guo Xiang stands on the earthly and integratist side of things; his ideal is to be in the world while steadily communicating with heaven above and the Tao within. He develops the vagueness and openness of the *Zhuangzi* into a more organized, more practical system, just as Heshang gong interpreted the *Daode jing* to integrate a medical worldview and practices. In both cases, the ancient philosophers have been made more accessible to religious practitioners; they were transformed from highly theoretical documents to living inspirations.

CHAPTER FOUR

The Immortalization of
Philosophical Taoism

SHAMANISM AND IMMORTALITY

In a different line of development, the philosophy of Laozi and Zhuangzi gradually merged with shamanism and the belief in immortality. Shamanism is a complex religious phenomenon that has first been described by nineteenth-century anthropologists in the context of Central Asian and Siberian tribes. The word "shaman" itself is of Tungus origin.

Shamanism refers to a form of tribal religion in which the central figure is a person—usually male in Central Asia, and female in Korea and Japan—who has close contact with the sacred. The sacred appears in the gods of heaven, earth, and nature, in the ancestors of the tribe, or in a variety of spirits, animal or otherwise, who populate the universe. Shamans are experts in certain techniques of ecstasy that allow them to travel freely to the otherworld. They enter the ecstatic states with the help of music and dance, or less frequently through taking psychedelic drugs or alcoholic beverages. The shamans' travels usually have one of four distinct purposes. They may go to present the sacrifices of the community to the highest god or because they wish to find out the cause of and possible cure for an illness. They may also serve as psychopomps and guide the soul of someone recently deceased to the realm of the dead. Or they enter the higher spheres in order to learn the secrets of the universe.

Shamans usually have spirit assistants, who appear in human form of the opposite sex, as animals, birds of prey, or powerful beasts (Sternberg 1925). Traditionally shamans are selected because of their specific constitution and ecstatic abilities, which are first manifested in extraordinary behavior or sickness. Shamans undergo initiation on two levels: a supernatural initiation in dreams and visions of the otherworld, in which they often experience the complete dissolution and reconstitution of themselves; and a human initiation through instruction in the lore and legends of the community, which enable them to find the unknown lands beyond and identify their inhabitants properly.[1]

The earliest evidence for shamanism in ancient China appears on the oracle bones that Shang rulers used in communicating with their ancestors. They inquired to divine the outcome of various planned activities or to find methods for healing diseases. A diviner on behalf of the king would heat the bottom of carefully prepared grooves and hollows in the scapulae of cattle or the plastral shells of turtles. The resulting cracks were then interpreted by a prognosticator, often the king himself. He would decide whether the judgment of the higher powers was favorable or not.

According to Chang Kuang-chih, the actual practice of divination possibly included direct mental or verbal contact with the otherworld. Like shamans, the diviner or the king himself seems to have visited the gods and ancestors in the realm above. "Music and dance were apparently part of the ceremony. Alcoholic drinks were possibly involved" (Chang 1983, 55).[2]

In addition, the animal designs on numerous bronze vessels suggest representations of the animal spirit-helpers who assisted the shamans in their heavenly excursions. A passage from the *Zuozhuan* (Mr. Zuo's Commentary) makes this relatively clear. As Chang paraphrases it,

> the Hsia cast the bronze tripods and put the images of the *wu* [animals] on them so that living people would realize which animals were helping people to cross from earth to heaven and which animals were unhelpful and even harmful. . . . among animals are some which are capable of helping the shamans and the shamanesses in their task of communicating between heaven and earth, and the images of these animals were cast on ancient bronze ritual vessels.
>
> (1983, 64)

Shamanism was crucial to politics in ancient China. All wisdom and knowledge was believed to lie with heaven, so proper communication with the otherworld was an essential base of political power. During the Shang, the king himself was the head shaman, assisted by numerous religious figures, some of whom could be more properly called "shamans" than others (Chang 1983, 45f). These assistants in due course became specialists of the otherworld in their own right. They were called *xi* if male, and—more commonly—*wu* if female. Arthur Waley describes them as follows:

> In ancient China intermediaries used in the cult of Spirits were called *wu*. They figure in old texts as experts in exorcism, prophecy, fortune-telling, rain-making, and interpretation of dreams. Some *wu* danced, and they are sometimes defined as people who danced in order to bring down Spirits . . . They were also magic healers and in later times at any rate one of their methods of doctoring was to go, as Siberian shamans do, to the underworld and find out how the Power of Death can be propitiated. Indeed the

functions of the Chinese *wu* were so like those of Siberian and Tungus shamans that it is convenient . . . to use shaman as a translation of *wu*.

(Waley 1955, 9)

Shamanism in the Chuci

One of the clearest textual documents regarding shamanism in ancient China is the *Chuci* (Songs of the South; Hawkes 1959). Even in this early text, two major forms are evident: shamans receive visits from the gods above; and shamans go on heavenly journeys to meet with divinities. These forms continued later in the form of poetry, incantations, and descriptions of far-off lands.

First of all, there is the technique by which the shaman induces the gods to descend and make themselves known to people. Frequently such encounters between a supernatural agent and a human being lead to a sexual relationship. They usually result in the shaman being left behind, full of unhappy longing for the deity.

A good example of this type of shamanistic encounter is found in the "Nine Songs" section of the *Chuci*. Here the Lord Within the Clouds is enticed to descend from his residence by a shamaness, purified by baths and heavily doused with fragrance. She dances for him, as he hovers above her, bright and majestic, with dragons as his steeds. He does not stay very long, though. Soon he is off again, whirling away into the clouds. The lady is inconsolable; sadness fills her heart (Hawkes 1959, 37). While the text does not describe the actual encounter in great detail, it confirms the basic pattern. Induced by the proper prayers and purifications, the god descends. He is willing to communicate with the shamaness, but soon ascends again to his lofty realm. She remains behind and sighs with longing.[3]

In the other form of interaction, the movement is reversed. Mortals actively seek out the divine. They pursue a union with the god or goddess on celestial ground and thereby transform into godlike figures themselves. This form in turn has two major subcategories: the temporary and the permanent. That is to say, when a human being, shaman or otherwise, sets out for an excursion to the otherworld, he or she may or may not return to this world. Seekers may attain the otherworldly state for good, or they may use their visit to bring knowledge and information back to earth.

When temporary, an otherworldly excursion results in a changed perspective regarding human life. After the return from the splendor and ease of heaven the practitioner sees all mundane existence as drab and dull. Like the shaman who was blessed by a divine visit, he or she remains full of unhappy longing, looking forward only to the next outing. When permanent, there is complete union with the sacred.

This results in a permanent personality change that irreversibly turns the human into a cosmic being, an immortal.

The *Chuci* contains examples for both these types of otherworldly excursion. Seekers commonly begin with a strong wish to leave this world, because they are dissatisfied with the political situation and their own professional standing. The "Nine Declarations" is a good example of the underlying feeling. Here a minister complains that he served his lord with complete devotion and yet was cast aside like an unwanted slipper. He has only one wish left—to get away from it all as fast and as far as possible. So he rides up high into the sky, seeking out gods and immortals, wishing to stay away, yet bound to return in the end (Hawkes 1959, 61–63).

The seeker's fundamental motivation is to escape from unhappiness. There is no powerful urge to unite with the divine and become one with the universe. Egoistically motivated, such seekers are bound to remain within the limited confines of their ego. They can only find temporary respite from their sorrows. This escapist spirit has given rise to much poetry in later generations. Ecstatic poets continued to search for a perfection that tended to elude them; the heavenly bliss they describe in their works was temporary and followed by a return to worldly sorrows. At the same time, the poets made important contributions to Chinese religion, not only with their metaphors and imagery, but also with their interpretations of otherworldly states.[4]

A good example from the *Chuci* for the permanent attainment of a heavenly state is the "Yuanyou" (Far-off Journey), discussed below. Here the seeker succeeds in taking up residence in the otherworld after traversing the known universe. He merges with the emptiness of the Tao and becomes an immortal.

Longevity and Immortality

The character for *xian*, "immortal" or "transcendent," consists of the graphs for "man" and for "mountain." Another variant appears in the *Shijing* (Book of Songs) meaning "to dance with flying sleeves." The *Shuowen* defines this as "living long and vanishing in flight" (8A.38b). The commentary to the *Shuowen* further details that the "man-and-mountain" variant means "to reach old age and not die," while the "dance-with-flying-sleeves" character signifies "to move away and enter the mountains." The obvious basic implication of the term *xian* is therefore twofold. It connotes, first, the idea of a takeoff, a separation from normal life, be it in an ecstatic dance or by going into the mountains; and, second, the notion of longevity and the complete avoidance of death.

The belief in immortality can be traced back to two phenomena originally not only unrelated but even contradictory: a strong wish for long life and an ascetic pursuit of the otherworld and altered states of consciousness (see Yü 1964). As early as the Western Zhou dynasty one finds the wish for longevity and a ripe old age in inscriptions and texts. Throughout Chinese history up to the present day, early death has been regarded as one of the greatest disasters possible. To live out one's heaven-given life span in peace and without violating the body given by one's parents is the foremost ideal and duty of every Chinese. Beyond that, permanence was envisioned by way of descendants who continued the ancestral sacrifices and thereby the identity of the lineage and clan—more encompassing and more important than the individual. Also, a way to permanence, already mentioned in the *Zuozhuan* in a discussion of the phrase "die but not decay," was to become solidly established in the memory of later generations by words or deeds (*Zuozhuan*, Xiang 24; see Erkes 1953).

Ascetic pursuits of altered states are not well documented in pre-Han materials. The *Zhuangzi* affords some glimpses of trance states. Master Ziqi of South Wall, for instance, "sat leaning on an arm rest. He was staring up in the sky and breathing—empty and distant, as if he had lost his other" (chap. 2). Also, there is the classic description of "sitting in oblivion." The seeker destroys all notion of physical and psychological identity and becomes fully one with the Tao (chap. 6). In addition, the *Zhuangzi* mentions physical practices, such as "bear amblings and bird stretchings" (chap. 15), allegedly good for long life and higher visions.

In the Han, the *fangshi* engaged in otherworldly pursuits. They experimented with diets, drugs, alchemy, physical practices, and certainly also mental states (see Ngo 1976; DeWoskin 1983). The ancient state of Qi, modern Shandong, was well known for its magicians and ascetics. Its famous *fangshi* presented their arts to the imperial court, making them known in the higher circles of society.

At this time, the belief in a concrete land of the immortals first arose. It was located to the magic island of Penglai in the Eastern Sea or alternatively to the paradise of Mount Kunlun in the Western Mountains. This world of the immortals is a realm outside of and beyond the known world, beyond even the four seas that form its borders. It is usually described as a mountain surrounded by water. One finds palaces there, towers, and courts, made of glittering and nondecaying materials such as gold and jade. What is rare in this world is common there. Trees grow fruits that ripen only once in three thousand mundane years; birds with golden feathers nest in them. The lakes are made up of sweet dew or wine; there are no storms or natural disasters. Like the Tao, the land of the immortals cannot be understood by human faculties. It is beyond words and thought. None of our categories of time and space apply there. The residents of the land live forever and can appear at will anywhere in only an instant. They are here and at the same time someplace else; they can change their shape at will, fly in the air or dive into the water, in utter disregard of space and time.

According to beliefs current at the time, immortal materials could transfer immortal status to a human being when ingested. The First Emperor of the Qin (221–210 B.C.E.) and Emperor Wu of the Han (140–87 B.C.E.) sent out several expeditions to the Eastern Sea to obtain the elixir of life (*Shiji* 28; Watson 1968a). The shining example for these rulers was the Yellow Emperor, who supposedly ascended into heaven in broad daylight taking his family and household with him. He lost his slippers in the course of ascent. They were buried with great ceremony and worshiped as sacred objects.[5]

The major motif that connects both shamanism and immortality is the journey (see Hawkes 1974, 58). They are equally concerned with the way that leads out of the common world and into the realm of the sacred, into heaven or the land of the immortals—either temporarily or forever. The idea of travel, moreover, relates easily to the concept of "free and easy wandering" in the *Zhuangzi*. Mostly described as a state of ecstatic freedom, "free and easy wandering" is also frequently illustrated by metaphors of flight, of physical travel, of roaming beyond the Four Seas. Zhuangzi himself, for example, is said to be stomping through the underworld or leaping up into the heavens. He is beyond all such categories as north or south; he "dissolves himself in the four directions and drowns himself in the unfathomable" (chap. 17; Watson 1968, 187).

Upon closer inspection, two main types of journeys emerge: horizontal and vertical. There are journeys through the earth, to strange lands and places; and there are journeys through the air, to heaven and the paradises.

Journeys through Earth and Heaven

Traditional Chinese cosmology envisioned the earth as consisting of a central land mass surrounded by water on all sides and covered by the dome of the sky. The central land area was patterned in concentric squares, and the sky or heaven above was built of increasing layers or strata. Both were arranged in accordance with the number nine, the number of perfect yang and highest completeness.

The *Shujing* (Book of Documents) records the earliest division of the land into nine continents or provinces in its chapter on the "Labors of

Yu." The sage king Yu labored nine years to control the flood. At that time he traversed the known world, gave it structure, and named it.[6] The system was duly expanded and became a standard part of Chinese cosmology through the work of Zou Yan (ca. 305–240 B.C.E.). None of his writings survive. According to the *Shiji*, Zou Yan said that China made up only the eighty-first part of the world. But since it was located in the center of the nine-times-nine lands, it was the world's most pure and spiritual region. According to Zou Yan, each of the nine continents was surrounded by an ocean, preventing people and animals from crossing over. Around all nine of them there was a great universal, which connected the known world with heaven (Chan 1964, 247).

Both the nine provinces and the nine continents were arranged in a square of three-times-three, a magic pattern later associated with the *Luoshu*, the "Writ of the Luo River" (Major 1984, 146). Surrounding them on all four sides were the Four Seas, named after the four cardinal directions. These were infinite and bounded only by heaven, the round concentric dome over and above the solid land. Heaven and earth merged at the horizon of the seas.

In the center of the universe, different traditions located different sacred poles. The most popular were Mount Kunlun at the center of the world, Mount Duguang at the equator, and the North Pole in the middle of the sky (Major 1984, 136). Even within the middle country, the law of centrality ruled. The closer an area was to the central axis, the more powerful and auspicious it was. Other areas, arranged concentrically around it, were less fertile and fortunate.

The "Labors of Yu," for example, locates the royal domain in the center, followed by the lands of the tributary feudal princes and lords. Outside of this was the "zone of pacification," still subject to a certain impact of Chinese culture. Then followed the area of allied barbarians, and finally the zone of cultureless savagery (Legge 1969, 145–49; Major 1984, 142).[7] According to the *Huainanzi*, the basic grid of nine provinces was surrounded by three layers of outside areas: the distant regions, the outlying regions, and the *terrae ultimae*. These were imagined as additional squares projecting from the central body in the eight directions (Major 1984, 144).

A similar structure applies to the layers or levels of heaven. According to ancient mythology, as summarized by Henri Maspero (1924), there are nine levels of heaven, each separated from the next by a gateway guarded by tigers and other beasts. Altogether eight gateways—in the eight directions—connect heaven and earth. Other gates are found at the poles—a Cold Gate at the North Pole and a Warm Gate at the South Pole. In the golden age of antiquity, no obstacles kept the inhabitants of heaven and earth from intermingling freely. In later days, one had to rely on intermediaries to establish contact.

The highest level of heaven is called Ziwei gong (Palace of Purple Tenuity), commonly located to the constellation Beidou (Northern Dipper; Ursa Major). Here the Emperor of Heaven resides. The administration of heaven functions like that on earth. Various deities are responsible for managing wind, rain, clouds, stars, sun, moon, mountains, seas, and so on. The animals most common in heaven are the dragon, the phoenix, and the unicorn. They appear on earth only in times of extreme bounty, more often in the old days than in later times. Dragons in particular serve for divine transportation, as mounts or yoked to cloudy carriages. Heaven is a bright and cheerful place. Gods and goddesses are dressed in rainbow colors; the palaces sparkle with the gleam of gems; clouds are radiant with sunlight. In many ways the higher levels of heaven are very similar to the paradises of the immortals, and it is not surprising that immortals are found there as well—just as gods are occasionally located on Kunlun.

Strangers in the Wilderness

On the earth, the center was the best place to be. The farther one moved from the fertile, friendly middle country, the more hostile, uninhabited, and strange the lands became.[8] Traversing the lands, the traveler eventually arrived at the shore of the encircling seas. Continuing his journey beyond them, he would certainly reach heaven. In ancient Chinese accounts of journeys around the earth, however, heaven is not the primary goal. There were more direct ways of ascent by flight with the help of clouds and dragons. There was no need to go to the ends of the world first.

Instead, travels to distant lands promised rare gems and unworldly knowledge. The fringe lands abounded in obscure jewels and rare substances and they held a wisdom unadulterated by culture and consciousness. Maxime Kaltenmark even suggests that ancient ascetics and *fangshi* received some of their wondrous drugs and secret lore from aborigines living in the distant corners of the land (Kaltenmark 1953, 13).

At the same time, travel was highly relevant to religion and politics. In order to demonstrate his rulership, the king made regular circuits through the country. Mapping the world meant owning it; receiving rare objects as tribute from strange lands meant controlling them.

For the shaman, exact knowledge of the world was necessary to find his way around the regions beyond. The mystic, in imitation of these journeys, molded his own universe, physically and psychologically, by traversing distant areas. Later Taoist ritual followed the steps of the great Yu, paradigm for the possessive circuit of the earth.

The *Zhuangzi* clearly describes the journeys to the far ends of the world as an enterprise in spiritual freedom. Here a seeker wanders off to distant realms, where he meets a mysterious stranger who is able, but not usually willing, to teach him. The stranger is the archetype of the true wanderer in the beyond; he has attained perfection and as an immortal has joined the creative forces of the universe. One example is the story of Tian Gen, a seeker who goes off to the far north. There he meets a nameless man, whom he asks about ruling the world. The stranger first scorns his ignorance. He describes how he hobnobs with the creative energies of the world, how he rides beyond the six directions. When Tian Gen repeats his question, the stranger grudgingly advises him to make his mind simple and join his spirit with the vastness of the Tao. Only by following along with beings in perfect non-action can the world be governed (chap. 7; Watson 1968, 93–94).

The story effectively contrasts the helpless seeker for mundane wisdom with the assured and powerful master of the beyond. The fringe lands are more likely to be inhabited by immortals from the otherworld and by seekers who have attained the ability to go anywhere they please. The strangers in the wilderness may venture into the lands of no-country, they may go to not-even-anything, they may dissolve in the emptiness of the sacred. The seeker, once he has found his quarry, will integrate his new level of knowledge into his life on earth. He acts in true non-action; this greatly benefits the world.

The *Zhuangzi* tells two other stories of mystical journeys over land: "Knowledge Wandered North" and "The Yellow Emperor Visits the Great Clod" (chap. 24). Both ridicule the conventional knowledge of the Confucian sages. Knowledge itself is far from the truth, clear only to Do-Nothing-Say-Nothing and Wild-and-Witless. These two, residing in the dark realm of the Far North, on the banks of the Black Waters and the Knoll of Hidden Heights, do not have language. They cannot tell the truth to Knowledge. They know but do not speak (chap. 22). In the same vein, the Yellow Emperor sets out to ask the Great Clod about government. He takes along an entourage of six renowned sages. But, "by the time they reached the Xiangcheng wilderness, the seven sages had lost their way and there was nobody to ask for directions." A small, insignificant cowherd sets them right in the end. He is even able to point out that governing the empire is quite like herding horses: "Get rid of whatever is harmful to horses" (chap. 24).

Lu Ao and the Immortal

Another famous journey to the fringes of the world that results in a spiritual uplift is recorded in the *Huainanzi*. A collation of Taoist-oriented philosophical literature of the second century B.C.E., this work was concerned with the creation of a broad synthesis of Lao-Zhuang thought and contemporary cosmology.[9]

In a section that serves as an explanation of the *Zhuangzi* statement, "Little understanding cannot reach to great understanding" (1/1/10), the *Huainanzi* recounts the adventures of Lu Ao, a seeker of perfection who traversed the world. When he wandered to the Northern Sea and entered the Darktower Range, he met an immortal. "His eyes were deeply sunk, his hair was dark, he had a long neck and shoulders drooping like those of a bird. His forehead was broad, his chin small. He was dancing about and welcoming the winds of the various directions" (*Huainanzi* 12).

When the immortal noticed Lu Ao, he fled. Lu Ao went to look at him and found him curled up in a tortoise shell, eating crabs and oysters. Lu Ao introduced himself:

"I am Lu Ao. I have turned my back on the common folk and left all striving groups behind. I went away from all in order to find out what lies beyond the Six Harmonies. Ever since my young days I have been extremely fond of traveling, a trait which did not change with growing older. I wandered in the four directions, only the Far North I have not seen. Now I finally meet you here, could I hope you will be friends with me?"

Hearing this, the immortal smiled wanly. He said:

"Ah, you are from the Middle Country, are you not? You made quite a distance getting here! Here it is like shining together with the sun and the moon, like being among the ranks of the stars. It is the place where yin and yang begin to move, where the four seasons originate. It can only be described as the nameless; it is most mysterious and obscure."

Lu Ao marveled at these words. Eager to learn more, he continued to listen. The immortal had started out as an inspired traveler like Lu Ao. He had gone to the far ends of the world, south, west, east, and north, where he experienced the purity of the Tao, the end of all sensual perception. As he told Lu Ao,

"Below these places there is no earth; above them there is no heaven. One listens but does not hear; one watches but does not see. Farther afield it seems like the edge of the water: all is glossy and gloomy. On passing even beyond that, one can travel a thousand, even ten thousand miles in an instant. However, that far even I have not yet gone.

"Now, you have come here for the first time and yet you are already talking about reaching the far ends and finding out all about them. How can they not be far to reach, even from here? But since you are here now anyway, I will share the unknowable with you. Then I will wait for you above the Nine Heavens—because I cannot remain here much longer."

(*Huainanzi* 12)

Again the story effectively contrasts conventional knowledge with the vastness of the immortal mind that has reached complete oneness with the Tao. Unlike earlier texts, the *Huainanzi* describes the stranger as a classic immortal. He is a weird, birdlike creature who dances about. Both motifs, the likeness to birds and the dancing, are important in early immortality beliefs.[10] Both have shamanistic connotations and are integrated in the physical immortality practices of later times. Being like birds represents the ability to fly, proper to shamans as well as to immortals. They rise equally up into the sky and enter the far ends of the world. Also, even the earliest descriptions describe dancing as a means to dissolve obstructions and stagnation of vital energy. Movements of the body ensure the healthy circulation of the *qi*, not only within human beings but also in the entire universe. Here a congestion of *qi* appears as a drought: shamans' dances bring the life-giving rain (Despeux 1989, 238).

Shamans and immortals were masters over water and fire, they could control the elements and resided near the beginning of things. Lu Ao hears this firsthand. The immortal is where "yin and yang begin and the four seasons originate." Control is best exercised where things begin. Within the cosmology of the five agents, the latent state of nonexistence is associated with the North. The North is the direction of darkness, of winter, of what the philosophers call nonbeing. Here lies the highest potential of the world; here perfection and realization take place; here the ordinary world is fully overcome. A person venturing to the extreme North becomes an equal of the forces of the universe; he or she is "shining together with the sun and the moon" and attains powers usually reserved for celestials. Immortal and without bounds, such a person can traverse thousands of miles in an instant, see to the lands' ends, and recognize cosmological landmarks. On friendly footing with the creatures and spirits in residence there, the immortal ultimately ascends into the heavens and beyond. There he or she reposes in heavenly splendor, descending on occasion to engage in immortal enterprises on earth.[11]

The tale about Lu Ao is a typical explanation of a philosophical issue through a concrete story. Such exegesis is also found in the *Hanfeizi* and in other sections of the *Huainanzi*. Literary illustration serves to join the vision of ecstatic freedom as formulated in the *Zhuangzi* with the concrete journey that leads away from the ordinary world and into the fringes. The seeker eventually reaches utter darkness, a land invisible and inaudible like the Tao—areas where one looks for things but cannot see them, and listens to sounds but cannot hear them (*Daode jing* 14, 35; see Fukunaga 1970, 110). Like in the paradises of the immortals, here magical powers and the impossible are the order of the day. Ordinary sense experience and the sorrows of humanity have been left far behind.

The Travels of King Mu of Zhou

Another journey famous in Chinese history, mythology, and literature is the travel of King Mu to the Western Queen Mother, first recorded in the *Mu Tianzi zhuan* (Biography of King Mu). This text was found in 281 C.E., in the grave of a King of Wei who had died in 296 B.C.E. Written on bamboo slips, the text constitutes one of the oldest literary works of the time. Not all its parts are of equal antiquity, but it can be roughly dated to the mid-Zhou period (Mathieu 1978, 101).

All six chapters of the text are devoted to the description of the king's travels, his campaigns and the circuits he made around his lands. The purpose of his extended visits to border areas was threefold: to meet barbarian princes and join them in an exchange of popular customs and culinary practices; to learn about the organization and structure of the known world; and to introduce new and possibly fruitful plants and animals to the home country and gather strange and wonderful objects, including fancy gems and powerful talismans. The latter found their way into the king's palace as royal treasures; they symbolized the reach of his influence and indicated his power as a ruler. Among those treasures were numerous things later regarded as talismans in Taoism: strange stones, jades, gems, jewels, silver, gold, and also charts, such as the *Hetu* (River Chart).[12]

The travels of King Mu became legendary in due course and were embellished with spiritual motifs. As such, they appear in the *Liezi*, a text lost during the Han and reconstituted in the second or third century (Graham 1961). The *Liezi* is similar to the *Huainanzi* in that it explicates theoretical ideas of the *Zhuangzi* in concrete stories. Chapter 3, entitled "King Mu of Zhou," deals with the idea that life is a dream and encourages readers to refrain from passing judgment. Instead, people should give equal weight to all experiences, however strange or commonplace they may be. This, as A. C. Graham has pointed out, is a concept indigenous to China. Dream and wakefulness are equal. There is "no implication that it is either possible or desirable to awake from the dream" (1960, 59). The Buddhist preference for finding the true reality and stripping away all illusion is alien to this thinking. "The dominant feeling is not that life is futile, but that it can assume the marvelous quality of magic and dreams" (Graham 1960, 60).

Journeys allow people to capture this magical quality of life, if only for a short time. With the help of a visiting magician, reminiscent of the Han dynasty *fangshi*, King Mu is temporarily transported out and away from everything.

> The magician rose upward, while King Mu held on to his sleeve. He did not stop until they were in the middle of the sky. Then they reached the magician's palace.
>
> It was built of gold and silver, ornamented with pearls and jades. It rose above the cold and the rain. One could not tell what supported it. From afar it looked like a congealed cloud. All the eye saw and the ear heard, the nose smelled and the tongue tasted, were things unknown in the human sphere.
>
> The King felt that he was enjoying the mighty music of innermost heaven. He thought he was in the City of Clarity or on the Purple Star—palaces of the gods. When he looked down, his own palaces and arbors were like rows of clods and heaps of brushwood.
>
> (*Liezi* 3)

King Mu's experience of the otherworld closely resembles what later Taoist adepts find in their ecstatic explorations. The heavens are open to the human traveler; life on earth seems shallow and insignificant; a new level of existence is reached. But not for long. Though the king is under the impression that he stayed in the magician's palace for twenty or thirty years, when he comes back to himself, "he was sitting in his own palace as before, his attendants waiting at his side. He looked in front of him: the wine had not yet cooled, the meat was still moist."[13] Asked for an explanation, the magician tells him that he was on a journey of the spirit.

In an effort to make the magical experience permanent, the king duly sets out for more travel experiences, this time bodily. In the course of these journeys he meets the Queen Mother of the West. Here the *Liezi* takes up the account of the *Mu tianzi zhuan*. Not yet a goddess and queen of the immortals, the Queen Mother of the West is described as the ruler of a foreign kingdom near the Chinese border with whom King Mu exchanges gifts and poems. Eventually the king returns home and, in the end, dies like any ordinary human being.

The concrete travels of the ancient king are first described semihistorically as the exploits of a monarch hungry for more power. Later they are integrated into a spiritual framework and the journey becomes the concrete expression of the mystical quest. Stimulated by a short sojourn in the wondrous heavens above, the king sets out. He reaches the distant land of the Queen Mother of the West, located at the far end of the known world. Yet in the end he has to return to the fate of all humanity.

The "Far-off Journey"

A truly permanent attainment of the heavenly realm is described in another early text. The "Yuanyou" (Far-off Journey) section of the *Chuci* describes the seeker's progress to immortality. The text begins with the original motivation for the quest: the protagonist finds himself saddened by the world's circumstances and wishes to escape. Initially unable to find either tranquility or freedom, he then practices the non-action advocated in the *Daode jing*. This gives him calm and inspiration; he envisions the true ones of old and admires the powers of the immortals. Again he falls back to his own mortal self. In comparison with these marvelous creatures, how could he ever enjoy his petty little life?

New hope awakens; not the Yellow Emperor but the immortals Wang Qiao and Chisongzi (Master Redpine) are now his ideal.[14] The protagonist becomes an ascetic, fasting and meditating after the fashion of the *fangshi*. Lightened in body and freed in mind, for the first time he experiences an ecstatic journey that takes him to the Far South. There he meets Wang Qiao in person and receives his instructions: he must practice more to reach the tranquility of emptiness and the complete concentration of spirit.

Taking this to heart, he can soon begin to journey in earnest. Traversing the entire world in a single day, he collects its finest gems and lives on its purest essences. His body increasingly dissolves; his spirit stretches toward higher realms. His solitary progress turns into a majestic procession. Accompanied by dragons and celestial beings, he triumphantly visits the gods-on-high. Higher and higher up the route takes him, to the very end of the world in the cold darkness of the North. Going beyond all, he dissolves in the beginning of all things.

> Below, lofty openness—there was no more earth;
> Above, empty vastness—there was no more heaven.
> I looked, but my vision blurred—nothing to be
>   seen,
> I listened, but my ears were numb—nothing to be
>   heard.
> Going beyond Non-action, I reached Clarity,
> And became a close neighbor of the Great
>   Beginning.

(lines 87–89)

These lines resemble the words that Lu Ao's immortal uses to describe the far end of the world. They go back to the famous passage in *Daode jing* 14, where the Tao is called invisible, inaudible, and subtle. The "Yuanyou" as a whole depicts the classical quest of the seeker for perfection: beginning with discontent, it leads through quietistic withdrawal to ecstatic excursions into the heavens (see Maspero 1981, 414).

The "Yuanyou" has exerted a strong influence on the later tradition. In terms of its position as a piece of literature, it belongs to poetry and is a precursor of the *fu* (rhapsody) literature of the Han. In literary origin, the "Yuanyou" imitates and continues the "Lisao" (Encountering Sorrow) section of the *Chuci* (Hawkes 1959, 211–34). The "Lisao" is older and was probably written by Qu Yuan, the most prominent author of the *Chuci*. The "Yuanyou," on the other hand, mentions immortals popular in the Han and is thus dated to this period.[15] Both poems describe a journey and have numerous expressions and metaphors in common. But where the "Lisao" is full of sadness and sorrow and affords its protagonist only a temporary respite from mundane worries, the "Yuanyou" reveals a lightness in its ultimately satisfied yearning for joy and celestial pleasures.

As the *Huainanzi* does not just collect stories and metaphors from earlier sources, so the "Yuanyou" does not merely copy or plagiarize the journey of the "Lisao." Fully based on Laozi and Zhuangzi thought, the *Huainanzi* interprets the *Daode jing* in terms of contemporary cosmology as well as through the rapidly developing sciences, such as astronomy, geography, and medicine. Similarly, the "Yuanyou" is closely patterned on the "Lisao" and yet turns it into something quite different. It develops the notion of departing from the ordinary and wandering in the unknown into a transcendent celestial excursion. It thereby interprets in a new and more radical manner the free and easy wandering of the *Zhuangzi*.

Both—the travels of Lu Ao and King Mu, who journeyed to the world's far end to discover the land of the immortals, and the ecstatic journey of the "Yuanyou," which describes an excursion into the heavens leading to complete dissolution in emptiness—are expressions of the mystical endeavor. They describe the ideal progress of the seeker from limited human surroundings to the very origin of things. "Here is where yin and yang begin and the four seasons originate," the immortal tells Lu Ao. "I became a close neighbor of the Great Beginning," rejoices the protagonist of the "Yuanyou." Also, both contain shamanistic metaphors and are firmly committed to the terminology of the *Daode jing* and the *Zhuangzi*. Journeys through earth and into the heavens thus symbolize and illustrate the transformation of a human into a cosmic being.

CHAPTER FIVE

Ecstatic Explorations of the Otherworld

THE IDEAL OF THE GREAT MAN

Transformative journeys later appeared in two kinds of texts: in the ecstatic lyrics of escapist poets during the third to the sixth centuries; and in the meditation instructions of Shangqing (Highest Clarity) Taoism, which arose first in the middle of the fourth century. Both kinds of documents are heavily indebted to the ideas and terminology of Laozi and Zhuangzi; both deal with ecstatic journeys to the otherworld; and both describe immortal freedom as their ultimate goal.

At the same time, they develop the pursuit of perfection further. They describe the ideal of complete transcendence, of a permanent residence in the otherworld after the fashion of the "Yuanyou." Yet they also go beyond this in that they formulate a vision of complete control over the world, of standing at the heart of all knowledge, of reaching the pinnacle and central axis of the universe. The journey here is undertaken not only to reach the beyond but to take the entire cosmos into the traveler's hands. Perfection in ecstatic poetry and Shangqing Taoism thus came to mean the realization of the ideal of the Great Man.

The ideal of the Great Man is part of traditional Chinese thought. The term "great man" (*daren*) occurs first in the *Yijing* under the first hexagram *qian*, indicating "Heaven."[1] It is found in the oracle of the fifth line, which reads,

> The dragon soars into heaven;
> It is auspicious to see the Great Man.

Among the six lines of the hexagram, the fifth symbolizes the ruler. The Great Man therefore refers to the head of state, the king or emperor of China. This notion is consistent with the role of the ruler as the Son of Heaven, who stands at the pinnacle of human society and provides an immediate link with the ancestors and gods of the country. The Great Man of the *Yijing* thus takes up the Shang-dynasty role of the king as the head shaman. The later "Wenyan" (Words of the Text) commentary explains the expression.

The Great Man is one who is in harmony with Heaven and Earth in all his attributes. He is one with the sun and the moon in his brightness. He joins the four seasons in his orderly proceedings. He is in accordance with the spiritlike operations of providence with all that is fortunate and calamitous. He may precede Heaven, and Heaven will not act in opposition to him. He may follow Heaven, but will act only as Heaven itself would at the time. If Heaven will not act in opposition to him, how much less will ordinary people?

In this passage the Great Man has realized the freedom of "free and easy wandering" while at the same time working with heaven, like the sage of the *Daode jing*. Like the dragon, a symbol of the ruler, he can soar up into empty space at will and enter into heaven.

In Confucian materials, on the other hand, the Great Man is opposed to the "small man." The expression denotes the sage, the paragon of virtue, as opposed to an ordinary person. The term occurs only once in the *Analects*, denoting a kind of person who is superior to the gentleman and on a par with the sages of old:

Confucius said: There are three things of which the gentleman stands in awe. He stands in awe of the ordinances of Heaven. He stands in awe of great men. He stands in awe of the words of sages.

The mean man does not know the ordinances of Heaven and consequently does not stand in awe of them. He is disrespectful to great men. He makes sport of the words of sages.

(16.8)

In the *Mencius*, the Great Man is characterized more clearly as a sage. He is a paragon of virtue who has attained perfection of himself in accordance with Heaven, who is perfect in the virtues of humanity. Mencius says, for example, that the Great Man will never perform "acts of propriety which are not really proper and acts of righteousness which are not really righteous" (4B.6). He is at one with nature and has "never lost the mind of a child" (4B.12), thus spontaneously doing and speaking what is right (4B.11). Beyond that the Great Man, like the sage, has an immediate impact on his surroundings: as he rectifies himself, all beings are rectified through him (7A.19).

The *Zhuangzi* characterizes the Great Man as the possessor of the state. As such, he cannot be a mere being, but must be greater and more powerful than all living things of the world. Not content to live merely with other beings, the Great Man then soars above and beyond the known; all alone he reaches the peak of realization. Nevertheless, the Great Man is still there for the world. Like the stranger in the wilderness he will answer questions and help human seekers on their way. He may grasp another's hand and take him on an excursion into the nothingness of no-beginning: "[The Great Man] passes freely in and out of the boundless; he is as ageless as the sun and the moon. His face and body merge with the Great One; like the Great One, he is without self" (28/11/65).

The Great Man represents the integration of ecstatic freedom and political order in the figure of the cosmic individual. He continues the ideal of the sage of the *Daode jing*, who was at the center of all life, the mediator among heaven, earth, and humanity, and also the ruler the world. The *Zhuangzi* connects this ideal with the freedom of the ecstatic journey and with the vision of an immortality "as ageless as the sun and the moon."

In another passage of the *Zhuangzi* that points toward later developments and may go back to a later member of the Zhuangzi school, the Great Man is described as a cosmic sage. He is one with the universe, free from all bondage, and yet sees all, knows all, and never dies (see Graham 1989, 204). He embraces heaven and earth but is without definite social connections. He neither holds office nor becomes famous in the world; like the Tao he is beyond the definitions of language (chap. 24).

Sima Xiangru's Daren fu

The first of a series of outstanding poems featuring the ideal of the Great Man is the *Daren fu* (Rhapsody of the Great Man) by Sima Xiangru (179–117 B.C.E.).[2] A native of Sichuan, Sima Xiangru became notorious for eloping with the daughter of a wealthy merchant. When her father cut them off, they opened a wine house, and the poet and aristocrat served behind the counter. Soon the father relented, happily, and Sima Xiangru went on to write his elaborate poems, which earned him a court appointment.

His *Daren fu* is among his few surviving works, and is an outstanding representative of Han dynasty *fu* literature.[3] He wrote the poem to eulogize the "Great Man" Emperor Wu in his aspirations to immortality. Already the *Shiji* is aware that a shift in the meaning of "immortal" has taken place. It says that what the emperor meant by these "ruler-type immortals" was quite different from all those contemporary practitioners of immortality who "make their residences in the mountains and swamps and look rather emaciated" (*Shiji* 117.3056).[4] Emperor Wu was famous for his ambition to attain immortality. He venerated the Yellow Emperor and reportedly once said: "Ah, if I only could become like the Yellow Emperor, I would leave my wife and children as easily as casting off an old slipper" (*Shiji* 28.1394).[5]

Heir to the *Yijing* as well as to Lao-Zhuang thought, the *Daren fu* also draws heavily on the "Yuanyou." In fact, the two are astonishingly similar in conception, structure, phrasing, even down to single expressions.[6] In both texts, the protagonist yearns for the transcendent reality of the spirit immortals and deplores the ordinary world of dust. In both poems, he has mastered the order of the world, and ecstatically soars up into the Great Void. The beginning of the *Daren fu* runs thus:

> In this world there is a Great Man
> Living in the middle continent.
> His abode extends over ten thousand miles,
> Yet never suffices him to sojourn even shortly.
>
> Grieved at the world's unpleasant state,
> He easily rises and soars away.
> He rides an immaculate rainbow streaming down,
> Mounts cloudy ether and floats upward.

This is patterned closely on the first lines of the "Yuanyou," just as the end of the *Daren fu* is almost identical with that of the earlier text.

> Below, lofty openness—there was no more earth;
> Above, empty vastness—there was no more heaven.
> He looked, but his vision blurred—nothing to be
>   seen,
> He listened, but his ears were numb—nothing to be
>   heard.
> Striding on emptiness and nonbeing, he ascends
>   even farther,
> Transcending all, he is without friends and alone
>   survives.
>
> > (*Shiji* 117.3062)

More than that, this ending reverts to the *Zhuangzi* in that it quotes Guangchengzi's famous words in his dialogue with the Yellow Emperor: "I will leave you now. I will enter the gate of the limitless and freely wander through the wilderness without bounds. I will join the radiance of the sun and the moon and become one with the eternity of heaven and earth. . . . All people exhaust themselves and die. I alone survive" (27/11/43).

Through these last words the Great Man of the poem is related to the Yellow Emperor whose example Emperor Wu wanted so badly to follow. With the allusion to the flight into heaven, however, the similarities of the "Yuanyou" and the *Daren fu* end. In the "Yuanyou," the protagonist pursues the cultivation of the Tao; he enters deep trance states and finds serenity and tranquility, spontaneous realization in non-action. Once on his journey, he is carried farther and farther out of this world. He continues to wander far and easy throughout the heavens, emulating the examples of ascetic—and perhaps emaciated—immortality-seekers. A conscientious student of the Tao, he learns the secrets of immortality, purifies himself and attains ultimate bliss in emptiness.

Unlike the hero of the "Yuanyou," the Great Man in Sima Xiangru's *Daren fu* is not a learner or a seeker. He is the emperor of an empire that spans the world, self-assured and strong, who knows that the world is his by rights. He does not practice longevity techniques in seclusion, nor is he plagued by despair and doubts. In full control over the universe and with a strong sense of rulership, he sets out to arrange things according to his pleasure. He equips a magnificent chariot, drawn by radiant dragon steeds. He freely summons stars and deities for his entourage, easily commanding all the powers that be. He embarks on a triumphant circuit throughout the universe, sure of his honored reception everywhere. Led by the five cosmic emperors, the imperial procession is followed by a host of spirits, gods, and immortals.

Inspecting the entire world in all directions, he eventually proceeds upward, always having gods and spirits do as he bids. Like the protagonist of the "Yuanyou," the Great Man of the *Daren fu* has the River God dance for him while celestial maidens play their zithers; but unlike the "Yuanyou" seeker, he exerts stern justice on the otherworldly personages if it so pleases him.

> At times when the sky turns gray and threatens
> darkness,
> He summons Pingyi, messenger of the gods,
> Makes him chastise the Lord of the Winds
> And punish the God of Rain.

(Shiji 117.3060)

No place is too far or too exalted for him to reach; nothing stops him from taking what is his by right. Eventually he reaches Kunlun and visits the Queen Mother of the West, emulating the travels of King Mu. Turning then toward the North, the direction of all origins, he samples the drug of immortality. Then he enters the Dark Pass and goes through the Cold Gate. His senses work no more; he vanishes from the world. Thus the Great Man finally spirals upward into emptiness and goes beyond all.

The Great Man of the *Daren fu* is first of all the ruler. He is one who knows all and has the moral right to power over the cosmos. Joining metaphors of the ancient pursuit of perfection in the cosmic figure of the Great Man, Sima Xiangru praises the attainments of a living emperor. The idealized Emperor Wu undertakes his exploits of the otherworld to gain complete power and control. Only when this is reached can he enter emptiness, the center of cosmic potentiality. In the "Yuanyou," the pursuit of seclusion and tranquility was still the basis of spiritual attainment. The *Daren fu*, on the other hand, sings of a powerful and triumphant tour of imperial inspection. The seeker is no longer a mere human being aspiring to perfection, but the Great Man, born to perfection, who realizes his full power over all in ultimate transcendence at the beginning of things.

Ruan Ji's Daren xiansheng zhuan

A later successor to Sima Xiangru's *Daren fu* is Ruan Ji's (210–263 C.E.) *Daren xiansheng zhuan* (Biography of Master Great Man). Born in a time of great political change and instability, Ruan Ji pursued an official career in the service of the Sima clan, the ruling family of the Jin dynasty. Repeatedly disappointed in his political ambitions, he turned away from official life and spent his time writing poetry, drinking, and making merry. He is well known as one of the so-called Seven Sages of the Bamboo Grove, a group of eccentrics and drugtakers who attempted to create a perfect and secure private society in the face of chaos and upheaval in the world at large.[7]

Ruan Ji's major work is his collection of poems entitled *Yonghuai shi* (Poems of Innermost Thoughts); but his work on the Great Man has been described as the "philosophical autobiography of the author" (Fukunaga 1970, 111; see Holzman 1976, 185). Here he contrasts a superhuman life with different ideal lifestyles of his time. Master Great Man is an eternal and universal being, beyond the rules and patterns of the world. He can be everywhere and move at the speed of lightning; he has true knowledge of all and power over the forces of nature. Encompassing the male and the female, he is yet free from egoistic yearnings or regrets and walks unrecognized among the common people.

Master Great Man meets three different people: a stout Confucian who expostulates on the merits of perfecting one's virtues and serving the state; a hermit who scorns all official involvement and sees only his solitude as noble; and a wood-gatherer who emphasizes the relativity and transience of all things and thus attains contentment with whatever he may be doing in any given moment.

Master Great Man, and through him the poet, rejects all three ideals of life. He denounces the Confucian view as rigid and limited, tied to narrow definitions of what is good and evil, virtuous and depraved.

He tells his challenger, "in antiquity, heaven was once below and the earth above. They kept turning over and were not yet stable. At that time, how could you not have lost your rules and models [based on heaven and earth]? How could you have found them preordained?" The Great Man finds the Confucian's views as narrow-minded and limited as those of "lice in a pair of trousers." He rejects the hermit's position as a form of self-deception. Although he claims to be entirely free from the values of the world, he is yet strongly tied to them. Ultimately an egoist, the hermit judges things by scorning what others do. He is neither calm nor divinely indifferent. The Great Man, to the contrary, never worries about his personal well-being and the judgment of others. He views the entire universe as his rightful domain. Making all things equal, he does not distinguish between right and wrong, nor does he evaluate things according to good and evil.

The wood-gatherer, finally, presents him with a vision of simplicity and contentment. Answering him, Master Great Man breaks into a song, which is closely patterned on Sima Xiangru's *Daren fu*. The song of the Great Man describes the only true life possible: the free and easy wandering and ultimate ascent into the heavens and beyond. It begins:

> Heaven and earth dissolve,
> The six harmonies open out,
> Stars and constellations tumble,
> Sun and moon fall down.

> I leap up and farther up,
> What should I cherish?
> My clothes are not seamed, but I am beautifully
>   dressed;
> My girdle has no pendants but is ornate naturally.

> Up and down I wander, fluttering about:
> Who could fathom my eternity?

In contrast to the *Daren fu*, the imperial nature of the Great Man has been privatized by Ruan Ji. It imitates the earlier poem yet also develops the ideal. Ornaments and beauty come naturally and do not have to be attached from without. The Great Man is free within, not outwardly recognizable as the emperor. No one will know where he stays—he is no longer the ruler, at the center of affairs, but one who has successfully escaped from the vicissitudes of the world, official and otherwise. He is chief, but in his heart and away from the world.

This escapist attitude has been described as typical for the politically unstable and insecure time in which Ruan Ji was writing (Balasz 1948, 1964). His friends and fellow poets of the time induced ecstatic experiences through music and drugs, especially the notorious Han-shi san, or "Cold Food Powder" (see Wagner 1983). They wrote poetry of freedom and escape, applying the *Zhuangzi* concept of free and easy wandering in the sense of getting away from it all. In their own way they continued the mystical tradition in their desperate search for a better world within.[8]

In many ways, though continuing the *Daren fu*, Ruan Ji's work thus goes back to the *Yuanyou*, which also begins with the wish to escape from sorrow and unhappiness. As the Great Man's song has it,

> Then I leave and float into the distance,
> Set up a carriage of clouds and spread a canopy of
>   *qi*.
> I soar about without a steady perch
> Beyond even the expanses without bounds.
>
> I raise a comet as my banner
> And strike the resonance of thunder.
> I open up the pillar of heaven and set my carriage
> To amble through the open richness of the Nine
>   Wilds.
>
> I sit in the Central Continent and look back once,
> Gaze to the majestic mountains and turn around.

The text takes up earlier images and phrases, yet changes their implications. Where a poor immortality-seeker strove for the freedom of the otherworld and the rightful ruler of the world exercised his complete freedom over all, now an unhappy civilian makes a lucky escape. The political and official side of things is radically negated; Ruan Ji's hero is "not matching his virtue with Yao's and Shun's, nor pitting his merit against Tang's and Wu's" (Holzman 1976, 202). All inconveniences of physical existence are finally overcome:

> Heat and cold don't harm me; nothing stirs me up.
> Sadness and worry have no hold on me; pure energy
>   at rest.
> I float on mist, leap into heaven, pass through
>   all with no restraint.
> To and fro, subtle and wondrous, the way never
>   slants.
> My delights and happiness are not of this world,
>   how would I ever fight with it?

Ruan Ji's version of the Great Man's journey is an outburst of his desperate and never-ending yearning for the true world of "loneliness and vastness," for a complete freedom from all mundane involvement by soaring up high and away from it (Fukunaga 1958). He yearns for Great Purity, for peace of mind and quiet. No longer a circuit, the journey has become linear; it leads away and only away. Strange sights and creatures on the way are only appreciated in relation to the protagonist's happiness and thus in terms of the distance already placed between him and his sufferings. Neither sage nor ruler of this world, the Great Man is a creature entirely of the beyond.

In this escapist poetry, ecstasy and withdrawal from society no longer mean an ascetic effort to learn from the otherworld. Rather, they create a free space for a kind of countersociety, in which everything that induces temporary forgetfulness is welcome—drinking, singing, music, drugs. The religious dimension of physical, emotional, and mental purification recedes in this literature while the motif of flight is pushed to the foreground, coupled with the panic-stricken look back and the dread of any future return to mundane realities.

Motivated by anxieties and sorrows, induced by drugs and other stimuli, the escape remains temporary. Ruan Ji and his fellows inevitably face the sad return. The freedom they dream of remains a dream; the ecstasy they find is but a moment's respite. They do not realize complete oneness and the dissolution of all ego in the Tao. They glimpse the realm of the immortals above in ecstasy, gaining short-lived respite for themselves. Still, they share the mystical ideal of the tradition. The denial of any egoistic concerns made in Master Great Man's reply to the hermit is a case in point. Envisioning the journey of the Great Man as leading to inner contentment and heavenly perfection, ecstatic poets develop and transform the ancient ideals of Chinese mysticism. They are heirs of the concepts and metaphors of Laozi and Zhuangzi, but at the same time their preoccupation with escape and their particular means of attaining otherworldly states set them apart in a lineage of their own.

Immortality through Wine and in Nature

The exotic lifestyle and powerful writings of the poets in later centuries stimulated the positive evaluation of an easy, carefree life with wine, women, and music in Chinese popular religion. The image of the immortal as a happy-go-lucky fellow or lady who sits around with a group of like-minded companions playing chess, striking the zither, or drinking wine has its roots with them. The strange immortal creatures of the Han, half animal, half human, who in Shangqing Taoism are replaced by ethereal and refined gods and goddesses, were thus transformed into wine-bibbers in Chinese folklore.[9]

The earliest and most explicit formulation of this idea is the description of the Great Man by the eccentric Liu Ling (d. ca. 265 c.e.), another of the Seven Sages, in his *Jiude song* (In Praise of the Virtue of Wine).

There is Master Great Man—

He takes heaven and earth as a single morning
A thousand years as one short moment.
The sun and the moon are windows for him,
The Eight Wilds are his garden.

He travels without wheels or tracks,
Sojourns without house or hearth.
He makes heaven his curtain and earth his seat,
Indulges in what he pleases.

Stopping, he grasps his wine-cup and maintains his
    goblet;
Moving, he carries a casket and holds a jar in his
    hand.
His only obligation is toward wine,
And of this he knows abundance.

The noble princely courtier
And the official in seclusion
Come to hear my song,
To deliberate its worth.

Waving with their sleeves, pulling up their robes,
Anger in their eyes and gnashing with their teeth,
They explain to me the rules of ritual and order,
Raise for me the lances that show what's right and
    what's wrong.

But the Master thereupon
Holds up his jar to them and goes on with his
    wine,
Cherishing his cup to the last bit of the lees.
With ruffled whiskers, he sits, legs spread apart,
The yeast becomes his pillow, the sediments his
    mat.

Utterly free he is from yearnings and from
    worries,
Always happy and full in his contentment.
Without ever moving he gets drunk,
Then, with a start he sobers up.

Listens quietly, but does not hear the rolling of
    thunder,
Watches intently, but does not see towering Mount
    Tai.
Unaware of the cold biting the flesh he is,
Unmoved by the afflictions of covetousness.

Looking down he watches the myriad beings bustling
    about
Like tiny pieces of duckweed that float on the Han
    and Jiang.
The two fighters stand as servants to his side,
Relating to him like the caterpillar to the sphex.

(Wenxuan 47)

At first sight, this description of the Great Man seems to reflect Liu Ling's own way of life. He was well known for his continuous drunkenness as well as for his refusal to wear clothes because, he claimed, heaven and earth were his residence, and his house was sufficient for a garment.[10] Then literary similarities become obvious. Like the *Zhuangzi*, Liu Ling powerfully contrasts the divine poise of the Great Man with the petty concerns of the two court gentlemen, ironically described as "fighters." Like the "Yuanyou" and its successors, he praises the transcendence of the Great Man, who goes beyond all sense experiences and roams far above the bustling mass of humanity. What sets Liu Ling apart from the tradition is his insistence on the "virtue of wine," the major vehicle for the Great Man's attainment of higher spheres. He sticks to his wine-cup and knows no other duty than drunken ecstasy.

The notion that drunkenness is akin, if not actually related, to the perfect state of the true person is not new, though. Already the *Zhuangzi* says that when a drunken man falls from a carriage, he will do himself no harm. Immersed in utter forgetfulness, he did not know he was riding, he does not know he has fallen. He is unworried and serene, and thus stays whole in body and mind (chap. 19).[11]

But where the *Zhuangzi* uses drunkenness as a metaphor for the perfection of forgetfulness, Liu Ling seems to take it literally. His ideal is the happy-go-lucky immortal with his wine flask, often a gourd symbolizing the microcosm.[12] This potbellied figure, prominent in later folklore, has come a long way from the ancient shaman-king, the sage of the *Daode jing*, or even the free and easy wanderer of the *Zhuangzi*. These ideals of old have led to the ruler-immortal of the Han dynasty, who in turn has given way to the ecstatic escape of the politically harassed individual. The execution of power over the world was duly replaced by the delight of merrymaking and wine-bibbing away from society. The ideal of oneness with the world developed into a vision of freedom from the world and the escape from it all. For the poets, wine, drugs, and drunkenness were accepted means toward attaining that vision.

Not only creators of the happy wine-drinking immortal, the poets were also the first actively to draw a connection between nature as landscape and the ideal of free and easy wandering. In particular, Wang Xizhi (ca. 307–363 C.E.), Sun Chuo (ca. 310–390 C.E.), Tao Yuanming (365–427 C.E.), and Xie Lingyun (385–433 C.E.) found respite from their earthly plights by immersing themselves in nature.[13] Before, nature had represented the opposite of culture, simplicity versus complexity, tranquility versus involvement. Now, nature symbolized the ideal of transcending both, and the means of becoming one with the Tao. The idea of naturalness developed (see Mather 1969).

Going along with natural so-being, Guo Xiang's ideal, originally meant the recovery of oneself as one had been spontaneously in the Tao. It was the pursuit of primordial purity and a reorganization of life away from desires and emotions and toward the simplicity of the Tao. It had nothing to do with either sensual letting-go or nature as landscape. With the ecstatic pursuits of the poets, naturalness came to mean going along with whatever happened, including emotions and desires. It was believed that one was most natural when experiencing all ups and downs—but primarily the ups—intensely. The sense of living life to its fullest was then linked with nature as landscape and the sensual enjoyment of the delights of a cultured, leisurely existence.

This line of interpretation continued the Hedonistic tradition, or Yangist school, as documented in the *Zhuangzi* and the *Liezi* (chap. 7). A major exponent of later Hedonism was Xiang Xiu, another of the Seven Sages, whose commentary to the *Zhuangzi* remains only in citations, especially in Zhang Zhan's commentary to the *Liezi* (Fukunaga 1964). But his criticism of Xi Kang's *Yangsheng lun* survives and expresses his views quite clearly (Henricks 1983, 31–37). He proposes to experience life as intensely as possible, to pursue all the happiness that can be afforded by the senses. He says,

> Where there is life, there are feelings. Feelings are part of nature. To cut them off and put them outside means to become just like an inanimate object. What good, then, is it to be alive at all?
>
> Moreover, people have cravings and desires. They delight in glory and detest disgrace; they delight in leisure and detest hard work. All these reactions are only natural.
>
> (*Nan Yangsheng lun*)

Realization for Xiang Xiu means to appreciate and savor the feelings of being alive. He criticizes the efforts of longevity-seekers who deny themselves all sensual gratification in order to prolong a merely physical existence. He asks: What good is a life I cannot enjoy? His attitude differs from the classic ideals of perfection, which claimed that the only life worth enjoying was the purified and tranquil sojourn on earth in as much alignment and contact with the Tao, the spirits, and the potency of heaven and earth.

The poets thus developed their own interpretation of the mystical pursuit of perfection. On the one hand, they expressed their ideas in the terms of Laozi and Zhuangzi, they partook in the elevated vision of the mystics, and they described ecstatic journeys to the realm of the immortals. On the other hand, they used wine and drugs for the attainment of higher states, thus gaining a temporary respite from their worldly plight, not a lasting personality transformation through oneness with the Tao. They sought to enjoy the pleasurable moments of life to the fullest, immersed themselves in nature as landscape, and enjoyed the satisfaction afforded by the senses. Their Hedonist claims as much as their lyrical exploits set them apart from the other forms of early Chinese mysticism, which were more withdrawn in outlook and more philosophical in diction. Yet the poets also represent a form of mysticism that had a lasting influence on Chinese religion and folklore.

MYSTICISM AND IMMORTALITY IN SHANGQING TAOISM

Shangqing or Highest Clarity Taoism—also known as Maoshan Taoism, after the seat of the headquarters of the sect—began in 364 C.E. with a series of revelations granted to Yang Xi (330–? C.E.), a medium residing in Jurong near Nanjing. The revelations were written down by two brothers Xu, who then spread the new teachings in the area (Robinet 1984, 1:108). They were welcomed heartily by the local aristocracy, who found in the newly discovered heavens a rank and nobility they had lost on this earth (see Strickmann 1978). They learned all about the organization of the thirty-six heavens above and practiced visualizations and ecstatic meditations to experience the higher planes. The Shangqing Canon, which survives to a large extent in the Taoist Canon (see Robinet 1984), consists of the original texts revealed to Yang Xi together with later collections and apocryphal scriptures of the late Six Dynasties and Tang.

For a long time, Shangqing beliefs and practices remained within the framework of those few clans residing in the Nanjing area. Toward the end of the fifth century, Shangqing Taoism became the leading Taoist school of China. It owed this position mainly to the efforts of Tao Hongjing (456–536 c.e.) and continued to gain strength and influence throughout the Tang dynasty (Strickmann 1978, 1981). In the course of this development, Shangqing Taoism incorporated certain parts of other religious teachings then current: the Taoism of the Lingbao school on the one hand, and Buddhism on the other.

The texts of Lingbao Taoism were compiled by Ge Chaofu, a descendant of Ge Hong, in the last years of the fourth century. His goal was to raise the position of his ancestor Ge Xuan in the heavenly hierarchy, which had been established on the basis of the Shangqing revelations after 364 c.e. Ge Chaofu included not only the Shangqing texts themselves in his new set of scriptures but also drew heavily on the library of his ancestor Ge Hong, on Han dynasty correlative thought, and on Buddhist sutras (Bokenkamp 1983, 445). Of all Taoist schools, Lingbao is the most ritually oriented, and much of Shangqing ritual goes back to its influence. The Buddhist impact on Shangqing Taoism, on the other hand, is apparent in its sophisticated meditation theories and practices as well as in a heightened emphasis on the development of wisdom. Within this framework of religious integration carried by aristocratic families, a higher spirituality and a well-organized mystical synthesis first begins to develop.

The Shangqing Cosmos

The cosmology of Shangqing Taoism shares its foundations with the cosmology of ancient China. First of all, it subscribes to the idea of the Tao, also described as the Great Ultimate, the One, or the center of the universe, the potency responsible for the creation and continued existence of the world. The One creates the two forces yin and yang, constituents of all change and transformation. The world is further structured according to the three and the five: the three vertical levels of heaven, earth, and humanity; and the five horizontal agents of wood, fire, earth, metal, and water, associated with the four cardinal directions and the center as well as with the five sacred peaks and the five planets (Robinet 1984, 1:130).

Shangqing cosmology strongly emphasizes the directions. The East is the place of origin; the West stands for decay and decline. The Center controls everything, while the North and South represent the extremes of death and everlasting life. The North in particular houses the underworld with its courts of judgment and divine palaces. Known as Fengdu shan or Luofeng shan, the underworld is ruled by the Great Emperor of Demon Administration, in whose entourage many of the mythological heroes of old have found a place. He is the head of so-called Underworld Governors and their staff of Good and Radiant Demons, who may advance to the position of governor themselves after four hundred years of faithful service. They rule and control the Lower Demons, the Killer Demons, and the Malicious Demons. All these serve there to be rectified in their ways, and have to be guided with great force (see Robinet 1984, 1:137–38).

The South, on the other hand, is the region of everlasting life, the place of purification and rebirth. Known as the Southern or the Red Palace, the Southern Court, the Red Fire Palace, and sometimes also called Red Hill or Cinnabar Hill, the South is one of the desired paradise-style meeting points of the successful aspirants to immortality and the celestial powers, be they stars, gods, or immortal administrators.

Beyond the basic division into One, yin and yang, and the three and the five, Shangqing Taoism has several sets of eight. There are the eight meeting points and the eight winds of the directions, as well as the eight seasonal festivals of the solstices, the equinoxes and the beginnings of the seasons.[14] These are the times when the gods come down to inspect life on earth. Moreover, there are the eight luminaries, groups of deities residing in the three major energy centers of the body, the cinnabar fields in the head, the chest, and the abdomen. Altogether twenty-four radiant divinities, these gods correspond to the twenty-four energies of the year and the twenty-four stars of the zodiac (Robinet 1984, 1:129; see also Andersen 1980).

The number of completed yang in Chinese cosmology is nine. To express the wholeness and integration of the system, Shangqing Taoism also has various sets of nine. There are nine palaces in the head, the upper Cinnabar Field among them. There are nine major constellations in the sky, and there are nine stars of the Northern Dipper—four to form the Scoop, three for the Handle, and two invisible stars (Robinet 1989, 173).

The Northern Dipper represents the Tao or the One in the center of the sky and is thus parallel to Mount Kunlun on earth. Both form the central axis of the universe, regulating and controlling everything. According to geographical accounts, Kunlun communicates with the original energy of the universe and radiates its power through the five agents. It regulates the heavens and adjusts yin and yang and can truly be called the root and nub of heaven and earth.[15] Beyond its function as a universal center and *axis mundi*, Kunlun is also one of the paradises or palaces of heaven, traditionally described as high mountains surrounded by deep water. More specifically, Kunlun Mountain "rises thirty-six thousand miles above the surrounding plain. Its top has three corners, is ten thousand miles wide and shaped like a hanging bowl" (*Shizhou ji* 10b). Immortals here reside in the Heavenly Walled City, a magnificent metropolis covering an area of a thousand square miles, full of golden terraces and jade towers. Here the Queen Mother of the West holds court, surrounded by hosts of realized administrators, gods, and immortals.

The Queen Mother of the West, queen of the immortals, is among the many deities Shangqing has inherited from classical Chinese mythology. There are also the Arbiter of Destiny with his extensive staff of record-keepers, the Jade Emperor, the Emperor of Heaven, and many others (Robinet 1984, 1:126). The altogether thirty-six Shangqing heavens originally developed from the nine heavens of the classical system, but later received names and a structure influenced by Buddhism. They are arranged vertically and house a celestial administration of twenty-seven ranks of immortals, realized ones, and sages. The heavens, like the sacred scriptures, are direct emanations of primordial energy; they are the true sources of life.

According to the tenth-century encyclopedia *Yunji qiqian* (Seven Slips of a Cloudy Satchel), the highest heaven is the Galaxy of Grand Network with its capital of Mystery Metropolis, also known as the Jade Capital. The thirty-five heavens beneath Grand Network divide into four groups, following the Buddhist notion of the Three Worlds. The lowest six heavens are located in the World of Desire; the following eighteen are in the World of Form; the four heavens above them are in the World of Formlessness. That makes twenty-eight planes within the Three Worlds. The next four heavens are called "Brahma-Heavens"; they are followed by the Three Clarities—Jade Clarity, Great Clarity, and Highest Clarity, to name them from bottom to top.

Even heavens within the Three Worlds are beautiful. As one rises through them, one finds life longer and more pleasant; precious materials and fanciful objects grow in abundance. However, anyone residing within the Three Worlds is still subject to reincarnation, and has not yet attained full immortal status. The Brahma-Heavens are the abode of realized beings; they house the gods and parts of the celestial administration. Only the Three Clarities house immortals proper, dividing them into altogether twenty-seven ranks. The Galaxy of Grand Network, finally, is the residence of the Tao in its purest form. It houses the Highest Venerable Lord and the sacred celestial scriptures (*Yunji qiqian* 3.6ab).

The scriptures are identical with the potency of all creation: uncreated, direct, primordial. Their recitation gave the gods, equally primordial, the power to furnish being from emptiness. Not just powers of creation, the scriptures are also the forces of survival. When the world comes to an end—as it does periodically—only the scriptures survive. The word *jing*, used for "scripture" in Taoism, thus evokes a new and more powerful meaning: the "going through" of the original graph becomes the "eternally surviving" of the religion. The scriptures continue to change along with the transformations of the world, sometimes accessible, sometimes hidden. They direct and pattern the life of the world and are immediately responsible for all human developments. World and society, originally created from the sacred word, end when the scriptures vanish, but may be saved by a new revelation. Shangqing eschatology is thus concerned with the cyclical revival of the scriptures. Its messiah, the Latterday Sage, is not a personal savior but the herald of a new revelation of the texts that alone have the power to save and create (Robinet 1984, 1:138).

Deities who reveal the true words to humankind include the Heavenly King of Primordial Beginning—not to be confused with the Heavenly Venerable of Primordial Beginning, the central deity of Lingbao Taoism—the Great Lord of the Tao, the Lad of Great Tenuity, the Four Realized Ones of the Great Ultimate, Master Li the Latterday Sage, and the Green Lad (Robinet 1984, 1:127). Altogether the gods in the universe are as innumerable as the divinities residing in the human body. Many heavenly deities take up their residence within the individual while at the same time being at home in their starry palaces (see Schafer 1977). Parallel to the cosmos at large, the body is a complete replica of the world and of the divine realms in the stars (see Kohn 1990a).

Organized strictly hierarchically and very well mapped, the Shangqing cosmos is colorful and multifaceted. Though continuing their language, it does not share the obscurity and vagueness of the *Daode jing* and the *Zhuangzi*. In many ways it inherits, continues, and develops the journey reports of old—both to the wondrous barbarian lands of the fringes on earth and to the vast otherworldly realms.

Shangqing Practice: Ecstatic Excursions

The aim and practice of Shangqing Taoism is aimed at perfection in the Tao.[16] As Isabelle Robinet has pointed out, "the active Taoist undertakes a certain representation of the universe, of the body, and of himself or herself. This representation comes alive, it becomes visible to the mental eye and is perceived by the inner being of each and every adept" (Robinet 1989, 159). Shangqing practitioners pursue a new integration of self and Tao, body and cosmos. The aim of their visionary and ecstatic practices is to reorganize their consciousness. From ordinary people, practitioners develop into cosmic beings. No longer limited to their earthly environment, they increasingly make the heavens their true home, wander freely throughout the far ends of the world and soar up into the sky. The mind at one with the rhythmic changes of creation, they go along with all and thereby continue to exist eternally. They develop "a new personality of cosmic dimensions, where the physical and the imaginary body, the individual and the cosmos, are intimately merged, where the ordinary human being has become a true Taoist saint, such as described by Zhuangzi" (Robinet 1989, 160).

Shangqing practice begins with the understanding that the human body is a microcosm of the universe. The inner organs or orbs of the body are systematically aligned in time and space with the ends of the world, the stars, and the seasons. Adepts visualize the five orbs and the divinities residing in the body as described in the *Huangting jing* (Yellow Court Scripture) and the *Laozi zhongjing* (Inner Scripture of Laozi).[17] At the same time, they actualize the basic potency of the universe. On the basis of perfect alignment in body and mind, Shangqing visionaries set out on an ecstatic journey. It takes them either to the far ends of the world or up into the sky. In the world, they reach the polar areas at the periphery of the inhabited regions to find mythical beasts and precious objects, presented by local residents with deep veneration. Truly imperial in their progress, adepts thus take control over the world through their presence in its corners. Also, they absorb its different energies, or "sprouts."

The sprouts are the essences of the clouds; they represent the yin principle of heaven and are manifest in human saliva, where they nourish and strengthen the five orbs. Very tender, like the fresh sprouts of plants, they assemble at dawn in the celestial capital, from where they spread all over the universe until the sun begins to shine. Turning like the wheels of a carriage, the sprouts first reach the heavenly gates, from where they descend to the world, settling on the five sacred mountains ruled over by the five emperors of the five directions.

Adepts visualize these sprouts as colored balls of energy, in accordance with the direction from which they arise. Slowly the sprouts come closer and closer, shrinking in size and approaching the practitioners, who carefully guide them to their mouths, swallow them, and direct them to rest in the proper orbs (Robinet 1989, 165). The sprouts contain the entire potential of being in its nascent state. To gain their fullest power, one must absorb them at dawn, when everything awakens to new life. Like the sovereign who takes nourishment from the "essence of all that is alive in the universe" (Granet 1950, 395) by feeding on the delicacies of the four corners of the world, the Taoist consumes the universe in its most subtle form.

Further adapting themselves to the powers and movements of the universe, adepts then align their movements faithfully to those of the heavenly bodies in the sky, especially to the sun and the moon. Going along with their rhythm, they try to reach the celestial meeting places at the equinoxes and the solstices, when the sun and the moon are there themselves. The meeting places are like the immortals' paradises. Again adepts take charge of them by absorbing some of their products, their essences, deeply into themselves.

Traveling to the far ends of the world and meeting the sun and the moon is a form of going-along with rhythmical change. These practices harmonize adepts with the temporal and physical movements of the cosmos. Once perfectly aligned, adepts are ready to move on. They then approach the central axis of the world, and establish themselves in the quiet center around which all the world revolves. To do so, adepts invoke, visualize, and visit the Northern Dipper in many different ways.

The Northern Dipper is *axis mundi* of the Shangqing system. Already the *Shiji* describes it as the governor of the four cardinal points, the power that separates yin and yang and determines the four seasons. The Dipper balances the five agents and arranges the divisions of time and space (Robinet 1989, 178). To find access to the Dipper, adepts may visualize its stars descending and surrounding them for protection. Thus enveloped by the Dipper, they become the center of the Center, the nub of all-there-is (Kohn 1981, 142). Or they may visualize themselves ascending to the Dipper and pacing on it, following the way in which the great Yu once gained control of the earth. Again they establish themselves in the center; they become its rulers. Adepts may also visualize the divinities of the Dipper entering into their three Cinnabar Fields in a set order and on precise dates. Or they may sleep in the Dipper, sketched, as it were, on their sleeping mat. In either case, the Dipper comes close to them, becomes part of them, as they become part of its centrality and power. By all these and many other methods (see Robinet 1976, 1979, 1989), Shangqing practitioners realize the ultimate transcendence of the Great Man. They merge with the root of all beginning, and enter the emptiness of highest potentiality.

Mystical Conceptions

Shangqing Taoism continues the Lao-Zhuang tradition in many ways, particularly obvious in its terminology. As Isabelle Robinet has pointed out, Shangqing texts take up many terms and phrases especially from the *Zhuangzi*. Examples are "true man," "Great Clarity," "Great One," "freedom from affairs," "fasting the mind," "making all things equal," and "sitting in oblivion" (Robinet 1983a, 63). On a conceptual level, the relationship is more subtle. Shangqing Taoism transforms Zhuangzi's ideas to represent a different form of Chinese mysticism.

First, rather than seeing continuous transformation as the nature of all things, Shangqing Taoism insists on the quiet source at the center of all changes. Next, it continues the tendency to define and delineate the relationship between human beings and the Tao, going beyond Guo Xiang and integrating Han dynasty cosmology into its system. Third, Shangqing Taoism inherits the ecstatic journey to immortality and its imperial development in the ideal of the Great Man. Altogether, the structure of the progress to perfection differs considerably.

First, unlike the *Zhuangzi* but like Guo Xiang, Shangqing Taoism defines the ways of the universe. In contrast to Guo Xiang, however, who preaches perfect accordance with all, Shangqing Taoism goes on to teach its adepts to establish themselves at the quiet center of all. This establishment is at the same time the highest possible alignment with the universe as demanded by Guo Xiang, yet it represents a different outlook on the ideal human state. The basic assumption that all life is change still holds true, but unlike the *Zhuangzi* or Guo Xiang, Shangqing Taoism integrates the concepts of the *Daode jing* insofar as it assumes an underlying unmoving source from which the change springs: the Tao, the Great One, the substance of the cosmos. The *Zhuangzi*, too, knows the image of the revolving circle with its empty center, the eye of the storm, where the seeker should establish himself and let everything around him go on as it pleases. Where the *Zhuangzi* emphasizes the endless empty circle, Shangqing Taoism places its stress on the center and explains it in mythological and cosmological terms.

Another point of difference is that Shangqing Taoism integrates the correlative thought of the Han dynasty and thereby defines the nature of eternal change in terms of time and space. The seasons, the movements of the planets, the far ends of the world, the central axis of the universe—all these serve to structure a system of cosmic change, to make it accessible to the human mind and body. Shangqing Taoism further claims an immediately analogous relationship between the body and the cosmos. The individual is already part of the universal structure; he or she has only to realize that deities reside within to become an active participant in the vibrant universe. The *Zhuangzi*, to the contrary, does not specify how human beings relate to the cosmos, except to say that they are part of the continuous change that is all-there-is. Guo Xiang introduces his concepts of share/inner nature and principle/fate to explain how people are linked with the Tao. Shangqing Taoism draws on cosmology and mythology to fill the gap. New opportunities for practice and attainment emerge.

A third major difference regards religious practice. The human mind, all three agree, is trapped the way it is. It should be made no-mind and cosmicized; it should be reorganized to take in the true nature of the cosmos as defined by the tradition. But where Zhuangzi advises complete oblivion in order to attain perfect happiness, and where Guo Xiang demands that people go along in complete fulfillment of their fates, Shangqing Taoism, true to the vision of the Great Man's journey, advises its adepts to take control and become the true ruler of the universe. Ecstatic excursions in Shangqing Taoism in their own ways follow the triumphant circuit of the Great Man. They lead to immortality—not only as perfect harmony on earth and residence in the otherworld but also as the true possession and control of the source of all life. The ego is dissolved in favor of the Tao. But while Zhuangzi wishes to see the ego in oblivion and Guo Xiang wants it replaced by a sense of impersonal flow, Shangqing Taoism aims to expand it to embrace the cosmos at large.

The ultimate state of perfection is thus described as a going-beyond in the *Zhuangzi* and a going-along in Guo Xiang. In both it is essentially formulated in terms of movement, of ecstasy reached through a process of increasing oblivion, which in turn is explained in terms of withdrawal and as a process of enstasy. In the *Zhuangzi* and Guo Xiang, in other words, enstatic immersion leads to ecstatic freedom. Shangqing Taoism in its formulation of the process can be described as exactly the reverse. Here an ecstatic outward movement leads to enstatic quietude. By way of expanding outward, of ecstatically going along with the rhythm of time and space, the unmoving center of all is reached. The final state is characterized by quietude and tranquility; it is an eternal resting with the source of the cosmos, mythologically described as taking up an immortal position in the hierarchy of the otherworld.

CHAPTER SIX

The Impact of Buddhism

EARLY CHINESE BUDDHISM

When Buddhist scriptures first came to China in the first and second centuries C.E., the Chinese interpreted them as an alternative teaching of longevity and immortality. Soon they realized that these texts were based on an intellectual and philosophical tradition of their own, but they still translated them with the help of Lao-Zhuang terminology. In the fourth century the first Chinese aristocrats became Buddhists, both monks and lay supporters, yet only with Kumārajīva and Huiyuan, in the early fifth century, did the intellectual and scriptural tradition of Chinese Buddhism begin a life of its own. By that time, however, it had irretrievably incorporated certain native Chinese—especially Lao-Zhuang—concepts and had, in turn, made an irreversible impact on the Chinese tradition.[1]

The main exponents of the early Chinese integration, adaptation, and interpretation of Buddhism, of whom we have knowledge, were:

1. Zhi Dun (314–366 C.E.), an aristocratic monk, who introduced Buddhist religious activities into the higher circles of society;
2. Xi Chao (336–377 C.E.), a lay activist, whose *Fengfa yao* (Essentials of Venerating the Law) laid down the basic rules and strategies to be followed by aristocratic Buddhist householders;
3. Dao'an (312–385 C.E.), the leading Buddhist figure of northern China, who interpreted the Buddhist notion of emptiness through Wang Bi's concept of original nonbeing;
4. Huiyuan (334–416 C.E.), the "founder" of Chinese Pure Land practice and defender of the Sangha's rights not to bow to the emperor;
5. Sengzhao (374–414 C.E.), a Buddhist thinker who interpreted the notion of wisdom (*prajñā*) through the Taoist concept of unknowing;
6. Daosheng (ca. 360–434 C.E.), a student of Kumārajīva, who is sometimes described as a forerunner of Chan Buddhism.

Much has been said about these important thinkers.[2] To clarify the impact on the native Chinese mystical tradition, suffice it here to discuss only one of them in some detail, looking also at some of his writings to gain a glimpse of the style and outlook of the time: Zhi Dun, the first aristocratic monk of the Chinese tradition, who in many ways was a precursor of the indigenous Chinese mysticism to come.

Zhi Dun and Guo Xiang

Zhi Dun, also known as Zhi Daolin, came from a gentry Buddhist environment that he never left, despite his position as a monk. He spent much time in the mountains of Zhejiang, where he founded two monasteries. To his aristocratic friends, his Buddhism was obvious mainly in his monkish attire, his shaven head (greeted with much suspicion and wonder), and his observance of the five precepts, then severely criticized because they prevented him from continuing his family line. His philosophical and religious ideas were linked closely with the Dark Learning interpretations of the *Daode jing* and the *Zhuangzi*; he especially took note of Guo Xiang's philosophical system.[3]

For Guo Xiang, the Tao is existence as such; to reach mystical oneness one has to go beyond the specific delimitations imposed on it by the human mind. For Zhi Dun, transcendence leads beyond matter, *se*, a translation of Sanskrit *rūpa*. Matter is ultimately empty, because it arises as part of the chain of dependent origination (*pratītya samutpāda*); it does not exist in itself. Nevertheless there is an entity underlying matter. "Heaven's truth is the original world," says Zhi Dun (Hachiya 1967, 84). He sees the mystical process not so much in the elimination of "thirst" (*drti*)—passions and desires—but as a return to truth. Buddhist cessation is not his goal, but rather the heavenly principle of Lao-Zhuang.

The truth of heaven, however, is most manifest in the true teachings of Buddhism, and here especially in the ten stages of *prajñā*, wisdom or insight. Yet even these true manifestations have to be overcome; even they are nothing but the "traces" of the truth. People must go beyond the traces by an act of forgetting, again a Taoist note in Zhi Dun's system. The degree to which any given individual is able to attain the subtler truth depends on his fate, here not described as the "bones of immortality," but as the "karma" that one has inherited from former lives. Still, Zhi Dun perpetuates Guo Xiang in that the former defines his notion of karma by means of Guo Xiang's concept of share (*fen*)—now no longer the share one is given by the Tao, but the share of life accumulated through past karma.

Inner nature, the psychological correspondence to cosmic share in Guo Xiang, consequently differs in Zhi Dun. Guo Xiang postulated that inner nature was an aspect of the Tao and therefore necessarily pure and good. Zhi Dun admits the possibility that inner nature could also be evil. The evil in inner nature has to be fought to attain purity; it is not sufficient merely to discover one's natural oneness with the Tao. He says, "Someone asked, 'Should everyone who follows inner nature be considered a free and easy wanderer?' Zhi Dun replied, 'Not so. The inner nature of [the tyrant] Jie and of [the robber] Zhi consisted of destruction and harm. To take following inner nature for true realization means that they too were free and easy wanderers' " (*Gaoseng zhuan*, T. 50.348b). A religious lifestyle is thereby justified. In order to attain the "truth of heaven" one must purge oneself of desires, cut all attachments to family and state, and fully submit to the precepts of the order.

Zhi Dun's treatment and development of Guo Xiang is symptomatic for the impact that Buddhism had on early Chinese mysticism. He added three major points, which forever altered the outlook and practice of the mystical tradition. He insisted that all things were empty due to the law of dependent origination, thus newly defining the relationship between the Tao and beings; he believed that inner nature was developed from karma and therefore contained evil seeds that needed active purgation; and he propagated a specifically religious lifestyle in a distinctly monastic setting.

The Mystical Path

Zhi Dun describes his vision of the mystical path in the *Zuoyou ming* (Inscription to the Right of [the Teacher's] Seat). Contained in his biography in the *Gaoseng zhuan*, this text served as an exhortation to his disciples.

INSCRIPTION TO THE RIGHT OF
[THE TEACHER'S] SEAT

Be diligent, be diligent!
Perfect Tao is endless.
How could it be obstructed?

You have lost your old home, your spiritual
    endowment,
Blurred and deluded you float about the Three
    Worlds,
Blind and unseeing you suffer under an eternal
    yoke.

In distress you labor to amass outer goods,
The obscure mind ever agitated within.
Greedily you hasten about, full of hope and
    thirst,
Thinking of far-off gain and forgetting your
    exhaustion.

A human lifetime, one generation
Is but a dewdrop falling.
My self is not mine, not me,
And yet—who fashioned it to be?

The accomplished one harbors virtue
And knows only in quiet is he lofty,
Only in serenity can he achieve purity,
And rinse off all fetters in a pool of trance.

Carefully he guards the enlightened prohibitions,
With ease he fulfills the holy rules.
He soothes his mind with spirit and with Tao,
Wards off all yearning in non-action.

Withdrawn to threefold concealment,
He cleanses himself from the six ailments,
Dissolves the five *skandhas* into emptiness and
    oneness,
And merges the four limbs with the abysmal void.

Not an attribute, yet explaining attributes,
Utterly other and yet not separate:
The wonder of awakening!

Again, he darkens his knowledge
And, freely yielding to the currents,
Moves along with all beings.

Passing through this, he goes on
Without yearning, without deliberation;
Sincerely he follows awakening as his father,
His will is that of a small child.

(T. 2059; 348c10–19)

For Zhi Dun, the mystical attainment is the realization of Perfect Tao, an expression taken from the *Zhuangzi* (27/11/29). He describes its pursuit in three basic stages of development. First, he outlines the basic conditions of humanity, the reality that beginning seekers face when they examine themselves. Next, he details the path, from monastic discipline to the practice of the trances, and on to the dissolution of the self in emptiness. Third, he deals with the experience of enlightenment and the life that the accomplished sage leads afterward, free from conscious deliberation and like a small child. In all three stages Zhi Dun merges Taoist and Buddhist expressions and ideas. In a few cases he also succeeds in joining both in one term. The result is a newer and richer vision of the pursuit of perfection.

The Deluded Mind

Zhi Dun first admonishes beginning students to be diligent. He emphasizes that the Tao is never obstructed, that all problems people face on the path are their own. His disciples should see what their present state of mind is. He compares them to "a man who left home in his youth and has forgotten the way back" (*Zhuangzi* 6/2/79), a Taoist way of deploring people's separation from the Tao. He also borrows the expressions "blurred and deluded" and "blind and unseeing" from the *Zhuangzi*. But instead of using them to refer to the ineffability of the Tao, Zhi Dun uses them for the deluded minds of people erring through the Three Worlds.

Resorting to purely Buddhist doctrine, Zhi Dun then paints a vivid picture of the futile life spent in continuous death and rebirth. Distressed, people only hanker after outer goods; greedy for more wealth, they rush about exhausting their bodies and agitating their minds. By good deeds, they may be reborn in better circumstances; still, life after life they must struggle along their way. The more distant perspective helps seekers to realize that one life is but a drop in an ocean. They begin to ask: For what? For whom? Who is this self?

In questioning the "self," literally the "personal body" (*shen*), Zhi Dun combines both Buddhist and Lao-Zhuang concepts. The doctrine of no-self (*anātman, wuwo*) harmonizes well with the questions regarding the "True Lord" in the *Zhuangzi* (chap. 2). The body consists of a combination of limbs and organs—which of them is really me? Which of all the parts of myself is the true ruler over the rest? Who or what created me? What constancy is there and what purpose? These questions raise the Taoist issue of body and ego identity and simultaneously prepare the disciples for the Buddhist doctrine of no-self. Life's delusions, the errors of the mind, become painfully obvious.

Practice in the Monastery

Stimulated by the realization that life is short and that there is no self worth laboring for, the mystical progress begins. Practitioners become "accomplished ones" (*daren*), an old Chinese expression for someone close to sagehood, someone who penetrates and pervades the deeper reaches of the universe (*Zuozhuan*, Zhao 7; *Liezi*, chap. 7). According to Zhi Dun, accomplished persons withdraw from social involvement into the tranquil and serene setting of the monastery. They submit willingly to the "enlightened prohibitions"—the five precepts to abstain from killing, stealing, telling lies, sexual misconduct, and intoxication—and the "holy rules" that regulate daily conduct in the monastic community. They engage in meditation practice that leads to the trances or absorptions (*dhyāna*, *chan*) that, in turn, allow liberation from the fetters of mundane existence.

With calm spirit and in pure Tao, perfecting non-action and deeply withdrawn, practitioners attain purity. They are liberated from the six ailments and become healthy in body and mind. This notion reflects the Chinese preoccupation with the body and the integration of medical therapy into religious practice. In Taoism, to enter the realm of the Tao, one must be in good physical condition; one must be perfectly healthy—only then can one alter one's personality and dissolve the ego.

The six ailments develop due to the six energies of yin and yang, wind and rain, dark and light (*Zuozhuan*, Zhao 1). They will do no harm when one is perfectly in accordance with them. Taoists strive for complete alignment with the six energies by means of diets and gymnastics. According to the later system, practitioners withdraw from the world to perfect their accordance after they have purified themselves and before they enter meditation (*Tianyinzi*; see Kohn 1987a, 11).

Here the process is not so clearly defined. Meditative seclusion and exercises lead to physical well-being; health in turn allows deeper purification of the mind. Zhi Dun emphasizes the physical aspect of mystical attainment, since he himself was known as an accomplished master of gymnastics and nourishing life. In his *Taiqing daolin shesheng lun* (Great Clarity Discourse on Protecting Life by Master Daolin; DZ 1427, fasc. 1055), he details his recommendations regarding lifestyle, living quarters, and diet; and gives instructions in massages, gymnastics, and breathing exercises. He was also among the putative authors of the *Yangsheng yaoji* (Essential Compendium on Nourishing Life), now extant only in citations (see Sakade 1986). And he had a hand in compiling the *Daoyin jing* (Gymnastics Scripture; DZ 818, fasc. 568), another important ancient text on physical therapy. Zhi Dun, moreover, seems to have played a serious role in the tradition of Chinese gymnastics. As a practicing Buddhist he presumably had close contact with Indian travelers and residents of China, who taught him so-called Brahmanic techniques that he duly integrated into the native repertory (Despeux 1989, 231).

Once liberated from the six ailments, mystical seekers turn their attention to the mind, more precisely to its five *skandhas* or "heaps of desire"—matter, consciousness, perception, sensations, and volition. The *skandhas* are not solid entities, but fleeting energies (*dharmas*, *fa*) that arise and pass away in an instant. Observing the mind's activity as determined by the five *skandhas*, practitioners dissolve the apparent solidity of mental processes and their ego identity. This leads then to complete mental dissolution in "emptiness and oneness," an expression from the *Zhuangzi* that evokes the idea of cosmic chaos and total forgetfulness. Emptiness and oneness is the beginning of the universe, to which the Taoist mystic eventually returns. The mental dissolution is complete when the physical body merges with the "abysmal void." This again recalls the Tao, described as an abyss in the *Daode jing* (chap. 4).

While the setting and practice are predominantly Buddhist, Zhi Dun's vision of the final state is heavily indebted to the Lao-Zhuang tradition and acknowledges the Chinese concept of body-mind continuity.

Ultimate Realization

To discuss the experience of awakening, Zhi Dun therefore takes recourse to Lao-Zhuang terms. "Not an attribute, yet explaining attributes" (*feizhi yuzhi*) is a quotation from the *Zhuangzi*: "To use an attribute to explain that attributes are not attributes is not as good as using a nonattribute to explain that attributes are not attributes. To use a horse to explain that a horse is not a horse is not as good as using a nonhorse to explain that a horse is not a horse" (4/2/31). Zhi Dun refers through the *Zhuangzi* to the Chinese logician Gongsun Long and his statements that "A white horse is not a horse" and "Attributes are not attributes in and of themselves." He thereby applies traditional Chinese logic to express the ineffability of the enlightenment experience. He calls it a "wonder," going back to descriptions of the Tao in the *Daode jing* (chap. 1).

Zhi Dun also envisions the liberated person in indigenous Chinese terms. The sage, the perfected, darkens his knowledge by taking precautions against too much thinking—a very important procedure in the later tradition. Also known as "forgetting the forgetting," or moving "from the mysterious into the doubly mysterious," this is clearly described in the *Zuowang lun* of the eighth century (Discourse on Sitting in Oblivion; DZ 1036, fasc. 704): "[Awakened] insight is a function of the mind, and when the mind functions much it will be labored. When one first realizes a little insight one is very happy and deliberates a lot. Thereby spirit and energy are drained away . . . and it becomes very difficult to perfect the Tao" (14b).

Once immersed in unknowing, the sage returns to being active and recovers his life in the world. For Zhi Dun, enlightenment or awakening should not be clung to; it is a passing stage of life. After the experience, the perfected one moves along with all beings in the state of perfect accordance so elaborately described by Guo Xiang. Free from all desire and conscious thought, he is at one with whatever comes his way. He becomes like a small child, at least so far as his volition is concerned. Again Buddhist and Taoist concepts join together well. The fifth *skandha*, volition or reaction, which produces karma and is responsible for people's "thirst," is dissolved. At the same time, the mind becomes like that of an infant, allowing perfect harmony with the Tao and unlimited physical energy, as already described in the *Daode jing* (chap. 55).

The realization of the childlike mind, free from volition, is in turn the gateway to free and easy wandering, the ecstatic freedom of the perfected. Zhi Dun describes it in the sole passage that remains of his commentary to the *Zhuangzi*.

Free and easy wandering refers to the mind of the perfected. When Zhuangzi talks about the Great Tao, he uses the analogy of the Peng bird and the quail. Because the Peng's life is without obstruction, the bird is free from all limitation in the realm beyond the body. The quail, on the other hand, because it lives in the near and scorns the far, it is limited and obstructed in its mind.

The perfected one rides the truth of heaven, soars aloft, and wanders boundlessly in unfettered freedom. He treats beings as beings without being treated as a mere being himself. He is not self-satisfied in his wandering. Mystically one with the universe, he does not act purposefully. [Like the Tao] he is not hurried, yet moves swiftly. He goes everywhere in his freedom. He is truly a free and easy wanderer.

The sage or perfected one is like the Great Man: he goes beyond beings and is no longer regarded a mere being. One with the Tao, he is swift without hurrying and arrives without moving; he possesses complete freedom over the material and spiritual world, and is full of happiness and satisfaction.

Zhi Dun's mystical methods thus demand a higher commitment and a more formal organization. They differ substantially from the quietistic simplicity of the *Daode jing*, the chaotification of the *Zhuangzi*, Guo Xiang's ideal of perfect accordance, and the escapist ecstasy of the poets. Nevertheless Zhi Dun also remains faithful to the indigenous tradition. He emphasizes the physical dimensions of mystical oneness and conceives of enlightenment and the life of the perfected in the terms of the ancients.

Buddho-Taoist Interaction

To understand the further development of indigenous Chinese mysticism, one must place the growing relationship of Buddhism and Taoism in proper perspective. One can roughly distinguish three levels of interaction, each characterized by specific literary forms and thematic concerns.

First, an indigenous salvational and communal religion developed. The Taoism of the Lingbao School and of the later Celestial Masters integrated much of Buddhist terminology, cosmology, pantheon, and doctrine. Next, Buddho-Taoist debates were staged to establish the prevalence of one teaching over the other, sponsored often by foreign emperors who wished to legitimize their rule. Here Taoists criticized Buddhism with its rule of celibacy as an enemy of the Chinese people and destroyer of the state. Buddhists countered by associating organized, communal Taoism with the rebellion of the Yellow Turbans, and characterized it as a minor sectarian teaching that could only attain the full status of a religion by plagiarizing Buddhist ideas and practices. Third, the tradition of Chinese mysticism integrated Buddhist terms, concepts of body and mind, as well as practices of meditation, continuing on its way to a full mystical synthesis.

Early Chinese mysticism is intimately linked to these various forms of Buddho-Taoist interaction. On the one hand, the mystical synthesis, like salvational Taoism, incorporates Buddhist doctrine and worldview on many different levels. On the other hand, some of the foremost mystical thinkers play important roles in the Buddho-Taoist debates. More than that, the major mystical text before the Tang, the *Xisheng jing* (Scripture of Western Ascension), is set in a quasi-polemical narrative and draws heavily on the current Buddho-Taoist mythology of the time.

Buddhist Influence on the Lingbao Scriptures

The fifth-century Taoist master Lu Xiujing (406–477) first cataloged the Lingbao scriptures in his *Xuanjing mulu* (Bibliography of Mystery Metropolis). Not extant in the Taoist Canon, this bibliography survived among the Dunhuang manuscripts (P. 2256). With its help, scholars have reconstituted the old Lingbao corpus in its original form.[4] The texts center around the original Lingbao myth as formulated in the *Wupian zhenwen chishu* (Perfect Script in Five Tablets, Written in Red; DZ 22, fasc. 26). Stephen Bokenkamp summarizes it thus:

> Arising from the primordial Brahman-ether, this scripture was secreted in the Five Marchmounts to await the completion of five kalpas, when it was finally deemed time for the Heavenly Worthy of Primal Origin to bestow it on the Most High Lord of the Tao for promulgation to mankind. Now it reposes in the Palace of Purple Tenuity in the Mystic Capital.
>
> (Bokenkamp 1983, 437)

About one-half of the Lingbao corpus contains revealed heavenly scriptures; the other half consists of instructions and explanations. The latter elucidate the arcane content of the scriptures and detail the concrete procedures necessary to fulfill their message. According to the orthodox Lingbao tradition, Ge Xuan of the third century, the great-uncle of Ge Hong, author of the famous *Baopuzi* (Book of the Master Who Embraces Simplicity),[5] was selected as the major promulgator of sacred scriptures on this earth. He was "singled out after a discouraging cycle of rebirths because of his devotion to the Tao and his Amitābha-like vow to effect the salvation of humanity" (Bokenkamp 1983, 438).

In historical fact, however, Ge's descendant Ge Chaofu compiled the Lingbao scriptures on the basis of the Shangqing revelations in the last decade of the fourth century. Ge Chaofu was not content with the celestial rank of Ge Xuan in the Shangqing pantheon and created his own system to elevate Ge Xuan to a prime position. The main sources of the Lingbao scriptures include the original Shangqing revelations, the library of Ge Hong, and translations of Buddhist scriptures. The original Shangqing revelations were responsible for the celestial orientation of Lingbao Taoism, its visualization techniques and several of its highest deities. The library of Ge Hong helped to include much Han-dynasty correlative thinking as well as ancient lore on talismans and charts.

Buddhist scriptures contributed the arcane "Brahma-language" to name the heavens and shroud esoteric formulas. In addition, they provided visions of cosmology, the concept of karma and retribution, the five precepts, and the bodhisattva vow. In concrete terms, the Buddhist texts used most frequently by Ge Chaofu were translations by Zhi Qian of the third century, a popular Buddhist among Jiangnan aristocrats (Bokenkamp 1983, 466).

Analyzing a large selection of early salvational Taoist texts, Erik Zürcher found four different ways in which they integrated Buddhist materials: formal borrowing, conceptual borrowing, borrowed complexes, and pervasive borrowing (Zürcher 1980).

Formal borrowing includes stylistic patterns like superlatives and large numbers; metaphors like the Heavenly Lord radiating a divine light; and stock phrases, found especially in standardized beginnings ("Thus I have heard . . .") and endings (in verses known as *gāthas*) of the texts (Zürcher 1980, 101).

Conceptual borrowing refers to the integration and transformation of Buddhist doctrine in Taoism. Here we have, for example, *"prajñā* wisdom," the "wheel of the law," the "dharma body of the Buddha," the idea and practice of *"samādhi* concentration," and the notion of "emptiness," as well as the system of the "three vehicles," so aptly used in the compilation of the earliest Taoist Canon (Zürcher 1980, 113).[6]

Most importantly, Buddhism contributed the whole complexes of cosmology, morality, and karma to salvational Taoism. In cosmology, Taoism integrated the ten directions, the Western Paradise, a multiplicity of heavens and hells, and the idea of the repeated renewal of the world in so-called kalpa cycles. On the level of morality, there are not only the classical Buddhist precepts but also the supreme virtues and the idea that humankind will be saved through the bodhisattva. In terms of karma and rebirth, Lingbao Taoism borrowed another huge complex relating to the ideas of personal responsibility, individual penitence, and possible rebirth on the grounds of one's former deeds and thoughts (Zürcher 1980, 121–41; see also Bokenkamp 1983, 469).

Salvational Taoism borrowed very little in the area of body-mind interpretation or the "Perfection of Wisdom." These more philosophical dimensions of Buddhism, on the other hand, strongly inspired Taoist thought and made a serious impact on the Chinese mystical tradition, as will become clear presently.

Pervasive influence, to mention Zürcher's last category, is hard to pin down. It is felt but not found in recognizable Buddhist terms or concepts. Among the potential areas for this are personal revelation, periodicity of time, the law of moral retribution, the positive effect of good works and charity, and the worship of texts, as well as numerous meditational techniques, visualizations, trances, and others (Zürcher 1980, 88). Many of these are not clearly defined as either Buddhist or Taoist. Yet they are among the most essential features of the early Chinese mystical tradition as it approached its heyday in the Tang.

Debates among Buddhists and Taoists

When Buddhism first came to China, the belief arose that when Laozi left China he traveled far west and eventually founded Buddhism in India. This belief explained the similarities of the teachings (Zürcher 1959, 291). It turned polemical around the year 300 c.e. when a certain Wang Fou compiled the earliest *Huahu jing* (Scripture on Converting the Barbarians). Here Buddhism is represented as a much-inferior version of the original Taoist teaching; its precepts become the means to civilize uncouth savages.

In the fourth century, Chinese literati integrated Buddhism in an encompassing "harmony among the three teachings." The chief exponent of this integrationist view was Sun Chuo (ca. 310–390 C.E.), who combined Confucian social responsibility, the Lao-Zhuang ideal of contemplation, and Buddhist enlightenment.[7]

In the fifth century, the first wave of court debates took place in south China. The Taoists Zhang Rong and Gu Huan were its chief exponents. Zhang Rong, in his *Menlü* (Instructions for My Followers; T. 2102; 52.39b–41b), made the "helpless attempt to gain acceptance at court for his creed by placing it on the same level as Buddhism" (Schmidt-Glintzer 1976, 112). Following Sun Chuo's line of reasoning, Zhang Rong contended that both teachings were fundamentally identical. Both court factions should therefore have equal say in matters of state. The Buddhist Zhou Yong countered this argument by referring to the association of Taoism with the rebellious Great Peace of 184 C.E. Contrary to this lowly heritage, he claimed Buddhism was lofty and of high quality.

Gu Huan, in his *Yixia lun* (On Barbarians and Chinese) of the year 467 C.E.,[8] argued that Buddhism was quite suitable for the barbarians, while Taoism was the proper teaching for the Chinese. Barbarians and Chinese were as different as fish and birds, so their worldviews should be irreconcilable too. His scheme divides the two teachings as follows:

Buddhism	*Taoism*
barbarian	Chinese
concerned with	concerned with
salvation of the spirit	longevity of the body
secondhand	original
involves no filial piety	very filial
contains abstruse ideas	concrete, practicable
complex	straightforward

Gu Huan was critical of Buddhism and ranked it lower than the native Chinese teaching, yet he allowed it its place in the scheme of things. It was a barbarian teaching and thus suitable for the uncultured tribes beyond Chinese borders, but as such it had its value and, though definitely unfit for Chinese consumption, needed not be extirpated altogether.[9]

In the sixth century, a second round of debates—now growing increasingly polemical—was staged at the Northern Wei court. In 520 C.E., the Taoist Jiang Bin and the Buddhist Tan Muzui argued the seniority of their teachings in the presence of the emperor. They concentrated on the problem of dating. If Laozi went west to convert the barbarians and become the Buddha, he must have left China earlier than the recorded birth of the Buddha in India. To best all Buddhist claims, the Taoists produced the *Laozi kaitian jing* (Scripture of Laozi Opening the Heavens), not identical with a text of this title still extant in the Taoist Canon today. Showing that this scripture was apocryphal and not a revealed text, the Buddhists emerged victorious from this phase of the debate and thereby gained influence at court (see Kusuyama 1976).

In 569 C.E., the next set of debates took place under the reign of Emperor Wu of the Northern Zhou, known as a partisan of Taoism who also sponsored the first Taoist encyclopedia, the *Wushang biyao* (Essential Secrets of the Most High; Lagerwey 1981). He organized a big conference on the advantages and disadvantages of the three teachings. As a Buddhist source records it,

> On the fifteenth day of the third month of the year 569, the emperor summoned meritorious monks, renowned Confucians, Taoist masters, as well as various civilian and military officials to the palace. All in all there were more than two thousand people.
>
> Before His Majesty they were to give measure of the three teachings in learned dispute. Confucianism was first named leading with Buddhism as its follower. But as the highest of all Taoism was acknowledged, since it alone went beyond even the nameless, transcending the ultimate of heaven and earth.
>
> However, the dispute at this conference was very confused. Participants tended to become agitated in defense of their personal preferences. In the end they parted without reaching any definite conclusion.
>
> (*Guang hongming ji* 8, T. 2103; 52.136a18–23)

The emperor ordered several reports on the proceedings but remained dissatisfied with the findings of the learned assembly. He then asked several specialists to summarize pertinent arguments on the subject. The *Xiaodao lun* (Laughing at the Tao; T. 2103; 52.143c–152c) and the *Erjiao lun* (On the Two Teachings; T. 2103; 52.136b–143c) were duly submitted in 570 C.E. But both ranked Confucianism and Buddhism above Taoism. The extremely polemical *Xiaodao lun* was burnt on the spot. The more conciliatory *Erjiao lun*, which defines Buddhism as the inner and Confucianism and Taoism as the outer level of one universal teaching, was graciously shelved away.

In the seventh century, the third and—for the time being—last phase of the Buddho-Taoist debates took place in the early Tang.[11] Less involved with the power needs of a non-Chinese ruler, the discussion summarized earlier arguments and extrapolated them in a more sophisticated, even scholastic, fashion. The classics of the debates were written at this time, including the *Poxie lun* (On the Destruction of Falsehood; T. 2109) of the year 622 C.E.; the *Bianzheng lun*

(On Discerning Truth; T. 2110) of the year 626 c.e.; and the *Zhenzheng lun* (On Examining Truth; T. 2112) of the late seventh century.[12]

Early Chinese mysticism grows in this fruitful period of mutual Buddho-Taoist borrowing and criticism. The heaviest borrowing took place in the salvational and communal Taoist schools, which under Buddhist influence soon began to establish monasteries and an organized canon of their own. The stage for criticism, integrative and polemical, was largely the imperial court. The debates were a rather academic exercise, aimed at securing dominant influence on state politics.

Taoist mystics flourished between the two. They were intellectuals who searched for a personally relevant understanding of the universe and pursued mystical states, intensely private and theirs alone. Yet they also found much inspiration and guidance in the newly established centers of the communal movements, venerated their scriptures, and followed their practices. Mystical writers of the Late Six Dynasties were also ritual masters and contenders in the court debates. They wrote mystical treatises and commentaries to the ancient philosophers, but their interpretations breathed practical religion and interaction with Buddhism.

THE SCRIPTURE OF WESTERN ASCENSION

The *Xisheng jing* is the first mystical Taoist text that integrates Lao-Zhuang philosophy, the pursuit of immortality, the motif of the journey, and Buddhist doctrine. It is today extant in two Song-dynasty editions—one by Chen Jingyuan (1025–94), the other by the Song emperor Huizong (r. 1101–26)—but dates originally from the fifth century.[14] The edition by Chen Jingyuan contains five commentaries, of which the one by Wei Jie (497–569) is the earliest. A retired scholar-official and active mystic of the sixth century, Wei Jie's life provides interesting insights into the background and concrete setting of early Chinese mystics. Other commentaries include the work of the seventh-century philosopher Li Rong and a number of less well known individuals.

The *Xisheng jing* is divided into thirty-nine sections. It claims to report the oral instructions that Laozi gave to Yin Xi, the Guardian of the Pass, when he transmitted the *Daode jing*. The text opens with the motif of the journey and evokes the conversion of the barbarians. It says:

Laozi ascended to the West to open up the Tao in India. He was called Master Gu. Skilled at entering non-action, without beginning or end, he exists continuously. Thus steadily ascending, he followed his way and reached the border.

Yin Xi, the Guardian of the Pass, saw his [sagely] energy. He purified himself and waited upon the guest. Laozi transmitted the Tao and the Virtue to him. He arranged it in two sections.
[Laozi said]: "I will tell you about the essentials of the Tao."

(*Xisheng jing* 1.1–1.7)[15]

All the remaining sections of the text begin with the words "Laozi said." The last section concludes the scripture. Laozi announces his immediate ascent to the immortals and vanishes. As the text narrates this dramatic event,

Suddenly Laozi was nowhere to be seen. The office building was illuminated by a brilliance of five colors, simultaneously dark and yellow. Yin Xi went into the courtyard, bowed down and said:
"Please, dear spirit man, let me see you once again. Give me one more rule, and I can guard the primordial source of all."
He looked up and saw Laozi suspended in midair several feet above the ground. He looked like a statue. The image appeared and disappeared; it was vague and indistinct and seemed to waver between young and old.
Laozi said: "I will give you one more admonition; make sure you get it right: Get rid of all impurity and stop all thoughts; calm your mind and guard the One. When all impurities are gone, the myriad affairs are done. These are the essentials of my Tao."
Then the vision vanished. Yin Xi did not know where it had gone. He cried bitterly and worshiped it in remembrance. Then he retired from office on grounds of illness. He gave up all thinking and guarded the One, and the myriad affairs were done.

(39.5–14)

From a traveler toward the Western regions, Laozi has therefore become a successful immortal who, his mission on earth completed, ascends to his true home in the heavens above. The pursuit of immortality together with the motif of the journey effectively frame the teachings of this mystical scripture.

The bulk of the text consists of Laozi's instructions to Yin Xi. It can be divided into five parts of about seven sections each. The structure of the text is cyclical. The discussion never develops in a linear and straightforward way, but different themes merge into and circle around one another in a kind of dancelike movement. The text is rather repetitive and often seems contradictory in its statements. But its very vagueness and apparent intellectual confusion turns the text into a living model for the quality of aliveness of the written word. In a new awareness of the qualities of the mystical process, the language of the *Xisheng jing* itself becomes a direct representation of the ascending movement toward the Tao.

Though circular, there is yet an ascending movement from one part to the next. The text begins by describing Laozi's ascent to the pass in the Zhongnan mountains. It continues to spiral upward in five cycles of teaching and ends, like a wisp of smoke, in the ultimate ascent to Heaven. The *Xisheng jing* literally ascends: it pauses, it moves on, it looks back, it glimpses the steep path ahead, it rejoices in the view, it sympathizes with the people down below, it returns in the end. It is not purely a literary document, but stands as a living example of the path of the mystic.

Cycles of Ascent

The first cycle (sects. 1–7) outlines the setting, in which the instructions take place, and summarizes Yin Xi's practice. It also delineates the foundations by discussing the relation of human beings to the world, of sense experience to knowledge, of body to mind, and of true teachings to false ones. The cycle begins with Laozi's ascent to the West and ends with his promise to teach ascension to the world.

In teaching, language is a necessity. Yet, as the *Daode jing* already stated, "Who knows does not speak; who speaks does not know" (chap. 56). How to reconcile the necessity of speaking with the impossibility of doing so knowingly? Laozi explains this statement:

> It can be compared to the knowledge of sound. One becomes conscious of sound by plucking a string. Though the mind may know the appropriate words, yet the mouth is unable to formulate them. Similarly the Tao is deep, subtle, wonderful; who knows it does not speak.
> On the other hand, one may be conscious of sounds, voices, cries. One then dampens the sounds to consider them within. Then when the mind makes the mouth speak, one speaks but does not know.
>
> (1.15–1.19)

Only by carefully concentrating on the Tao can one develop a certain intuition for it. However, that remains ineffable: one knows but cannot speak. At the same time, the conscious mind may experience and classify certain experiences. They can be put into words but do not ultimately represent the experience as such: one speaks but does not know. The predicament requires a new way of dealing with language, a gradual development of language from the ordinary to the more Tao-like. To begin with, Laozi clarifies that there are various ways of speaking about the Tao. It is emptiness and nonbeing, but it is also a choice between various forms of mystical practice: "The Tao in its words may be said to be either true or untrue. The untrue Tao teaches you to nourish the body, the true Tao teaches you to nourish the spirit. Spirit realized, the Tao pervaded: you can freely be gone or exist in this world" (7.3–7.5)

According to the *Xisheng jing*, only the cultivation of spirit will lead to immortality, while the body "is mere dust and ashes" (7.7). This rejection of physical practices and of the belief in physical survival is one of the unique characteristics of the *Xisheng jing*. Very soon, with Li Rong's commentary, gymnastics and breathing exercises become part of the mystical path.

The second part (sects. 8–14) outlines the mystics' progressive participation in the Tao. There can be no true knowledge of the Tao, but one can develop a working hypothesis, laid down in scriptures and precepts, and approach the truth by practice. The relationship of the active mystic to the written word is fundamentally antagonistic. Yet it develops as his spontaneous understanding grows.

To begin with, a practitioner knows that "all that is said in scriptures and precepts, all that is prescribed in laws and statutes, is powerful, awe-inspiring, and openly declared" (13.1). Because it is generally accessible, it is inferior to the Tao. Nevertheless, the Tao also has patterns that can be described. Beginners therefore study the scriptures. When they do not fully understand them, they should "just try to grasp their basic meaning and observe the precepts without fail" (14.6). This integrates disciplined monastic practice as an initial step of the path.

Then adepts proceed to practice meditation. They "observe all things as manifestations of the Tao and visualize the spirits in meditative imagination" (12.1). As a result they "will establish freedom from desires and no longer know the difference between ordinary and meditative thought" (12.5). This in turn leads to sageliness. Mystics are free from longing and remain in perfect simplicity.

The cycle takes the student—the reader as much as Yin Xi—from the understanding that all is part of the ineffable Tao to the realization that one can become one with it by accepting the premises of Taoist doctrine and following the master's instructions. The ascent leads to the understanding that meditation does not replace theoretical knowledge but leads to a higher state in which one knows intuitively by not knowing.

Mystical Attainments

The third cycle (sects. 15–22) intensifies theory and practice. We learn how the world began. Laozi said: "Emptiness and nonbeing bring forth nature; nature brings forth the Tao; the Tao produces the One; the One produces the myriad beings. The myriad beings embrace the

One and come into being; they attain the subtle and wonderful and come to life" (15.1–15.2).

People think and feel within a living cosmos. Their spirit represents the Tao within. Self-consciousness, on the contrary, increases the distance to the Tao. Laozi says, "What gives me life is the spirit, what kills me is the mind. Mind and conscious intention are afflictions to me. Thus, if I am of no-mind, what would I know?" (17.2–3). To attain the ideal state of no-mind, one should "recollect the time when one was not yet born: then one did not have a personal body" (17.4). The personal body develops physically through the accumulation of energy (*qi*) and blood, psychologically through consciousness and ego-identification. Dissolving the personal body and the conscious mind, mystics return to their primordial body—a replica of the universe—and to original spirit, the pure agent of the Tao.

According to the *Xisheng jing*, spirit and body are cosmological forces that existed from the primordial beginning. The purpose of the universe lies in the perfection of spirit with the help of material bodies (sect. 22). The abstract cosmology of spirit and body is unique in this text. It supplements the classical cosmology of the Tao cited above and reveals the text's dominant concern with the human mind.

In the fourth cycle (sects. 23–31), the mystic ascends to sagehood and becomes fully one with the Tao. Beyond the world and yet in it, the sage is free from all harm.

> The sage cherishes the subtle and wonderful, embraces roughness and simplicity and never dares to act deliberately or in any way interfere or contend with the world.
>
> There may be wild beasts, but they will not attack him; there may be wasps and scorpions, worms and snakes, but they will not bite him; there may be soldiers and weapons, but they will not injure him.
>
> Because he has accumulated virtue and pervades the mystery, none in the world can do him any harm.
>
> (27.4–27.6)

The sage has all the magical powers of the immortals and will eventually ascend to heaven. But he is also the ideal ruler of the *Daode jing*, who channels the power of the Tao, and the sage of the Confucian tradition, whose major concern is social harmony and the moral perfection of humanity. The sagely ruler teaches and helps all beings, acting in accordance with heaven. He controls his own destiny but must never try to control others. Free from worldly strife, "the sage rests in non-action and no-affairs; he only desires to keep the people of his country at peace" (25.8).

The fifth cycle (sects. 32–38) returns in many ways—to the theme of participation, to the root of life, to the beginning of the world, to the theme of returning itself. The sage as all else, as "heaven and earth, water and fire, the myriad beings, high mountains, and deep ravines" (36.1), has his place of origin to which he now returns. The return takes place in a complete loss of conscious awareness. It is a deathlike trance state, in which the body is unmoving and the mind is enveloped in darkness. The text describes it as follows: "The four limbs are stiff, there is no-mind within. I reach the innermost flourishing of the myriad beings, the non-ultimate to which all nature returns" (38.7–38.10).

This complete dissolution in the Tao comes as a result of long practice and mystical training. It is a state of utter harmony of the spirit and indicates a joyful and willing return to the latency of human existence. Everybody will return likewise, whether they know it or not. However, in most cases people think of this return as death and loathe it. Instead they should consider the return as part of the ongoing cosmic transformations and realize that death is as much a part of the Tao as is life—maybe even more so, since death, like the North in the cosmic journey, represents a more original level of participation, a higher potential of oneness.

The text then concludes with Laozi's ascent into heaven and Yin Xi's return to his practice in the world. Life, suspended for five spiraling cycles of teaching, goes on in its course: the heavenly to the heavenly, the worldly to the worldly. But the interaction, the instructions, have changed the quality of both. Laozi, the divine sage, has fulfilled his worldly destiny; Yin Xi, the human aspirant, has begun to realize, in theory and practice, the development of cosmic life.

Throughout the ascent, language has continued to change. The text itself uses words differently, makes its readers aware of the differences between ordinary consciousness and the perspective of the Tao. Section 37, for example, redefines "good." Laozi first says that he does not know good or evil. Then he claims that "the Tao is supported only by good people." The same word "good" is used to refer to two entirely different things. As mystics are freed from the classifications of ordinary life, the subtler levels of good and evil become manifest. They use the same word, yet their understanding has shifted from the goodness of everyday life to the goodness of the eternal Tao.

Buddhist Influence

The Xisheng jing continues Lao-Zhuang philosophy in a framework of religious Taoism and the belief in immortality. At the same time it reveals much Buddhist influence. First of all, there is the framework narrative, according to which Laozi is identical with Master Gu, interpreted to refer to the Buddha. Also, the setting evokes the conversion of the barbarians. Laozi is said to be "skilled at entering non-action," a phrase that could refer equally well to nirvāna. The use of *wuwei* in this double sense is typical of the philosophical integration found in the *Xisheng jing*.

Buddhism pervades the text, but there are also instances of conceptual borrowing. Buddhist concepts merge seamlessly with the worldview of the text. The four Indian elements, for example, appear (5.3), but are immediately set in correlation with the four seasons. The three conditions (*sanye, trividha-dvāra*) of body, speech, and mind occur several times, but are interpreted in Chinese fashion. Originally part of the Tao, they are naturally pure, spoiled only through human carelessness. Carelessness, then, is specifically linked with greed (*tan*), a translation for *rāga*, "passion." Again, the doctrines of causation and rebirth play an important role in the text, which connects them easily with the indigenous concept of fate. In one place it says, "In former lives one did not study or ask questions, so in this life one once again lives in the common world" (9.4).

A strong preference of mind or spirit over body is the least Taoist feature of the *Xisheng jing*. It discounts physical longevity techniques and vigorously denies the possibility of immortality in the body. At the same time, the purified mind, once having entered nirvāna, can and will ascend into the heaven of the immortals. The overall cosmology is Taoist; the strongest detectable impact of Lingbao Taoism is Laozi's statement that "I have been moving along for years amounting to kalpas" (9.10). This again is related to the mystic's ascent. Laozi, not unlike the Buddha of the Theravāda tradition, is more the exemplary seeker and model for his followers than a cosmic deity. He undergoes suffering to attain nirvāna and suffers to help humankind.

Many terms are used in a double sense. The word *se* refers to both visual stimulation and matter (*rūpa*); *fan* indicates both *kleśa* and general troubles and afflictions; *shen* is the self as cultivated in the Confucian and Taoist traditions as well as the *ātman* denied in Buddhist doctrine. No-self (*wushen, anātman*) is interpreted as the state before one was born, again giving a native tinge to a foreign concept. The three periods of time and all conditions pertaining to the body are critically examined by means of *guan*, a mixture of traditional visualization and insight meditation techniques (*vipaśyanā*) (12.1). Following the precepts (*jie; sīla*) is recommended so long as the practitioner has not grasped the teaching spontaneously, but—as do Buddhist texts—the *Xisheng jing* warns against becoming too attached to outer forms of behavior (13.1). Unknowing (*wuzhi*), the ultimate state of mind, is also based on both the *Zhuangzi* and Chinese Buddhist interpretations of *prajñā*.

The mystical tradition as documented in the *Xisheng jing* therefore continues the philosophical heritage of Lao-Zhuang, Guo Xiang, and early Chinese Buddhist thinkers like Zhi Dun. It also integrates Confucian ideals of moral rectitude and social responsibility, inherits the salvational vision of Lingbao Taoism, and contains visible Buddhist elements.

The Mystic's Life

The *Xisheng jing* claims the status of a revealed text and therefore does not name an author. It can be dated to the fifth century on the basis of its concepts and structure, but most of all because its first commentary was written by Wei Jie of the sixth century (497–569 c.e.). His biography is an instructive example of the situation in which Chinese seekers of perfection found themselves at the time. Zhao Daoyi's *Lishi zhenxian tidao tongjian* of the thirteenth century (DZ 296, fasc. 144; 29.4a–5b) gives a lucid picture of an aristocrat-official of northern China in the sixth century who turned into an active Taoist mystic and philosopher. According to Zhao Daoyi, Wei Jie or Wei Chuxuan was born in 497 c.e. in a village near Chang'an in Shaansi. He was very bright and loved books. At the age of fourteen, in the year 510, he began official service in the Palace Library under Emperor Xuanwu of the Northern (Toba) Wei (r. 500–516). He was advanced upon the accession of Xuanwu's successor, Emperor Xiaoming, and again in 528, when Emperor Xiaozhuang ascended the throne. At the early age of thirty-two he already held the office of a provincial prefect.

Wei Jie's administrative district was the area of Mount Song in Henan. There he became the friend and disciple of Zhao Jingtong, a Taoist master about whom nothing further is known. In 534, when the Toba empire was divided after much factional fighting, Wei Jie decided to abandon his career in favor of a quiet life in the mountains. He gave illness as the official reason for his retirement. Under Zhao Jingtong, Wei Jie practiced a combination of Celestial Master practices, Shangqing meditation, and Lingbao ritual. As Zhao Daoyi has it: "From his teacher he received the numinous scriptures, divine methods, and secret formulas of the Three Caverns." After graduation, his master sent him off to the southern peak of Huashan in Shaansi as the place predestined for his particular *qi*.

In his new residence Wei Jie continued to practice Taoism for thirty-five years until his death in 569. He followed a dietetic regimen of sesame, fungus, sulphur, cinnabar, and realgar to strengthen his health and ensure longevity. A scholar and philosopher, he devoted much time to writing commentaries on established Confucian and

Taoist classics. He had a strong interest in the *Daode jing* and the *Yi-jing*, to which "he devoted special treatises."

His collected works, which came to more than eighty scrolls, also contained commentaries to religious Taoist texts, of which unfortunately only his commentary to the *Xisheng jing* survives. His death in 569 was accompanied by the auspicious appearance of a brilliant cloud. He knew of the event in advance and could properly prepare himself, finally announcing, "I shall ascend and leave."

Wei Jie's life exemplifies the career of a sixth-century Chinese mystic. Born and raised in the Confucian system, he was thoroughly familiar with the philosophical works of all mainstream Chinese culture. Rising at a young age to high official status, he gave up his political involvement, partly because the political situation was deteriorating, but also because he found the Taoist's teaching stimulating intellectually and spiritually. He practiced the various techniques, learned to nourish his body and to meditate on the various manifestations of the Tao. Later returning to philosophical speculation, he wrote a number of commentaries. In his work on the *Xisheng jing*, which closely follows the worldview of the text, he integrated the various teachings then current to suit his individual outlook and understanding (see Kohn 1991).

In many ways, Wei Jie was representative of the Chinese mystics who left behind philosophical and technical writings. They all came from a literati background and were often involved with official careers. If lucky, they might have continued to serve their ruler in a government position. Neither Sima Xiangru nor Guo Xiang left official service. In the late Six Dynasties, however, political instability and the ideal of monasticism encouraged mystics to retire from service and withdraw to the mountains. There they studied as a group of like-minded associates, integrating traditional health techniques, especially gymnastics and diets, with more spiritual pursuits, such as visualizations and insight meditation, with the correct handling of talismans and the performance of Buddhist rituals.

But most of all, those mystics who left behind written accounts of their accomplishments were and remained literati. The religious life in those days, far from being bound by confessional limitations, encouraged individual selections and specialization. Thus any Taoist or Buddhist, though trained in the standardized ways of his school, was never just the representative of one specific teaching only. Mystics can thus be described as the more intellectually specialized among a large group of religious seekers of various denominations, frequently not too rigidly defined.

CHAPTER SEVEN

The Tang Synthesis

IN THE TANG dynasty, the mystical synthesis of Lao-Zhuang thought, shamanistic ascension, and Buddhism came into its own. Three major developments took place.

First, the formulation of the mystical process and its attainments became more sophisticated. Strongly influenced by Buddhist Mādhyamika, *Daode jing* interpretation after the fashion of Twofold Mystery flourished especially in the seventh century. This fashion represented an attempt to clarify and elucidate mystical oneness in intellectual terms. It was rather esoteric and shows inclinations toward scholasticism.

Next, the impact of Buddhism continued and became stronger. Cosmology, meditation methods, and mystical stages turned more obviously Buddhist. The *Daojiao yishu* (The Pivotal Meaning of the Taoist Teaching; DZ 1129, fasc. 762–63) of the late seventh century incorporated a veritable cornucopia of Buddhist doctrine in Taoist guise. It established an integrated system truly harmonizing the teachings.

Third, physical practices were accepted fully as part of the mystics' path. Diets and drugs, gymnastics and breathing exercises, all the health and longevity techniques of Chinese medicine, developed into an important segment of the ascent to the Tao. Masters like Sun Simiao and Sima Chengzhen of the seventh and eighth centuries compiled detailed instructions leaving no doubt about the integrated path they envisioned.

TWOFOLD MYSTERY

Twofold Mystery (Chongxuan) was the dominant way of interpreting the *Daode jing* in the seventh century.[1] It was not a school in the sense of a sect or an exclusive group; nevertheless, its representatives developed a sense of belonging to it, often expressed in their adoption of the character *xuan* as their middle name: Cheng Xuanying, Huang Xuanyi, Che Xuanbi, to give a few examples (Sunayama 1980, 36; Fujiwara 1980a). The fashion also included Emperor Xuanzong of the eighth century, an ardent Taoist in more ways than one (see Benn

1987). In the seventh century, there were three major Chongxuan thinkers: Liu Jinxi, Cheng Xuanying, and Li Rong. They all were involved in the Buddho-Taoist controversies at court and wrote commentaries to the *Daode jing* or other works central to the understanding of Twofold Mystery.

The Thinkers

Liu Jinxi was a resident of the Qingxu guan (Monastery of Clarity and Emptiness) in Chang'an. Du Guangting dates him to the Sui dynasty, a time when he seems to have completed his major works. He defended the Taoist faith in the debates under Emperor Gaozu (r. 618–27) and died around 640. He left an anti-Buddhist tract entitled *Xianzheng lun* (On Illuminating Truth), an essay on Laozi, and a commentary to the *Daode jing* (Robinet 1977, 103). His most famous and sole surviving work is the first section of the *Benji jing* (Scripture of Original Time).

An important philosophical and mystical text, the *Benji jing* appears first in the early Tang dynasty and survived in Dunhuang.[2] The term *benji* is taken over from Buddhist literature, where it occurs, among other instances, as the title of the translation of the *Samyuktāgama sūtra* (T. 99; 2.240–43). *Benji* refers to the state before universal creation, illustrated in an ancient Indian origin myth. According to this myth, being developed from nonbeing through the formation of a cosmic egg, which split into heaven and earth. Chapter 4 of the *Benji jing* recounts this myth (Wu 1960, 8; Kaltenmark 1979a). Buddhists were prone to citing the text as a prime example of the Taoists' ruthless plagiarizing of their sutras. According to the polemical *Zhenzheng lun*, they claimed that Liu Jinxi was among its authors (Wu 1960, 11).

The *Benji jing* is what one could call a Māhayāna Taoist scripture. The Tao is a cosmic deity and resides in heaven, answering questions posed by various followers. Following the concepts of Twofold Mystery, the text is highly sophisticated and engages heavily in philosophical speculation along the lines of the Mādhyamika. Frequently cited in Tang-dynasty Taoist materials, it became less popular later. Its essential doctrines were summarized in one *juan*, now contained in the Taoist Canon (DZ 1111, fasc. 758).

Cheng Xuanying was another famous author of Twofold Mystery. Originally from the Guangdong area, he was summoned to the capital in 632 (*Xin Tangshu* 59). In 636 he actively participated in a Buddho-Taoist controversy in Chang'an. At that time Emperor Taizong established the priority of Taoism due to the descent of his family from Laozi. In 643 Cheng Xuanying became abbot of the Xihua guan (Monastery of Western Florescence). In 646 he was asked to inquire into the authenticity of a newly discovered manuscript of the *Sanhuang wen* (Writ of the Three August Ones; see Fukui 1952). Cheng refused to accept its third-century origins and advised the emperor to have it burned.

Following this, the *Daode jing* officially became the highest Taoist scripture (Sunayama 1980, 126). In 647 the emperor ordered Cheng Xuanying to translate the *Daode jing* into Sanskrit together with the Taoist Cai Zihuang and the famous Buddhist traveler Xuanzang (ca. 602–64; *Fodao lunheng*, T.2104; 52.386c). Little is known about Cheng's later years. He fell from grace and died in far-off exile around 670. Cheng Xuanying's works are mostly commentaries. He wrote on the *Daode jing*, the *Zhuangzi*, the *Duren jing*, and the *Yijing*.

The third among the better-known Chongxuan philosophers of the seventh century was Li Rong. Also known as Renzhenzi, he came from Sichuan, where he became a Taoist at an early age. Like Liu Jingxi, Li Rong actively participated in the Buddho-Taoist controversies and appeared at court in the years 658, 660, and 663 (*Fodao lunheng*; T.2104; 52.387c). Li Rong also appeared as a poet and member of the literati elite. Several poet-officials, such as Lu Zhaolin and Luo Binwang, wrote for him. Li Rong seems to have been a well-liked guest in officials' residences. Like Cheng Xuanying, he wrote commentaries—his works on the *Daode jing* and the *Xisheng jing* still survive.[4]

The thinkers of Twofold Mystery represent a new and different kind of mystical Taoist. In earlier periods, mystics were primarily recluses who left society and practiced esoteric techniques on isolated mountains. Prominent Taoists of the early Tang, to the contrary, were accredited well at court and held considerable intellectual influence in their time. They had close and friendly connections with members of high officialdom and repeatedly appeared in the imperial debates. This indicates that they moved in the highest circles of the period, were in fact Taoists of the court, like Du Guangting in a later age (see Verellen 1989). Although different in status and social integration, the major protagonists of Twofold Mystery were sincere and worthy heirs of the mystical tradition as it continued to unfold. Like their Six Dynasties predecessors, they were deeply involved with the philosophy of Laozi and Zhuangzi, yet at the same time represented a religious environment suffused with Buddho-Taoism and pursued the ascent to the immortals above.

Levels of Truth

The expression "twofold mystery" goes back to the line "mysterious and again mysterious" of the *Daode jing*. Cheng Xuanying explains it thus: "Mysterious means deep and profound. It is also an expression for being without obstructions. The two minds of being and nonbeing, the two visions of outcome and subtlety all spring from the one Tao. They arise together, but have different names, yet they are part of the one Tao" (chap. 1; Yan 1983, 303; Robinet 1977, 108).

"Mysterious" in Chongxuan philosophy moreover appears as a verb in the sense of "to make mysterious." Read like this, "mysterious and again mysterious" is parallel with "decrease and again decrease" (chap. 48). To decrease means to eliminate desire. As the *Daode jing* says, "Let there be no desire so that the subtle may be observed" (chap. 1).

One discards all desires in two steps, following the structure of the basic statement "mysterious and again mysterious." As Cheng has it,

> Practitioners must first discard all desires, then proceed to discard the state of no-desires. Only then can they truly accomplish twofold discarding of all and wondrously merge with the Tao of Middle Oneness. Beings and ego looked upon in equal fashion, mental states and wisdom both forgotten— when someone makes such a state his principle of government, then everything will be well ordered.

> (chap. 3; Yan 1983, 315)

The process outlined here consists in a double obscuring, a double decrease, a double forgetfulness (*jianwang*). First one eliminates all mental states (*jing*), the illusory visions of the mind erroneously regarded as real. Then one abolishes wisdom (*zhi*) or mind (*xin*), the inherent function of the mind as such (Fujiwara 1980b, 659; Zhao 1982, 10). Twofold Mystery therefore aims at the transformation of the ordinary mind into true wisdom; then, however, even true wisdom is given up in favor of neither mind nor no-mind. This is called reaching the Tao of Middle Oneness, which results in a state of radiance and resurging activity.

> On the outside the sage will not have any mental states that would be desirable; on the inside he will not have a mind that could do any desiring. Mind and mental states are both forgotten, thus the mind as such becomes no-mind. Where there were mental states and illusions before, later there is only the emptiness of mind. Yet even though the mind as such is no-mind, it shines forth in numinous radiance.

> (chap. 3; Yan 1983, 313)

With these ideas Twofold Mystery continued the indigenous mystical tradition but explained it in terms of Mādhyamika, also known as the Three Treatises School. Founded in the second century by the Indian thinker Nāgārjuna, it made a strong impact on Chinese Buddhism in the fifth and sixth centuries. Jizang (549–623) outlined his ideas in his *Erdi zhang* (On the Two Levels of Truth).[5] He claimed that one developed truth by passing through three distinct stages.

The first stage leads from the worldly truth of ordinary people to the absolute truth realized by the sages. Practitioners realize that all things are ultimately empty because they have no intrinsic nature—their existence is co-dependent and relative. In a second stage, both ordinary thinking and the understanding of emptiness are realized as merely another form of worldly truth. Absolute truth is redefined as complete nonduality—neither being nor nonbeing. The third stage, then, explains that both duality and nonduality are worldly truth, whereas neither duality nor nonduality is the highest truth. Gradually all evaluation and conscious thinking is eliminated.

This structure of two levels of truth and its application to three stages of mystical progress leads logically to the analytical method of the "Four Propositions," already part of traditional Mādhyamika:

affirmation of being;
affirmation of nonbeing;
affirmation of both, being and nonbeing;
negation of both, being and nonbeing.
                                        (Robinson 1967, 57; Robinet 1977, 117)

Cheng Xuanying explains this in terms of Twofold Mystery applying the concept of the origin (*ben*) and the traces (*ji*). He says in his commentary to the *Zhuangzi*,

There are four levels of meaning:
First, the wonderful origin is empty and concentrated, one is serene and
    without movement.
Second, the secondary traces develop through impulse and response, one
    is active and not serene.
Third, origin and traces coincide, one is active and serene at the same time.
Fourth, origin and traces are both forgotten, one has discarded both move-
    ment and serenity.
                                        (DZ 745, 9.13b; Sunayama 1980a, 133)

Twofold Mystery thus integrates the basic concepts and analytical methods of Mādhyamika into the indigenous mystical vision of a progressive forgetfulness. Again, Cheng says in his *Daode jing* commentary, "Not only must one never develop desire toward being. One must neither even desire the simplicity of the nameless. First use non-being to discard being, then use being to discard nonbeing. Separated from both, being and nonbeing, this is the Tao of Middle Oneness" (chap. 37; Yan 1983, 446; Fujiwara 1980, 658).

The Taoist version of Buddhist Mādhyamika therefore links the two-truth theory with the elimination of desires and the attainment of a state of oblivion. As the sage proceeds toward greater oneness with the Tao, he undergoes various phases of movement and serenity, of ecstasy and enstasy.

Sagely Attainments

Passing through the stages toward higher understanding, the sagely mind gradually dissolves the interchanging relationship between movement and serenity. The development culminates in a peak of serenity. Yet this does not free the sage from social relations. Quite to the contrary; the intense serenity attained in the effort to go beyond being and nonbeing leads to a renewed state of movement: "In self-cultivation one discards movement and returns to serenity. Once the practice is complete, one rises again from serenity to movement. Going along with all living creatures, one moves without distorting serenity. Thus no harm or evil is done, one continues to practice within and without, and in fruitful interchange returns to oneself" (chap. 60; Yan 1983, 560). Egoistic concentration on the self is thus not the final stage. Rather, the sage turns away from "self-benefit" (zili; atmahitam) to serve for the benefit of others. Having attained completed enstatic serenity, the perfected Taoist returns to society and takes up his duty, urging people toward salvation.

Integrating Confucian doctrine, Twofold Mystery believes that human society is inevitably hierarchical. What is right for one is not right for another. Following Guo Xiang, Chongxuan claims that people have different inner natures and fates. It consequently uses Jizang's three stages to develop three classes of people, somewhat reminiscent of Confucius's four types of human beings: "Those who are born with knowledge are the highest type of people. Those who learn through study are the next. Those who learn through hard work are still the next. Those who work hard and still do not learn are the lowest type" (Lunyu 16.9).

Twofold Mystery distinguishes bright, medium, and dull beings. Each class has its own path of mystical realization. The bright can attain sagehood through the Greater Vehicle of sudden realization; the medium need the help of the sages—they have to practice hard, but will certainly attain the goal; the dull have to depend entirely on the written teachings and can only follow the Lesser Vehicle of gradual progress (Sunayama 1980a, 132; Zhao 1982, 13). The existence of dull people who have to be led and guided by the sages makes a hierarchical organization of human society a natural necessity. It underlines and justifies the differences in social structure, the differences in behavior and outlook among ruler and ruled. Cheng Xuanying outlines his political theories in his commentary to the *Zhuangzi*:

> The natural way of human relationships means that officials act purposefully and get involved with affairs. The lord, on the other hand, resides above them and only goes along with beings. He is in harmony with the way of heaven and realizes non-action.
>
> The position of the lord is venerable and lofty; he is guide and shepherd to his deputies. The way of the minister is humble and lowly; he exhausts his sincerity to serve his superior. Therefore the way of the lord is idle, the way of the minister is laborious.
>
> (chap. 11; DZ 745, 30.41ab; Sunayama 1980a, 130)

Cheng Xuanying thus continues Guo Xiang's vision of the world as the absolute. He claims that perfect happiness for all is reached when everybody perfectly fulfills inner nature. The lord rules in non-action, the sages save people with compassion, the ministers serve the administration, and the people labor for their daily millet. Government as a whole becomes superfluous in this state of total social harmony.

Li Rong's Contribution

Although largely in agreement with Twofold Mystery as formulated by Cheng Xuanying, Li Rong in some instances goes beyond the worldview of his contemporaries and predecessors. He interprets the Taoist path in a more detailed, more idiosyncratic way.

First of all, Li Rong equates the ideal mental state of the practitioner with the so-being of nature. He makes a more subtle distinction between knowledge, wisdom, and insight, a distinction easily adapted by later Taoist masters. In his commentary to the *Xisheng jing*, Li Rong defines two main approaches to enlightenment and three different levels of knowledge. One may reach out to enlightenment by analyzing the world around oneself or by observing the realities within. Either way one will find that one's conceptions of the world are mere constructs without reality and that one's personal identity is not permanent. Sageliness then follows in three stages—knowledge, wisdom, and insight. First, the sage knows good and evil and applies this knowledge correctly; second, he acquires the wisdom that all conceptualizations are constructs with no reality of their own; and third, he gains the insight that his self is impermanent—he "embodies no-self" instead of being someone or something (*Xisheng jing* 9.1).

Li Rong also contributes to a more sophisticated understanding of the role of the sage. For him, the sage is a realized person who has the pleasure and the duty to lead others to salvation. The way in which the sage goes beyond ordinary forms of life is not by a mere rejection of worldly values, but by subtly distancing himself from them. He realizes that most values of the world are distorted and abused for egoistic purposes and abandons fame and punishment, benevolence and righteousness. Showing to others how one can live in harmony with the Tao and how good fortune always comes to the good, the sage sets the pace for further advancement and purity. The more powerful his position within society, the wider his radius of influence spreads. Incorporating the notion of the Great Man, Li Rong yet goes beyond it. He insists that everyone who wishes to follow the Tao needs an enlightened teacher. Like the *Xisheng jing*, he accepts the necessity for words, teachings, and scriptures. Then he proceeds to evaluate newly the relationship between Tao and world, principle and teaching, meaning and words.

In a third contribution, Li Rong describes the practice of the Tao in more detail and places a stronger emphasis on the physical cultivation of energy and the body. In his *Xisheng jing* commentary, he says, "In the Tao of self-cultivation, one has to practice gymnastics and harmonize the respiration. Only when one has attained high suppleness of the body, one turns to visualizing the Three Ones and can guard the One in meditation" (12.2). Gymnastics and breathing exercises allow the body to be open and its *qi* to circulate freely. Li Rong relates this state of suppleness and health to the beneficial residence of the spirits within. A beginner must use physical methods before he or she can enter the more meditative stages. This clear integration of physical practices in the mystical progress is not found before Li Rong. His work thus sets the theoretical stage for the full-fledged practical synthesis of the masters to come.

Taoist Mahāyāna

Buddhism continues to play an important role in the mystical synthesis of the Tang. Taoist soteriology embraces increasingly larger sections of Buddhist thought and doctrine. Not merely Mādhyamika structures and ideas, it also makes use of Prajñāpāramitā argumentation, Yogācāra and Huayan analysis of the mind, frequent references to the *Vimalakīrti nideśa sūtra*, and Tiantai Samatha-Vipaśyanā or calm and insight meditation practice.

More than that, Taoist mystical thought is found more and more in Mahāyāna-style scriptures. Here the highest deity of the Tao teaches Taoist principles to a host of sages, immortals, and ordinary folk. The style of the texts, formerly limited largely to philosophical discourse and commentary literature, changes through a stronger integration of Lingbao and Shangqing scriptures to include more cosmic and mythological levels. At the same time, ritual actualization of the teaching is more strongly emphasized, and the philosophy becomes increasingly scholastic. Taoist teaching adopts the formalized divisions of Buddhist doctrine; the divisions in turn are imbued with more subtle cosmic and esoteric meaning.

In the Tang synthesis, foreign and indigenous forms merge together further. There are more detailed definitions; procedures one could only guess at before are now spelled out formally. The approach to perfection and oneness with the Tao is more organized and more elaborately described. Tang texts are more accurately dated and supply more information on Taoist cosmology and practice, while Buddhism persists as their major source of inspiration.

Master Haikong

The *Haikong zhizang jing* (Scripture of Master Haikong zhizang; DZ 9, fasc. 20–22) is a good example of a Taoist Mahāyāna scripture of the early Tang.[6] It deals with the life, work, and teaching of Master Haikong, a great sage who serves at the court of the Heavenly Venerable of Primordial Beginning (Yuanshi tianzun).[7] The very name of Master Haikong indicates his cosmic powers. As the text says, "His body is like an ocean (*hai*) and his mind is like the open sky (*kong*); his inner principle embraces all beings, and he is a storehouse of wisdom (*zhizang*)" (*Haikong jing* 1.2b; Kamata 1969, 84).

According to the text, Master Haikong resides near the court of the Heavenly Venerable in the City of Assembled Treasures, located in the Country of Ultimate Happiness. Master Haikong is very old but looks young. He has accumulated sagely powers and spends his time dissipating doubts and helping the living. He is highly esteemed by the celestial host as well as among worshipers on earth. His senior disciple is a Taoist called Dahui (Great Wisdom), a name adapted from the figure of Mahāmati in the *Lankāvatāra sūtra*. The disciple's role is mainly to elicit answers to basic questions regarding the Taoist path.

The text then proceeds to outline the teaching of Master Haikong. Not unlike the worldview of the *Daojiao yishu* described below, Haikong's main concept is "subtle thinking." This refers to the purity of the unmoving mind inherent in human beings from birth and a fundamental part of all existence. Subtle thinking, although already present, can and should be practically cultivated in the practice of the trances. This concept is close to the idea of Tao-nature (*daoxing*), a Taoist adaptation of Buddha-nature.[8] Tao-nature is in everything and yet must be realized through religious practice. One fully realizes it by "attaining a vision of Tao-nature," again an adaptation of the Chan Buddhist emphasis on "seeing nature" (*jianxing*). Rather than in enlightenment, the vision results, in Taoism, in one's "entering of the womb of Haikong's first vehicle." This in turn integrates the Buddhist concept of the "womb of Buddha-hood" (*fozang*; *tathāgata-garbha*; see *Haikong jing* 2.8a).

Before realizing Tao-nature and the womb of Haikong's vehicle, however, adepts must develop non-action as the basic pillar of Taoist practice. This leads to five distinct stages of Taoist attainment, so-called Tao-fruits (*daoguo*). First, they become earth immortals and reach immeasurable longevity in this world. Next, they attain the stage of flying immortals, explained as the attainment of transcendence due to right moral behavior. In a third stage, they reach self-dependence (*zizai*, *iśvara*), defined as the state of complete freedom from all obstruction, when the mind is utterly liberated from delusion.

As a fourth fruit of the Tao, they reach freedom from afflictions (*wulou*), the complete absence of all the outflows (*lou*; *āsrava*) of old karma. They are now ready to enter the paradise of the Pure Land. Finally, adepts reach perfected non-action, an adaptation of nirvāna, a state of complete serenity and nonbeing. The non-action of the fifth stage is therefore different from the non-action defined earlier as the underlying effort necessary for any level of Tao attainment. Because of proper efforts, wisdom arises and spirit pervasion is attained; adepts acquire the magical powers of omniscience, multilocation, radiance of light, and so on. In complete absorption, the Tao is finally realized.

The *Haikong jing* does not hide its indebtedness to Buddhist doctrine. It freely cites Buddhist texts, including the *Avatamsaka-sūtra*, *Sukhāvatīvyūha-sūtra*, and *Prajanāpāramitā* texts, as well as a long passage from the *Vimalakīrti-nideśa-sūtra*.[9] While conscious of the divisions of the teachings, Taoists would yet not consider themselves guilty of theft or plagiarism. Rather, they accepted any religious scripture available on the market and written in Chinese as part of a cultural heritage they shared equally with Chinese Buddhists. To them, any text was just one in a large pool of religious documents to be used freely as relevant and needed. This is evident from the fact that in many instances Taoists cite neither the most authentic versions of Buddhist texts nor the most recent translations available to them.

They are not concerned with the similarity of a Buddhist text to the original Sanskrit, but instead choose the version that makes most sense to them—a version that, more often than not, has been transmitted within their own religious environment for several generations (see Kamata 1968). The Taoists thought of themselves as guileless and without harm, and actively defended the originality of their teaching against Buddhist accusations of forgery and cheap imitation.

Fundamental Teachings

Such a defense gave rise to another highly sophisticated Buddho-Taoist synthesis contained in the *Daojiao yishu* (Pivotal Meaning of the Taoist Teaching).[10] This text purports to "clarify the teaching and methods of the perfect Tao, to indicate the pivot and essence of its overall meaning." It is dated to the late seventh century and was compiled by a certain Meng Anpai.[11]

The *Daojiao yishu* was written as a reaction to Buddhist criticism of the Taoist tradition. It wished to present the intentions and basic mysteries of Taoism to the Buddhists—the latter being called the "ones who laugh greatly" in reference to the *Xiaodao lun* (Laughing at the Tao). The *Xiaodao lun* of the late sixth century criticized and ridiculed various aspects of Taoism in altogether thirty-six sections, imitating the structure of the Taoist Canon. The *Daojiao yishu* betters this arrangement by dividing the major tenets of the Taoist teaching into thirty-seven sections (Yoshioka 1959, 310). As much a part of the Buddho-Taoist debates as it is Taoist philosophy, the text serves as an explanation and apology of the Taoist teaching.

The *Daojiao yishu* begins with a discussion of the Tao and the virtue, the root doctrines of Taoism. The Tao is the underlying cosmic ground, the mysterious and obscure principle of all-that-is. Virtue represents the path to the Tao, the mode of behavior in the world, the order for actual Taoist practice. The text identifies non-action as the final state of the Tao and defines it more precisely as the transcendence of body, mind, fame, and time.

Then the *Daojiao yishu* focuses on the role of the body, indicating the enormous importance attributed to physical practice and longevity in Taoism. At the same time, it connects this Taoist preoccupation with the Buddhist concept of the "body of the law" (*dharmakāya*). In Buddhism, this refers to the spiritual or true body of the Buddha, the essence of Buddhahood, and the absolute of the universe. In Taoism, the body of the law indicates the cosmic nature of the human body. It appears on two levels—as the original body of the Tao and as the body of its traces in the world.

The original body is restful and serene. It may be the pure body of the Tao itself, free from birth and death; it may be the body of truth as such, never aging and without obstructions; or it may appear as the body of rewards, full of the benevolence and goodness caused by the rewards of former lives. The more worldly body of the traces is ecstatic and flowing, a constant transformation of the Tao in the world. It may appear as the body of response, going along with everything; it may be the body of division, multiplying its shape to appear in many different places at once; or it may be the simple body of transformation, changing uninterrupted without end. Both types of bodies represent the Tao. The original body stands for the Tao in its pure, primordial state; the body of the traces shows how the Tao appears in this world.

Adepts have to realize both types of body if their Tao is to be complete. To do so they need the Three Jewels, an expression taken from the Buddhist jewels of Buddha, dharma, and sangha. Here the Three Jewels are the Tao, the scriptures, and the teachers, representing the fundamental necessities for attainment of the Tao.

Having received a physical body with cosmic potential and having learned about the Tao through scriptures and teachers, adepts will in due course experience the results of their practice and attain positions in the heavenly hierarchy of the immortals. Taoist attainment takes place in five stages.

First, practitioners develop the right mind and become active students of the Tao. Next, they submit fully to the Tao and reach deliverance from the corpse. Third, they find knowledge of the truth and attain the rank of earthly, heavenly, or flying immortal. Fourth, they attain transcendence and go beyond the Three Worlds to occupy a position among the twenty-seven ranks of immortals. Fifth, finally, they realize the highest Tao and utterly dissolve their selves in the eternal stream of the Tao.

Having thus summarized the necessary cosmological preconditions and prospective attainments of the Tao, the *Daojiao yishu* duly proceeds to outline the Taoist path in more detail. It begins by describing the structure of the Taoist Canon, from the first an adaptation of Buddhist models.[12]

Then the text describes the process of Taoist attainment. It begins by characterizing the human situation as divided between the two different and ultimately antagonistic worlds of sensual desire and the purity of the Tao—the animal and the divine in human nature. Since being human means that one has already fallen prey to sensual desire, Taoists must recognize their true situation and strive for complete union with the pure world of the Tao. In other words, they must seek liberation from the Three Worlds.

When practitioners first realize their predicament, they develop a growing intention for the Tao. This intention develops from being spontaneous and innocent to practical and ascent-oriented. In due course, intention is directed at the knowledge of truth, at transcendence, and finally at the highest Tao itself. These five levels of intention are parallel to the five levels of attainment described above. As practitioners move up the ladder toward immortality, their dominant mind-pattern changes. They need to be aware of that.

For practical purposes, adepts begin by developing the ten good attitudes, won first through complete avoidance of the ten evil deeds (*daśakuśala*). A literal integration of the ten Buddhist precepts, already actively pursued in Lingbao Taoism (see Bokenkamp 1989), this means that one must abstain from killing, stealing, lasciviousness, double-tongued speech, coarse language, lying, filthy language, covetousness, anger, and false views.

The elimination of these bad deeds in one's life allows the ten good attitudes to flourish. They are sympathy for all beings, social respect and kindness, true chastity, clarity and openness, soft-spokenness, truthfulness, purity, modesty, deep compassion, and proper notions. In this basic practice of moral behavior, adepts learn how good and evil work in everyday life. They gradually understand the universal law of cause and effect, and find acceptance of their past karma and the strength to continue the ascent to the Tao.

To understand their ongoing Taoist transformation properly, practitioners must know furthermore how their minds are structured, and contribute to pull them toward desire or the Tao. Taoist psychology is largely based on Buddhist ideas. The *Daojiao yishu* first explains the "five covers," an adaptation of the five *skandhas* or aggregates of consciousness. These are matter (*rūpa*), consciousness (*vijñāna*), perception (*saññā*), feeling (*vedanā*), and reaction (*samskāra*). The five covers, so called because they cloud and hide the purity of the spirit within, stimulate the "six feelings," desires and passions based on the six senses, including the mind. True to the *Daode jing*, sensual stimuli are rejected. The more they are allowed to run wild and control human behavior, the farther away one moves from the Tao.

Within the continuous transformations of the Tao, the birth and rebirth of the individual depend on the karma as produced through the three conditions (*trividha-dvāra*). The personal body, uncontrolled speech, and the immoral mind are solely responsible for all good and bad fortune one encounters in one's lives. Taken well in hand and properly purified, they can yet become assistants rather than obstacles to the Taoist path. They will help to avoid the ten evil deeds and accumulate the ten good attitudes, basic conditions for any further progress.

Results and Attainments

Once adepts have understood the basic structure of mind and karma, they will easily establish themselves in sound moral behavior and with the right kind of intention. Then they can begin to take constructive actions toward the Tao. They practice physical exercises and perfect their health by visualizing the deities in the body.

First they concentrate on the Three Ones, the three major deities who reside in the three Cinnabar Fields in the head, chest, and abdomen. These three represent the three fundamental forces that make up the human body, essence, spirit, and energy. When they are visualized and properly purified, essence turns into radiating wisdom, spirit becomes the agent to dissolve all bondage, and energy learns to distinguish outward appearance from true reality. When all three are cultivated jointly, practitioners can enter observation or insight meditation. They learn to observe energy and spirit, being and nonbeing, reality and emptiness. Developing both in concentration (*samādhi*) and insight (*vipasyanā*), adepts attain the higher stages.

In due course, they develop the six supernatural powers (*abhijñā*), attained in Buddhism when an arhat has reached the highest stage of absorption. These powers include supernatural vision, divine hearing, knowledge of others' thoughts, recognition of one's former lives, multilocation, and insight into the waning of evil propensities. Adepts also acquire the "six perfections," the Bodhisattva virtues that take the seeker across to nirvāna. They consist of charity, morality, patience, zeal, meditation, and wisdom. In addition, the Taoists' mind will embrace the four great pure powers of Brahma (*brahmavihāra*). Having completely lost all desires and traces of evil, their minds will be nothing but love, compassion, joy, and equanimity.

Moving onward from the mind, adepts set their eyes on the attainment of celestial rank. For this they must learn the correct cosmological understanding of the Tao. The Three Worlds (*triloka*) constitute the fundamental network of the universe. They are the World of Desire, the World of Form, and the World of Formlessness. These, as already adapted in the Shangqing cosmos, constitute the lower twenty-eight heavens. Above them, four heavens are reserved for true believers; then come the highest realms of the Tao. To be born in human form is only one possibility of altogether "five destinies" (*gati*) also including gods, animals, hungry ghosts, and hell-dwellers. Already greatly favored by their destiny, adepts have to be aware of all other beings in the universe. Increasingly their duty is to help in the salvation of all beings.

However lowly born, however highly advanced, all life in Taoist cosmology depends on primordial chaos. This is the Tao in its purest form. It is the latent creative state of the universe, when the original, incipient, and mysterious energies have not yet separated. In the true Tao, heaven and earth are still merged into one. Not merely the foundation of all cosmology, this is also the state to which Taoist adepts return in their mystical ascent to the Tao.

Moving from cosmology to philosophy, the *Daojiao yishu* emphasizes the need to understand the Tao properly. Drawing heavily on the system of Twofold Mystery, the text distinguishes first between principle and teaching. Principle represents the underlying absolute truth of the Tao. Teaching stands for its manifestation on earth, the form in which the Tao becomes accessible to suffering humanity. Thus linked to Jizang's theory of two truths, principle and teaching are also explained in terms of origin and traces. As the origin, principle refers to the underlying absolute (*uttara*) of the world, while teaching, its trace, is its skillful means (*upāya*). Adepts have to understand that they cannot approach principle except with the help of its outward manifestation in the form of teaching. However, once the essence of the teaching is grasped, all skillful means should be abandoned and forgotten.

Next, the text draws a similar line of distinction between mental states and wisdom. Where wisdom is the underlying spirit radiance of the Tao, mental states are the illusory projection of sensual passions and desires. Practitioners must not only recognize the truth about their minds but eventually go beyond both. They must come to forget both mental states and wisdom in double forgetfulness (*jianwang*).

Complete forgetfulness leads to the realization of perfect emptiness and ultimate so-being. Ultimate so-being or nature (*ziran*) is the spontaneous character of original nonbeing. Utterly free from self or other, it is without identity as being or ego. So-being is existence just as it is. Tao-nature, moreover, is at the nucleus of original so-being. Tao-nature is the serene source of all life, yet envelops the world in its entirety. It cannot be defined. Truly empty, it is neither empty nor not empty, nor is it *not* not empty. All beings have Tao-nature, but need to cultivate it to make it blossom fully and guarantee them union with the Tao.

Adepts have thus found mystical oneness. Wonderful rewards await them. They enter the "fields of blessedness," five paradises or pure lands (*sukhāvāti*) in the higher spheres of the Tao. The first pure land is the realm of all sentient living beings as they are endowed with unspoiled Tao-nature. The second is the realm of the Heavenly Venerable of Primordial Beginning, where adepts initially attain the Tao. The higher three pure lands, then, are the three classical heavens of

Taoism—Jade Clarity, Great Clarity, and Highest Clarity. Here the sages, realized ones, and immortals who make up the twenty-seven ranks of the heavenly hierarchy have their residence.

The *Daojiao yishu* concludes its comprehensive exposition with a discussion of more details, establishing the proper relationship between movement and serenity, impulse and response, being and nonbeing, and illusion and reality. In all cases it encourages adepts to move from the grosser to the subtler, from outer appearances to the absolute deep within. It also insists that adepts must eventually overcome both opposites in an act of double forgetfulness, defined along the lines of Twofold Mystery. It specifies the process of universal origination, the development of history, and the ideal life of the sage in some more detail, taking, as it were, the high-flying adepts back to their reality of the present moment. Still quite ordinary human beings, determined in their position and thinking by karma and history, they just begin to attempt their first halting steps toward the cosmic purity of the Tao.

Mystical Practice

In practice, these first halting steps mean seclusion from the world, purification through baths and fasts, a radical dietary change away from grains and heavy foods, and a new understanding of themselves, the world, and everything. Not all materials of the Tang dynasty are as abstract and cosmological as Twofold Mystery and Taoist Mahāyāna. Several eighth-century masters of the Tao—the Shangqing patriarch Sima Chengzhen (647–735), the alchemist and physician Sun Simiao (581–672), and the poet Wu Yun (d. 778)—have described the mystical ascent in great practical detail.[13]

Those of their works that have an immediate bearing on mystical practice are:

1. Sima Chengzhen's *Fuqi jingyi lun* (Treatise on the Essential Meaning of the Absorption of *Qi*; *Yunji qiqian* 57). This is a description of altogether nine distinct physical practices leading to a purification of the body and perfection of health: diagnosis of diseases, their treatment, taking care of the five intestines, avoidance of inauspicious and taboo times, drug taking, ingestion of talisman water, gymnastic exercises, absorption of *qi*, and the ingestion of the five sprouts or energies of the five directions (see Engelhardt 1987; Kohn 1988).
2. Sima Chengzhen's *Tianyinzi* (DZ 1026, fasc. 672). This text outlines the mystical process in five stages: fasting and abstention; seclusion; visualization and imagination; sitting in oblivion; and spirit liberation (see Kohn 1987a).

3. Sima Chengzhen's *Zuowang lun* (Discourse on Sitting in oblivion; DZ 1036, fasc. 704). This text describes the meditator's progress in seven steps: respect and faith; interception of karma; taming the mind; detachment from affairs; true observation; intense concentration; realizing the Tao (see Kohn 1987).

4. An inscription also called *Zuowang lun*, dated to the year 829. It was placed before a temple dedicated to Sima Chengzhen on Mount Wangwu, his lifetime residence (Wu 1981, 46a; Kohn 1987, 113). This text is similar to Wu Yun's *Shenxian kexue lun* (Spirit Immortality Can Be Learned; DZ 1051, fasc. 726–27; 2.9b–16a). It contains a condensed version of the later *Zuowang lun*.

5. The appendix to the *Zuowang lun*, the *Dingguan jing* (Scripture on Concentration and Observation; DZ 400, fasc. 189; *Yunji qiqian* 17; Kohn 1987, 125). This text specifies five phases of increased mental concentration and seven stages of physical transformation toward immortality.

6. Sun Simiao's *Cunshen lianqi ming* (Visualization of Spirit and Refinement of Energy; DZ 834, fasc. 571; *Yunji qiqian* 33; Kohn 1987, 119). This is the original basis for the *Dingguan jing*, the first text to list the five phases and seven stages. Beyond that, it also describes some preparatory measures—diets, breathing, and concentration exercises.

7. The *Neiguan jing* (Scripture on Inner Observation; DZ 641, fasc. 342; *Yunji qiqian* 17) by an anonymous author. Also from the mid-Tang period, this work includes more Buddhist references and places a stronger emphasis on cosmology and psychological definitions. It describes the human body as a replica of the cosmos and instructs adepts to reinterpret their identities (see Kohn 1989b).

All these texts have in common the fact that they describe the practical process of gradual refinement that Taoists undergo on their ascent to mystical oneness with the Tao. They outline the steps that lead to the mystical experience. There is first a harmonization of the body with the course of nature. Then adepts move on to the recognition that their everyday consciousness is constituted by delusions. Eventually they attain a concentrated mind, insight arises, and they become one with the Tao. This, then, means immortality and the transcendence of all (Kohn 1990b).

Aligning the Body with Nature

According to the *Fuqi jingyi lun*, practitioners first undergo periods of physical purification through fasting, bathing, and complete withdrawal from the world. They practice gymnastics and breathing exercises and continue to refine their diet, substituting vegetable and mineral drugs for the grosser nourishments of ordinary humanity.

Gradually they become perfectly healthy and develop a fine-tuned sensitivity to the changes of day and night, winter and summer. Thus, the body itself is aligned with the Tao.

First of all, practitioners withdraw from the world and set up camp in a secluded mountain spot, finding a teacher who instructs them in the proper ways toward the Tao. Then the actual practice can begin. Body and mind are emptied of old content and increasingly filled with the Tao.

The first step is to cure acute diseases and discomforts. Practitioners must also take good care to spot latent pathogenic tendencies and counteract them with drugs and exercises. To do so, they have to understand the structure and organization of the body. They learn the basic system of traditional Chinese medicine, centering around the five orbs—liver, heart, lungs, kidneys, and spleen, together with their associated sense organs, muscle types, spiritual forces, and emotions (see Porkert 1974). These five orbs are the places where the five cosmic agents assemble in the form of pure energies (qi). The more the body consists of these cosmic energies, the closer it is to the Tao.

Next, practitioners learn what *not* to do: exert the body by too much physical strain, harm the mind with too many emotions. Harmony of all physical and psychological forces and actions is necessary if progress is not to be impeded. They refrain from eating ordinary food and instead use more drugs that replace especially the five grains, but also anything hot and spicy. Normal nourishment, according to Taoist theory, causes people to decay and die, whereas drugs distilled from pure plants and possibly minerals will help them to live. The first reaction to the ingestion of drugs is a weakening of the body as it is cleansed and emptied of harmful and superfluous matter.

Then practitioners enter the more specialized practices, beginning with gymnastics and breathing. Physical and respiratory exercises frequently imitate the movements and habits of animals. An example is found in the famous "Five Animals Pattern," ascribed to the physician Hua Tuo of the second century. Loosening the body and shaking off old tensions, they provide a new flexibility and higher suppleness. Gymnastics serve in particular to harmonize the different energies of the body. They also stimulate the digestion and the blood circulation, and expel the remaining psychosomatic diseases (see Despeux 1989).

The physical practice of Taoist mysticism culminates in the absorption of qi or cosmic energy. Qi becomes more and more the main nourishment of the body. Adepts absorb the qi of the five agents by visualizing the five energies of the five directions as they enter the body from heaven through the nose. Similarly, the five tastes enter the body from earth through the mouth. Stored in the five orbs within, they make practitioners increasingly independent of outer air and the normal act of breathing. The inner *qi*, the pure seed of immortality within, develops once a certain amount of outer *qi* has been absorbed. The immediate effect of the practice is again a weakening of the body, which reacts to insufficiencies in its habitual nourishment. Soon, however, a period of adjustment and overall strengthening sets in.[14]

Physical practices prepare the body for eventual immortality. The body no longer depends on ordinary mundane nourishment; it no longer needs to breathe the air of this world. The adepts' very physical constitution is reorganized from a profane to a sacred level. As pure *qi*, the flesh and bones of the body become fully part of the Tao.

Restructuring Consciousness

In order to restructure their consciousness, adepts must actively control all desires and emotions. According to the *Cunshen lianqi ming*, they begin by practicing a preliminary concentrative meditation, which consists of fixing the attention on the lower Cinnabar Field in the abdomen (1b). Once they have attained full control over the conscious mind, they can begin to examine the phenomenal world by analyzing their physical and psychological makeup. In doing so, adepts increasingly realize that, body and mind, they are nothing but part of the Tao. There is no solid reality or identity anywhere; they are nothing but a tiny segment of the eternal flux of creation, the primordial energy of the universe.

This phase of the practice developed as an adaptation of Buddhist techniques of insight meditation into the realm of Taoist mystical practice (Kohn 1989b). As the *Zuowang lun* describes it, adepts learn that they are separate from the Tao because of their delusions, the conscious mental constructs they place on reality. Delusions are the reason why the primordial spirit is no longer at rest in the mind. Originally, at birth, spirit as the agent of the Tao worked through the human mind and governed life perfectly. But, because of the delusions created by conscious thinking, spirit is wasted on emotional entanglements and the uncontrolled exertions of the senses. Confused and defiled, human beings need to be taught how to recover the primordial state (*Zuowang lun* 3a).

Practitioners move toward primordiality when they realize the impermanent nature of the personal body. The personal body is not the body of flesh and bones, but the body one identifies with on the basis of conscious classification; it is the personality or identity of the individual. It has no reality of its own, nor is it permanent. Following the *Neiguan jing*, adepts should come to see their personal bodies or identities as part of the continuous transformations of the Tao, just as their physical bodies are replicas of the universe (3a). They should understand that any self, consisting of physical body in conjunction with conscious identity, is merely "borrowed from heaven and earth" (*Liezi* 1). The physical body, they see, undergoes the same transformations as all creation: it is bound to return to "dust and ashes" (*Xisheng jing* 7.7). The conscious identity, they realize, is unstable within itself: There is no true master of body and mind (*Zhuangzi* 4/2/17), nor do people have active control over its transformations (*Zhuangzi* 58/22/25).

Although both body and identity continue to change independently of one's desires, people are usually unable to let things go on changing as they please. Rather, as practitioners painfully realize, any attachment to the body, any reliance on the apparent solidity of a conscious identity, becomes "the reason why I have terrible vexations. If I did not have a self, what vexations would I have?" This famous citation from chapter 13 of the *Daode jing* appears frequently in Tang mystical literature. Li Rong comments on this passage as cited in the *Xisheng jing*:

> Having a self means having vexations and adversities. Frustrated by sight and hearing, tortured by taste and smell, one is subject to pain, irritation, heat, and cold.
>
> (7.8)

> As soon as there is a self, the hundred worries compete to arise and the five desires of the senses hurry to make their claims.
>
> (17.7)

Practitioners thus continue to distance themselves from their selves. Only when they have deeply realized the negative aspects of any sort of identity and learned to bewail their captivity in the clutches of the senses can they turn their attention to the heavenly qualities inherent in them. The simple shape of the body—unrelated to personal fondness—then appears as a pure replica of the cosmos. It is a "storehouse of inner nature," a "habitation of spirit," a "vehicle" or the "host" of the Tao (*Xisheng jing* 17.5). The Tao in the shape of numerous gods resides in the body like a ruler in his country (*Huangting neijing jing* 27.6). The body is the "vessel" of the Tao; one need only look inside to find the Tao right there (*Huainanzi* 11.7b). The Tao, the gods, original spirit, inner nature, and sometimes even virtue are the rulers and inhabitants of the body. They make the body come to life; they fill the cosmic replica with activity and power.

Adepts prepare to realize the Tao within. They understand that they are originally and unchangeably part of it. They visualize the body as a replica of the universe (*Neiguan jing* 1b) and identify with the Tao as it governs and inhabits the body. Thus they further loosen attachments to their limited physical, personal self and begin to develop a new and wider identity as part of the universe at large (*Zuowang lun* 15a; *Dingguan jing* 12b). Eventually they come to see themselves truly as spirit beings merely housed in a fragile physical framework, which will be subject to all the transformations the spirit transcends.

Realizing the Tao

Final realization, as described in the *Tianyinzi*, takes place on two levels. First adepts enter into deep oblivion, a trancelike state of complete immersion in the Tao to the exclusion of all else. Pure spirit, the one basic agent of oneself and the world, is now joined with the body as a replica of the universe. They guard each other so that no outside entity can interfere with the harmony and stability within. This state of harmony and stability is characterized by immobility, darkness, and a complete cessation of the senses (sect. 7).

Already the *Zhuangzi* describes this state: "I smash up my limbs and body, drive out perception and intellect, get rid of physical shape and abandon all knowledge. Thus I merge with the Great Thoroughfare" (19/6/92). Guo Xiang adds: "Practicing this forgetfulness, how can there be anything not forgotten? First forget the traces, such as benevolence and righteousness; then put that which caused the traces out of the mind. On the inside unaware of one's body, on the outside never know there is a universe" (DZ 745; 8.39a). The *Zuowang lun* describes the trance as "Intense Concentration." Using again the metaphors of the *Zhuangzi*, it says: "The body is like rotten wood, the mind is like dead ashes. There are no more impulses, there is no more search: one has reached perfect contemplative serenity" (*Zuowang lun* 12a).

On a second level, adepts undergo refinement to increasingly higher levels of purity. Coming out of enstatic immersion and the complete cessation of all physical, sensual, and mental functions, they go off and transcend all in ecstatic pervasion. The clearest description of how adepts gradually attain perfect ecstatic freedom is found in Sun Simiao's *Cunshen lianqi ming*. A very similar passage also appears in the *Dingguan jing* and in the appendix to the *Zuowang lun*. Here immortality is the result of five phases of mental concentration and seven stages of bodily transformation. The five phases are an exercise in concentration, an enstatic stabilization of the mind. The seven stages are a gradual increase in movement, openness, joy, light, even ecstasy, until the successful adept of immortality takes up a position next to the Jade Emperor of the Great Tao.

More specifically, practitioners start with the ordinary mind, characterized by plenty of agitation and no tranquility whatsoever. They gradually learn to calm the mind, until they attain first a little, then ever more tranquility. Eventually their minds are completely at rest; deep concentration is found. They reach the trance of oblivion.

From there they can enter the seven stages of the body. First, they experience a lightness and radiance in their bodies, reflecting the utter peace of the mind within. There is pure joy and exultation, complete freedom from emotions and the fetters of the senses. In a second stage, the limits of ordinary life are left behind. Adepts look young and vigorous, they feel strong in their bodies and peaceful in their minds. They attain first visions of the depth and mystery of the Tao.

From there, practitioners move on to become immortals. They can live for a thousand years and with spirit feet travel through all the power-spots of the globe. Accompanied by celestial lads, "they step high on mist and haze, while colored clouds support their tread." In a fourth stage, the immortals become realized ones by refining their bodies into pure energy. They win the powers of multilocation and invisibility. Frolicking about the universe, they spend their time hobnobbing with immortals and visiting the grotto heavens.

The fifth stage sees the refinement of energy to pure spirit. Realized ones become spirit beings. They change and transform spontaneously, free from all bounds. Their power can move even heaven and earth. In a sixth sage, the pure spirit is merged with the world of form. A spirit-being before, practitioners are now perfect beings. Pervading all existence in ecstatic freedom, they no longer have a definite appearance but change according to occasion.

The final, seventh, stage is complete transcendence. As Sun Simiao describes it,

> Going beyond all in one's body, one whirls out of normal relations and comes to reside next to the Jade Emperor of the Great Tao in the Numinous Realm. Here the wise and sagely gather, at the farthest shore and in perfect truth. In creative change, in numinous pervasion, all beings are reached. Only one who has attained this level of cultivation has truly reached the source of the Tao. Here the myriad paths come to an end. This is called the final ultimate.

> (*Cunshen lianqi ming* 3a)

The five phases of mental concentration and seven stages of bodily transformation exemplify the gradual purification and increasing subtlety of the adepts' minds and bodies as they attain the subtler levels of the Tao. The trance of utter oneness with the Tao in enstatic oblivion is an intense mystical union, during which all sensual activity ceases. The deep immersion then leads to an ecstatic freedom over all. Gradually passing through the stages of immortal, realized one, spirit being, and perfected being, mystics participate in all movements of existence. They are free to be or not to be, just as life itself may be latent or active, hidden or apparent. Ultimately, they take up their proper position in the heavenly hierarchy above.

Taoist mystical practice follows a clear threefold structure. Adepts move from refining the body to restructuring the mind, and ultimately attain oneness with the Tao. The three levels of body, mind, and Tao, together with their respective practices, systematically integrate the various traditions of early Chinese mysticism. The health and simplicity of the body goes back to the *Daode jing* and its interpretation along the lines of traditional Chinese medicine. The restructuring of the mind takes up Zhuangzi, Guo Xiang, and the Buddhist impact. The seven stages, finally, integrate the ecstatic, shamanic flight and cosmic vision of Shangqing Taoism.

The practices, although of rather different origins, join smoothly to form one integrated mystical synthesis. They carefully guide practitioners through different phases of their development, and nobody stops to ask whether they are not ultimately incompatible. The genius of early Chinese mysticism lies in this harmonious integration of widely different visions. The Chinese mystical synthesis is eclectic—in philosophy, in cosmology, and in practice.

Early Chinese Mysticism: An Evaluation

EARLY CHINESE MYSTICISM developed over more than a millennium. Its earliest traces go back to the *Daode jing*, several centuries before the Common Era; it culminated in the synthesis of the Tang in the seventh and eighth centuries C.E. Many texts, of which this volume introduces only a representative selection, document its development. Each of these texts is highly specific in its individual interpretation of the mystical path. Yet one can distinguish three major mystical types and textual traditions that continued to combine in ever-more-intricate ways:

First, the writings associated with the philosophers Laozi and Zhuangzi, together with their Dark Learning and later commentaries, represent a quietistic and naturalistic tradition, which integrated the cosmological theories and longevity practices of Chinese medicine.

Second, the ecstatic experiences described in the *Chuci*, by escapist poets, and in Shangqing Taoism make up the ecstatic and shamanistic tradition, which sought an active encounter with the deities and immortals of the beyond.

Third, the scriptures of Buddhism, both translated and Chinese, together with their indigenous commentators, stand for the tradition of insight meditation and a specifically Buddhist analysis and interpretation of body and mind.

Following these traditions in their historical development and understanding the dynamics of their interaction, a comprehensive chronological sketch of early Chinese mysticism became apparent. To evaluate the phenomenon more fully, a diachronic description of its major characteristics is in order. Several recurring themes can be distinguished. They are the Tao, the dualistic structure of human nature, the continuity of body and mind that leads to an integration of various practices, and the ideal of the Great Man.

The Tao, in its most ancient understanding, is best described as organic order. It is a whole surrounding and embracing everything, yet at the same time pervading all. The Tao corresponds to the Ground of the perennial philosophy. It underlies the universe and makes things be what they are. It causes the world to come into being and to decay again; it is the source of all being, from which all come and to which all return. The Tao is organic in that it is not willful; it is the natural so-being of things. Governed by the laws of nature, at the same time it is these very laws itself. Yet the Tao is also order. It is rhythmic and cyclical in its transformations, predictable in its developments. It can be analyzed and described in its ordered patterns—but these patterns are only its periphery, its outside, not its central essence.

Mystics aspire to both order and organic living, to harmony with the cycles of life and to oneness with its root. Depending on their background, mystics emphasize different aspects of the order of the Tao—be it the seasons, the interchange of yin and yang, the harmony of society, the movement of the stars and planets, or just their own needs for food and sleep. But their aim is to reach through order to the inner organism of the world, to its hub, its empty and vague center, which is the Tao in its essence.

The Tao consists of periphery and nucleus, yin and yang, darkness and light. Similarly, there is a dualistic structure of human nature. It partakes of the Tao in two ways. The Tao is the most within and at the same time the most without. People are within the Tao, because the Tao contains all. But the Tao is also within people, because they receive its spirit to be alive.

In addition, human nature deep within is closer to the Tao than the rational consciousness that governs ordinary life. Early Chinese mysticism distinguishes between the truth of the Tao and the sense-based consciousness that obscures and obstructs it. Discriminating consciousness keeps people from realizing that they are one with the Tao. Yet even this power of discrimination is part of the Tao, because consciousness is a basic human endowment.

At the same time, consciousness is opposed to the Tao, since it does not share in the Tao so fully as the spirit deep within. Spirit is natural; consciousness is artificial. Spirit is immediate; consciousness is mediated through the senses and through language. Spirit enhances oneness; consciousness thrives on dualism.

Human nature emerges as a complex hierarchy of inner and outer. Spirit is the most within, the true representative of the Tao that also is the most without. The senses and consciousness are outside of this, yet still within the human mind that contains both. Farther outside, then, is the personal body, the body that people identify with on the basis of sensual experiences and conscious evaluations.

Mystics strive to go to the very center of the mind. They wish to free the spirit within and make it radiate through themselves, dissolving the conscious mind and the personal body. Thus they practice methods that lead ever farther inward, transforming ego and identity in favor of the spirit. Then, empowered by spirit radiance, the movement reverts to an expansion toward the outside, suffusing the body, now felt as an impersonal replica of the cosmos, with the energy of the Tao. As spirit merges with the cosmic body, there is a return from darkness to light, from yin to yang, from enstasy to ecstasy, from duality to oneness, from earth to heaven. The basic dichotomy of human existence is overcome as inner and outer are merged in an ascent toward the radiance of heaven.

Body and mind in early Chinese mysticism, though clearly distinguished, are not seen as opposites. Rather, they represent different aspects of the same continuum of the Tao and have to be purified in equal measure. Both the conscious mind and the personal body dissolve in favor of pure spirit and the cosmic body. The cosmic body, free from all fetters and attachments, is as much a manifestation of the Tao as the pure spirit. As a replica of the cosmos, the body follows the cosmic rhythm spontaneously—the more it does so, the less it is affected by culture and consciousness. The body is therefore where the practice of mysticism starts. Without a proper vessel, the Tao has no place to develop. A strong and healthy body is thus the foundation for all further spiritual cultivation and mystical oneness.

Closely connected with this understanding is the continuous integration of various techniques into the mystical synthesis. Taoist mystical practice begins with medical and physiological practices, including diets, drugs, gymnastics, breathing exercises, and the like. Only when the body is ready can one reach for more spiritual attainments. The distinction between physical and meditational practices blurs. There is no difference between being nourished on the pure energy of the five sprouts and meditating on them by means of visualization. The technique is one. It frees the body from the need for food and develops the mind to see the energy structures of the world.

Within more specifically meditational techniques, further integration of practices occurs. Quietistic, concentrative exercises seamlessly join with ecstatic excursions. Both are then combined, without apparent effort, with the practice of insight meditation that leads to a reinterpretation of one's self in a cosmic context. From this creative and continuous integration of techniques—and their related worldviews—early Chinese mysticism gains its own particular dynamic. It provides the beauty and uniqueness of the mystical synthesis.

The accomplished mystic, finally, is the sage. Described as the Great Man, he is ruler, shaman, and sage merged into one. He returns to life in the world and serves his fellow beings as teacher, guide, and ruler. Early Chinese mysticism has thus a political dimension, which is based on the notion that since the Tao is order, the person who realizes it must bring order to the world. The accomplished mystic is thus a true human being, a perfected or realized one, who is whole within himself; easily communicates with the world above; and has a responsible role in the political and social order of his time.

These characteristics, though common to early Chinese mysticism in general, are not static. They change considerably over the times as they are interpreted differently in the literature.

Defining the Ground

To begin with, the *Daode jing* describes the Tao as the source of all being. It is nameless, formless, not beginning, not ending, ineffable, unknowable, transcendent yet immanent, weak yet powerful, original yet developed, subtle yet huge. It encompasses all opposites and yet is part of all. The accumulation of nonattributes is almost worthy of the *via negativa* of Christian theology and it is certainly reminiscent of the descriptions of Brahman in the Indian tradition. Nothing definite can be said about the Tao. It is vague and elusive, dark and obscure, existing before time and called at most the mother of the universe. In its undefined and original state, the Tao of the *Daode jing* thus remains unfathomable.

The vague and mysterious Tao, however, does not last long. Already Wang Bi, third-century commentator on the *Daode jing*, defines it. For him, the Tao is the One, nonbeing, or the Great Ultimate. No longer beyond all human understanding, the Tao becomes an opposite in a dualistic structure: the One as opposed to the two, nonbeing as opposed to being, the Great Ultimate as opposed to yin and yang. Original nonbeing, the central concept of Wang Bi, is the Tao defined. It is the latent phase of existence and, as such, part of the cycle of existence. It is no longer something mysterious and ineffable beyond and yet within everything.

Guo Xiang goes further in the same direction, although his conception of the Tao goes back largely to the *Zhuangzi*, where the Tao is still ineffable and undefined. Zhuangzi, as mentioned previously, tends to leave things vague. He explores possibilities rather than trading in definite assumptions. The only positive thing Zhuangzi says about the Tao is that it manifests itself in continuous change. What it is, where it comes from or where it goes, how one should talk or not talk about it, is not his concern. The major issue for Zhuangzi is the tangible reality of the Tao in the human world—and that is change.

Guo Xiang follows Zhuangzi. He begins by identifying the Tao as the flow of existence as such. He characterizes it as continuous change and transformation—a characterization that leads to his preoccupation with going-with-the-flow as the proper form of mystical realization. However, Guo Xiang also defines the structure of the Tao and the exact relationship that human beings have with it. The Tao is not vague and obscure, but has its organizing principle and is shared by all beings. Because of the impact of the Tao, all beings have a given fate and a specific inner nature. In realizing the Tao, seekers no longer plumb the hidden depths of the universe but proceed to recognize and accept the fate and inner nature that make them part of the Tao. The Tao is everything. It is neither the ineffable ground nor a mere part of existence. The Tao is all—even social hierarchy and conscious language. Therefore it is clearly visible whenever one takes the trouble to look.

A completely different understanding of the Tao arises in the vision of the belief in immortality. Defined first of all as the course of nature in the cosmological speculation of the Yin-Yang school and in the medical thought of the Han dynasty, the Tao is in due course taken out of this world and located to the stars and paradises of the immortals. The pure world beyond is the ultimate form of true life; the way to realize the Tao is the excursion to and eventual residence in the divine realms above. The ecstatic journey that samples the pure qualities of the Tao leads to the far corners of the earth, where the marvelous—the closest representation of the Tao in this world—is found. Then its takes the seeker to the heavens, the primordial and pure realm of the original Tao.

In religious Taoism, the definition of the Tao takes on an additional dimension. Here the Tao is personified in the god Taishang Laojun; the philosopher Laozi becomes a transformation of the Tao. Shangqing Taoism integrates the Taoist and the immortality seekers' vision. In the times of cosmic chaos, the Tao arises and manifests itself in the form of the gods, the heavens, and the scriptures. All these are uncreated, direct, primordial. Highest creative power rests with the scriptures. Their recitation gave the gods, equally primordial, the power to furnish being from emptiness. Not only powers of creation, the scriptures are also the forces of survival; they are the light that leads the seeker to mystical oneness. They give instruction, furnish maps and passports of the otherworld, and are themselves the spells that will open its gates.

The Buddhist impact on the understanding of the Tao maintains the concepts of Wang Bi and Guo Xiang while at the same time placing a higher emphasis on the human mind. It spells out a stronger dualism between the underlying Tao and ordinary people's discriminating consciousness. According to the Buddhist-inspired vision, the Tao is accessible to human beings as wisdom and Buddha-nature. It can be realized through years of disciplined practice, preferably in a monastic setting. The perfection of the Tao is the attainment of nirvāna, in the early stages translated as non-action. This is a state beyond all opposites, an ineffable and indescribable way of being. It is one and yet multiple, light and yet dark, immanent and yet going beyond. Through Buddhist influence, the Tao is graded and related to the concept of no-self, then defined as the state before one was born and described as complete liberation from the shackles of conscious, individual personality.

First integrating the various tendencies, the *Xisheng jing* and its commentators proceed to identify the Tao with nature. They describe it in terms of emptiness and nonbeing, as shapeless and ineffable mystery. The Tao is immediately responsible for the existence of life on earth, which develops originally from complete vacuity to natural so-being. The Tao is thus the constructive, life-giving aspect of nature. The bridge between the Tao and all-that-is is then provided by the One and the two, the Great Ultimate and yin and yang. It becomes apparent in the world as change and transformation, and is structured through the five agents. Beyond that, the Tao is most apparent in the *qi*, the cosmic energy of the world. Differences in energy quality and destiny allow people different approaches to the Tao. All individual differences ultimately go back to the karma accumulated in former lives. They have to be corrected by specific techniques of insight meditation and the development of wisdom.

The complex understanding of the Tao culminates in the *Daojiao yishu*, which integrates the traditions into one system. The Tao here is, first of all, the underlying cosmic principle, mysterious and obscure. It is apparent in the "body of the law" (*dharmakāya*) and, as such, represents the complexity of this world as well as the teachings of the sages. Beyond that, the Tao is the heavenly realm of the immortals, attained through the complete dissolution of self and consciousness in the eternal stream of life.

Forms of Dualism

In the *Daode jing*, the basic dualism is between the Tao and the world, between nature and culture, purity and defilements. The original Tao first produces the myriad beings, but then it is transformed—and nobody is quite sure why—into aberrations. The beings it brought forth go their own way and develop consciousness and culture. Their understanding of themselves opposes them to their source. The main agent of this degeneration is attachment to sensual experience, from which cultural sophistication and luxury develop. People increasingly disregard life's essentials. Involved in the hustle and bustle of this world, they turn their backs on the Tao. According to the *Daode jing*, human beings think that sensual enjoyment means happiness, but they are wrong. The superficial truth of this world is ultimately false;

real truth is only in the Tao, to which they can and should return through non-action.

In a more abstract way, Yan Zun expresses the same idea in his commentary. According to him, there are two levels of truth—an inner truth of the Tao and an outer truth of being in the world. One is truer than the other. The truth within is more powerful and eternal than the ever-changing reality of outside existence. In fact, outer reality is nothing more than a trace of the inner workings of the Tao. Wang Bi describes the same conflict in terms of nonbeing versus being. He relates being and nonbeing not only to culture and simplicity but also to agitation and tranquility, multiplicity and oneness, distance from and closeness to the source of all life.

In the *Zhuangzi* and in Guo Xiang, the dualism is centered clearly in the human mind. It is not so much actual culture or involvement in the world that seduces the minds of people. Rather, the structure of consciousness itself causes people to be alienated from their real inner truth, to live and think on a surface level of reality. In the *Zhuangzi*, the dualism is between the immovability of the circle's axis and the swirling movement on its periphery, between the absolute now and the past and future that trap the mind. Inner truth lies in the free and easy experience of the present moment. All thinking about it, all conceptualization, all language and knowledge, are false. They only appear to be true.

Guo Xiang follows this reasoning, but increases its complexity. He asserts that the Tao is not different from mundane reality, but includes language and knowledge. Zhuangzi advocates the complete freedom from words and ideas, the complete dissolution of all discriminating consciousness. Guo Xiang accepts consciousness as part of the Tao and places the dualism within it. He demands that people stop being trapped by words and ideas. They must take them for what they really are and never attach feelings to them. The dualism is no longer between inner truth and outside considerations but between two forces within the human mind. Discrimination is necessary and acceptable, but attachment to its values is not. Any personal identification with something conventionally called good or evil must be avoided. There are several levels of truth in Guo Xiang's thought. He distinguishes conventional ego-centered knowledge from the true Tao-based understanding of the world. But the boundaries have become more subtle and, almost in anticipation of Buddhist doctrine, have shifted to the inner workings of the mind.

The early Buddhists found it easy to accept Guo Xiang. They added further subtlety to the picture by contributing the doctrines of karma and dependent origination. The truth is further subdivided into levels of realization. According to Zhi Dun, truth appears, first of all, in the true teachings of Buddhism, and here especially in the ten stages of *prajñā*, wisdom or insight. But even wisdom is only a trace of the real truth of heaven, of the Buddha-nature deep within.

The Buddhist way of expressing the dualism of the mystical worldview finds its fullest formulation in the Two Truths theory of Nāgārjuna and Jizang, later integrated into Twofold Mystery. All ordinary thinking is faulty. But even when replaced by the understanding that "neither being nor nonbeing belongs to absolute truth," the ultimate is not yet reached. Rather, old conceptualizations have merely been replaced by subtler and slightly truer classifications. There is still a discriminating mind. Only when the mind of the mystic knows neither duality nor nonduality is it free for real truth.

A different expression for the same dualism of conventional knowledge versus the true understanding of the immortals is found in the travel stories in the *Zhuangzi* and the *Huainanzi*, later continued in ecstatic poetry and Shangqing Taoism. The search for the inner truth of the Tao becomes a journey to the far ends of the world and into the heavens. Just as the Tao is located in the paradises of the otherworld, so truth is now outside and beyond the known world. The only real way of seeing the world is through the eyes of an immortal. All ordinary human understanding is faulty and has to be abandoned.

The Tang synthesis combines these various interpretations. Ultimate truth is only in the heavens, but the consciousness of neither duality nor nonduality is as close as one will get while still on earth. One reaches out to ultimate truth by overcoming ordinary thinking, by abandoning the outer layers of the mind in increasing stages of forgetfulness. In learning about the Tao and the origin, of which conscious discrimination is a mere trace, one develops a way of thinking along the lines of Guo Xiang, Zhi Dun, and Twofold Mystery ultimately to overcome even this and attain complete oneness with the Tao, an ecstatic excursion to the immortals beyond.

Body and Mind in Integrated Practice

It is almost a truism nowadays that the Chinese tradition does not radically distinguish between body and mind. Yet it would be a gross simplification to assume that body and mind are one and the same in the Chinese tradition. There is a distinction between the two in idea as well as language, but they are not understood as fundamentally different in nature. As Maxime Kaltenmark described the situation,

> Chinese terminology reflects subtle differences between states of a more or less ethereal quality, but of one and the same principle lying at the foundation of all the complex functions of man. The gross conditions of the body

are as much included as are its finer essences and the higher mental states which make up holiness.

This then is the reason why one can say that the Chinese do not make a clearcut distinction between what we call body and mind. Their outlook is in general much more oriented towards life as an organic whole and ongoing process.

(Kaltenmark 1965, 655)

Nevertheless, as we have seen above, there is a dualistic distinction between states that favor ultimate truth and those that do not. The border is not between body and mind, but within the mind. The physical body, seen as the divine replica of the cosmos, is then placed on the side of the Tao.

For many mystical thinkers, the body does not play an important role. Zhuangzi and Guo Xiang and the mystics writing under the impact of Buddhism are concerned primarily with the mind, and exert much effort to describe its exact functioning. The most radical denial of the body is found in the *Xisheng jing*, which clearly denounces all attempts to nourish the body in the search for mystical union. "The untrue Tao teaches you to nourish the body, the true Tao teaches you to nourish the spirit" (7.4), it says, and emphasizes that "the body ultimately is mere dust and ashes" (7.7). Yet even the *Xisheng jing* makes a distinction between the body as a cosmic power and the body as personal identity.

The physical cosmic body is part of creation; it merges with the spirit to realize the Tao. The cosmic body belongs to the universal, yet it can only be nourished through concentration and visualization of the spirits residing in it. The personal body, on the other hand, is the product of the senses; it is an imaginary self built through discriminating consciousness and passions and desires. It is the source of all trouble, sorrow, and afflictions. The personal body must be abandoned, silenced, eradicated in favor of the cosmic body cultivated through the spirit. Only in a state of no-self, free from constructed identity, can the Tao and the spirit flourish. This, in turn, leads to long life and thus has a positive effect on the physical body. When this body returns to dust and ashes, the spirit immortal ascends into heaven.

This vision of the *Xisheng jing* goes back to two earlier and more straightforward concepts of body and mind. One, in the lineage of the *Daode jing*, sees the body as the natural state of humanity and physical being as the naturalness of the Tao. The other, part of the immortality belief, understands the body as a replica of the universe, which includes all the stars and gods and heavens (see Kohn 1991a).

When the body is the naturalness of the Tao, the mystical process is a return, a recovery of physical spontaneity. Abstention from conscious action and willful thinking is the method that leads there. The practice consists of cultivating quietude and tranquility; it is a withdrawal from the world and into oneself that easily accommodates the physical therapies of the medical tradition. Its aim is an enstatic withdrawal into oneself, complete natural simplicity in life and mind.

When the body is a replica of the universe, the mystical quest is the discovery of the universe within, a process that simultaneously takes the seeker to the far ends of the world outside and into the heavens. True realization of oneself as a physical being occurs in the identification of one's own body with the cosmos at large. The practice consists of visualizations and shamanic flights. The movement goes outward and away from all; it is an ecstatic exploration of the cosmos.

In the *Daode jing*, the major method to recover the Tao is non-action, reached through abandoning sageliness and wisdom, humanity and righteousness, skill and profit (chap. 19). It is a state of complete vacuity of thinking and being, a steadfast inner quietude and the return to the root (chap. 16). A simple way of living in response to the basic needs of the body brings one closest to the Tao.

The commentary by Heshang gong continues along the same lines. Integrating the medical understanding of the body as the conglomerate of the five agents and their energies, which reside in the five intestines or orbs, he insists that "skillful practice of the Tao searches it within the body and never goes to the halls or out of doors" (chap. 27). The body here is the major vehicle for the forces of the Tao, rising and falling in accordance with the seasons.

All mental activities are only an outgrowth of the physical. Heshang gong accordingly divides them along the same cosmological structure into five different forces, residing in the five orbs. He lists the spirit soul in the liver, the material soul in the lungs, the spirit in the heart, the intention in the spleen, and the will in the kidneys (chap. 6). For him, to approach the Tao is to return to the more visceral dimensions of one's being. One finds the Tao in the union and integration of the five agents within. For this, one practices breathing exercises that represent the activities of heaven and earth in the body.

In the ecstatic vision of the body, its true inner structure is identical with the organization of the universe. This concept is expressed most clearly in the origin myth that describes the transformation of the cosmic giant Pangu (*Yunji qiqian* 56.1b)—or, in another version, of Laozi—into the world at large.

> Laozi changed his body: His left eye became the sun and his right eye the moon. His head was Mount Kunlun, his hair the stars. His bones turned into dragons, his flesh into wild beasts, his intestines into snakes. His breast was the ocean; his fingers, the five sacred mountains. The hair on his

body was transformed into grass and trees; his heart into the constellation of the Flowery Canopy. Finally, his testicles joined in embrace as the true parents of the universe.

(*Xiaodao lun*, T. 2103; 52.144b)

One realizes this truth of the body by traversing the inner landscape and visualizing its various divinities in their splendid palaces, located simultaneously in the otherworldly realm in the stars and the human body (see Schipper 1978, 1982). The aim is complete acquaintance and eventual control over this true structure, from which one proceeds to union with the One, the central agent of the world. The One is the Northern Dipper; it also resides in the lower abdomen. To reach it, mystics visualize it within, they pull it down around themselves, or they ecstatically travel into the heavens. The true body is at the center of the universe and, at the same time, is the universe itself.

The Tang synthesis integrates these different visions of body and mind and their realization in mystical practice. A clear threefold structure emerges. Adepts move from refining the body to a restructuring of the mind, and ultimately to oneness with the Tao. The three levels of body, mind, and Tao, together with their respective practices, are closely parallel to Christian descriptions of mystical refinement through the purgative, the illuminative, and the unitive life. In the Chinese tradition, the three are, moreover, linked to the traditions of the *Daode jing* and ancient medicine, to the *Zhuangzi* and Buddhism, and to the ecstatic, shamanistic flight of Shangqing Taoism. The various practices associated with the three phases take care of the adepts first in terms of physical health and longevity. They then restructure their minds so that they come to see themselves as part of the Tao and lose all attachments to worldly things. The practices finally culminate in the ecstatic ascent of the individual to the Tao at the center of the cosmos.

The Political Dimension

Early Chinese mysticism did not grow in a strictly organized religious or monastic setting. Neither the ancient *Daode jing* nor the highly influential Guo Xiang had an organized group of followers. Rather, they addressed their ideas and visions to the intellectual elite in general and wished to influence society at large. They envisioned the accomplished mystic as a social being who would spread and radiate his qualities throughout the world. Placed thus at the pinnacle of society, they saw the sage as the ideal ruler, who continued the ancient Chinese ideal of the shaman-king as the chief intermediary between humanity and the cosmos. The accomplished mystic was duly stylized as the Great Man. Mysticism, never isolated from society, continued to develop a political dimension.

Already in the *Daode jing*, the sage is the ruler. However, unlike in later literature, the sage does not qualify as ruler because he is a sage; on the contrary, the ruler qualifies to be trained as a sage, because he is already at the center of human and cosmic affairs. Once the ruler has attained the One and has concentrated his vital energy, the Tao will begin to be manifest through him. He will bring peace and purity to the people. Wherever he goes and whatever he does in perfect non-action, all around him will be in cosmic harmony. There will be no more disasters or misfortunes; an ideal society will develop, made up of small farming communities that are entirely self-sufficient and eschew all luxury and sophistication (chap. 80).

Heshang gong, in his commentary to the *Daode jing*, presents a more cosmic dimension of the political aims. For him, ruling the country is parallel with, if not magically identical to, cultivating oneself. The creation of political order is structurally isomorphic with the cultivation of mystical realization and personal longevity. The sage governs the country just as he cultivates himself: by driving out attachments and desires and holding on to the Tao. Government becomes an extended act of self-cultivation. Strongly emphasized by Heshang gong, this concept too goes back to Chinese medical thought and the correspondences it perceived the political and the physical organization of humanity: "The heart is the residence of the ruler; spirit and clarity originate here. The lungs are the residence of the high ministers of state; order and division originate here. The liver is the residence of the strategists; planning and organization originate here. The gall is residence of the judges, judgments and decisions originate here" (*Huangdi neijing suwen* 3.1ab).

Nevertheless, the link of good government to self-cultivation has its major origins in the Confucian tradition. Already in the "Great Learning" chapter of the *Liji*, control of one's inner being is the key to good government. In Neo-Confucianism, attuning one's inner being to the cosmos leads to the perfection of virtue (see Taylor 1978). Cultivation of the inner self thus becomes part of the pursuit of good government and universal peace.

Guo Xiang is the first to integrate Confucian thinking into the mystical system. For him, language and social reality, hierarchy and ritual, are all part of the Tao. Thus, the perfect accordance with all-that-is must produce an ideal society. This develops not because of the benign influence of one sage, but through the increasing transformations of every individual member of the human community. If everyone attains the true and perfect state of going along with the Tao, there can be no more strife or disorder in the world. Everyone fulfills his or her share in the cosmic plan and moves in harmony with universal principle.

An ideal society without strife or friction develops; the Tao is realized on earth. The world is as it was originally meant to be, a realm of Great Peace full of harmony and unity. People find their inner truth and become true human beings. In this utopia, there are only useful and propitious situations; heaven and earth cease to suffer from calamities of any kind; there is food and drink in plenty; and everyone is healthy and lives for a very long time.

Guo Xiang's vision had a tremendous impact on later mystical thinkers, who frequently used his terms to describe their ideas. The utopian state of complete harmony for them was the reason why the world needed accomplished sages. No longer magical and shamanistic rulers, mystical sages became teachers and examples for humanity. They have gone ahead and can point to the way others still have to pursue. Buddhist doctrine greatly encouraged this understanding of the sage, since it describes the Buddha in just these terms.

As a political ideal, on the other hand, Guo Xiang's utopia never developed—fortunately, one might say, because of its inherent dangers. A despotic ruler might take it upon himself to represent the Tao in the world and decide personally what exactly the true place of everyone should be. Deterministic to a certain degree, as Confucian critics have pointed out (Chan 1964, 318), Guo Xiang's thought lends itself to a despotic and totalitarian system. In pursuing Guo Xiang's political vision, however, a despotic ruler would crush the very realization of individual freedom that is Guo Xiang's religious ideal. As Zhi Dun has said, an evil ruler might realize his inner nature by spreading evil and causing endless harm to the world. Both Zhi Dun's and the Confucian criticism of Guo Xiang's philosophy are justified, so far as its political implications go. They are right so long as they look at Guo Xiang primarily as a political, rather than a mystical, thinker.

With the important exception of the *Zhuangzi*, early Chinese mysticism therefore contains a strong political dimension. Yet it must never be mistaken for genuine political philosophy, which it neither is nor attempts to be. Mystics address their writings to fellow seekers; they base their ideas on a highly cosmological vision of the universe and aim at the religious realization of the individual in the Tao. Their political interest concerns the impact this realization has on society. They do not claim credit as political philosophers. Nevertheless, the very idea that the mystical union of an individual with the Tao should have a broad social impact is an important characteristic of early Chinese mysticism.

This political dimension takes on yet another form in the vision of the Great Man as expressed in the *Yijing*, the *Zhuangzi*, and later poetry. Not just emperor over the world, thanks to his birthright, the Great Man takes possession of the entire cosmos in an ecstatic excursion around and above the known world. Rather than mystic turned politician, here the politically powerful is turned mystic. The rituals and visions of the shaman-king of old and the Zhou king's circuits around his realm become metaphors for the realization of the mystic. Also, they became more than mere metaphors when Shangqing Taoists began to undertake such excursions in their ecstatic visualizations.

The Great Man turns the "Far-off Journey" away from the world into a triumph of taking control over everything. The poor religious seeker in his lonely meditation chamber transforms into the glorious possessor of all. He resides in the center of the universe, converses with gods and spirits, orders demons and jade maidens to his service, and calls the palaces of paradise his own. Merging the imperial with the immortal, the mystical loss of ego and dissolution into the Tao becomes a feast of power, a celebration of cosmic *I*-ness. The contradiction of later immortality beliefs is born here: Who, in the end, goes up and enjoys his or her position "next to the Jade Emperor of the Great Tao"? Whose will is being done in those ranks of the heavenly hierarchy? Who is this immortal self and what does it have to do with whatever self is mortal?

The contradiction is resolved in the Tang synthesis by distinguishing the no-self state on earth from the immortal personality above. An immortal is a being that emerges upon the end of the physical body and ascends to heaven in broad daylight. Still, the imperial sense of power and control, the right to rule inherent in the figure of the Great Man have left their traces. Mystical realization means power: power to radiate universal harmony in non-action, to teach the truth to fellow seekers, to reside in the higher spheres and make an occasional impact on the world. It means control over life and death, not only in the sense of psychological equanimity, but also as magic. The true one, the sage, will never be harmed by fierce beasts, is immune to the elements, and can traverse the ordinary world freely. As the *Daode jing* states,

> I have heard that one who is skilled at preserving
>   life
> Will not meet tigers or wild buffaloes when
>   wandering across country,

And will not be touched by weapons of war in
    fighting.
The wild buffalo cannot butt its horns against
    him,
The tiger cannot fasten its claws into him,
And weapons of war cannot thrust their blades into
    him.

(chap. 50)

In utter freedom, invulnerable from earthly hazards, the Great Man
surges above and beyond, a sage on earth, an immortal in heaven, a
blazing star shining like the pure Tao.

Notes

Introduction

1. For comprehensive recent discussions, see Schwartz 1985 and Graham 1989.
2. On these two early movements, see Eichhorn 1957; Kaltenmark 1979; Kandel 1979; Levy 1956; Seidel 1969a, 1984; and Stein 1963, 1979.

Chapter One

1. The dichotomy involves three distinct levels within human beings: sensual experience, rational consciousness, and the spiritual. None can be expressed by means of any other, which accounts for the absurdities and contradictions in religious texts: to express the spiritual with rational means must necessarily result in incongruence. See Wilber 1983.

2. I am in full agreement with Steven T. Katz (1978, 1983) in saying that all experiences are mediated. At the same time, I agree with Sallie B. King in claiming that mediation and cultural determination are not everything (King 1988). I take recourse to psychology in the study of mysticism to remedy the lack of our concrete understanding of how this mediation works—a lack deplored in the recent debate (Smith 1987; King 1988).

3. Other characteristics include timelessness, a sense of being grasped by something greater, a consciousness of oneness with everything, and the transcendence of the phenomenal ego. See James 1936, 371; Stace 1966, 44; Happold 1970, 45; and Bucke 1901. For a critical discussion of the ineffability and the noetic quality of mystical experiences, see Proudfoot 1985, 124–48.

4. As the level of excitement and quietude is regulated by brain chemicals, the notion that mystical experiences may be introduced through drugs seems plausible. At the same time, the experience alone only makes a mystic when the person continues to reorganize his or her life and consciousness. Thus, even though a distinct religious spirituality may not be so crucial as Zaehner (1961) claims in his critique of Huxley's mescaline-based conclusions (1954), the cognitive and active reaction to the experience is as essential to the phenomenon of mysticism as the mystical experience itself. For a discussion of various theories regarding mysticism, including Zaehner's, see Almond 1982.

5. For more detail on the workings of the different hemispheres of the brain and their relation to meditation and mysticism, see Ornstein 1972, 1973, 1980.

6. This is why mystics never have visions alien to their culture. A Christian mystic is not likely to encounter the Buddha, nor would an ancient Chinese interpret a strong motherly presence as an apparition of the Virgin Mary.

7. A similar distinction is made by Arthur J. Deikman when he describes the object self versus the observing self. The object self conceives of itself and the world as objects. It functions in the three distinct ways of thinking, feel-

ing, and acting, which are all based on measurements and comparisons, on the establishment of object-based categories and classifications. The observing self, on the other hand, is the inner root of a person's existence, the ultimate and transcendent sense of self deep within. It is there, yet it cannot be known, felt, or manipulated; it allows people to be receptive to the world around them, to perceive everything as flowing streams of energy, intensely alive and perfectly individual, yet ultimately interconnected in a cosmic whole. See Deikman 1982.

8. These three levels are also known as the Active, the Interior, and the Superessential or God-seeing Life (Happold 1970, 56). Evelyn Underhill distinguishes five stages: Awakening or Conversion, Self-knowledge or Purgation, Illumination, Surrender or the Dark Night of the Soul, and Union. Following the traditional threefold pattern, she also includes the conversion as an initial level and adds the stage of Surrender. This is a phase of loneliness and helplessness before the Unitive Life (Underhill 1911, 169–70). See also Ellwood 1980, 168 and Underhill 1980.

9. Evelyn Underhill defines the basic values of the Purgative Life as detachment: "By *poverty* the mystic means an utter self-stripping, the casting off of immaterial as well as material wealth, a complete detachment from all finite things. By *chastity* he means an extreme and limpid purity of soul, cleansed from personal desire and virgin to all but God. By *obedience* he means that abnegation of selfhood, that mortification of the will, which results in a complete self-abandonment, a holy indifference to the accidents of life" (Underhill 1911, 205).

10. For further details, see Huxley 1946; Russell 1963; and Schuon 1953. A recent defense of the perennialist viewpoint is found in Forman 1990.

CHAPTER TWO

1. The order of these two sections is reversed in the version found at Mawangdui. For a discussion and translation of this edition, see Lau 1982 and Henricks 1989.

2. For a detailed discussion of the dating of the text, see Lau 1982, appendix 1 and Graham 1990.

3. As recently reported, the birthplace of Laozi near Luyi has all but lost its religious significance. In an area still closed to foreign visitors, the temple serves now as a community center. The buildings still stand, but all statues were destroyed during the Cultural Revolution. See Mugitani 1989, 73–75.

4. One famous literary interpretation of the story is Bertold Brecht's "Die Legende von der Entstehung des Buches Taoteking auf dem Weg des Laotse in die Emigration," part of his cycle of Svendborg poems.

For a discussion of mythological developments within religious Taoism, see Kohn 1990a. Its impact on the mystical tradition is strongest in the *Xisheng jing*, mentioned below. A detailed analysis and translation of this text is found in Kohn 1991.

5. The translation is my own. For other versions and discussions of the text, see Lau 1982, x–xi and Fung and Bodde 1953, 1:170.

6. For details on the process of the deification of Laozi, see the outstanding works of Anna Seidel: 1969, 1978, 1978a. For an overview of the development of religious Taoism, see Kaltenmark 1969.

7. For a study of this deity, see Cahill 1982. A recent reevaluation of ancient sources and a comprehensive bibliography are found in Fracasso 1988. On the cults of the second century, see Seidel 1969a, 1984.

8. On this text and its description of Laozi, see Schipper 1978, 359 and Seidel 1969, 61. A similar statement is also contained in the *Shengmu bei* (Stele for the Holy Mother). This stele is located near a temple dedicated to Mother Li, Laozi's mother, in the sage's birthplace. It was there in the sixth century and is fully quoted in the *Shuijing zhu*. Kusuyama dates it to the year 153 C.E. (1979, 324).

A related passage is found in the first section of the *Laozi Daode jing xujue* (Introductory Formula to Laozi's Daode jing), another Dunhuang manuscript: S. 75, P. 2370. For recent editions, see Yoshioka 1959, 40–45; Ofuchi 1979, 509; Takeuchi 1978, 6:220–22; and Yan 1983, 265 and 273.

This text consists of four sections, dated differently. Section 1 is a eulogy on the cosmic Laozi. It goes back to the third century (see also DZ 723, fasc. 431; *Yunji qiqian* 1).

Section 2 tells the legend of Heshang gong, the Master on the River (see chap. 3); section 3 is a summary of Laozi's conversion of the barbarians. Both are dated to the fourth century.

Section 4 contains a description of Taoist meditation practices and is dated to the late Six Dynasties. For a discussion of this text, see Takeuchi 1978, 6:220; Yoshioka 1959, 40; Ofuchi 1964, 344–434; Robinet 1977, 24; Kusuyama 1979, 134; and Kobayashi 1986.

9. The translation is my own. For various ways of rendering the *Daode jing*, see—among many others—Legge 1962; Waley 1934; Bynner 1944; Lin 1948; Duyvendak 1951; Lau 1982; and Henricks 1989. A translation that includes later commentaries as well as a list of the most important commentators from the beginnings into the twentieth century is found in Ch'en 1981.

10. There is, for example, the expression "sitting in oblivion," which came to denote a very specific practice of Taoist meditation and named an entire school (see Kohn 1987). Moreover, numerous *Zhuangzi* terms and concepts were integrated into Shangqing Taoism (see Robinet 1983a).

11. For a detailed discussion and translation of parts of the text that takes these distinctions into consideration, see Graham 1981 and 1982. A translation of the *Zhuangzi* that relies heavily on Guo Xiang's commentary and Fukunaga's work is found in Watson 1968. Recent studies of the *Zhuangzi* include Mair 1983; Schwartz 1985; Graham 1989; and Allinson 1990.

12. A. C. Graham, following a passage in chapter 27 of the text, distinguishes three different kinds of discourse, based on different modes of thinking. There is, first, the "saying from a logding place," a kind of language based on universally accepted convention, on conscious discrimination and classifications. Next, there is the "weighted saying," a kind of discourse based on one's own personal experience and using language in a personally meaningful way. Third, there is the ideal kind, the "spillover saying," which indi-

cates a language that keeps flowing through changing meanings and viewpoints without obstruction or solidity. This kind of language is based on inner spontaneity; it is the characteristic of the sage, an indication of being at one with heaven (Graham 1989, 201).

13. The following discussion is based on Fukunaga 1946, 1978 and the English summary of his understanding of the *Zhuangzi* found in Knaul 1985. For another short description of Zhuangzi's mysticism, see also Maspero 1981, 421–26. For an analysis of the second chapter, see Graham 1969. For *Zhuangzi* mysticism as a return to Hundun or chaos, see Girardot 1983. For an analysis of Zhuangzi's thought as describing the transformation of the socialized self into the perfected self, see Berling 1985. For a discussion of the "Inner Chapters" as a philosophy of spiritual transformation, see Allinson 1990.

CHAPTER THREE

1. The Mawangdui manuscripts, found in two variants that scholars have designated A and B, are surprisingly similar to the standard edition. Still, they contain some important differences; they place the *Dejing* before the *Daojing* and change the order of certain chapters. Character variants are few and tend to elucidate the original meaning of the text. For detailed studies and translations of the texts, see Jan 1978; Lau 1982; W. Boltz 1984; and Henricks 1978, 1989.

2. A short sketch of Wang Bi's life is contained in the biography of Zhong Hui in chapter 28 of the *Sanguo zhi*.

3. Texts in the Taoist Canon (*Daozang*, abbreviated DZ) are given according to the number of the reduced sixty-volume edition (Taipei: Xinwenfeng; Kyoto: Chubun). These numbers coincide with those found in Kristofer Schipper, *Concordance du Tao Tsang: Titres des ouvrages* (Paris: Publications de l'Ecole Française d'Extrême-Orient, 1975). "Fasc." stands for "fascicle" and refers to the volume number of the 1925 Shanghai reprint of the original canon of 1445 (*Zhengtong Daozang*).

4. On Wang Bi's *Yijing* interpretation, see Bergeron 1986. His commentary to the *Daode jing* has been translated by Lin (1977) and Rump and Chan (1979). For a general discussion and partial translation of Wang Bi's works, see Fung and Bodde 1952, 1:179–89; Chan 1964, 314–24; Robinet 1977, 56–76; and Chan 1991. For recent stylistic studies especially of his *Laozi weishi lilue*, see Wagner 1980, 1986.

5. Summary and translations of the Heshang gong legend are based on the account in section 2 of the *Laozi daode jing xujue*, dated to the fourth century (see p. 179, note 8). For the original text, see Takeuchi 1978, 6:221; Ofuchi 1964, 348–49; and Ofuchi 1979, 509. A translation of some parts is found in the introduction to Erkes 1958.

6. The classical model of the humble emperor is Huangdi, the Yellow Emperor, who receives various teachings at the hands of celestial agents. He receives the political teaching of the cosmic sage Guangchengzi (*Zhuangzi* 11), the sexual techniques of the Dark Girl (*Sunü jing*), and the medical wisdom of

Qi Bo (*Huangdi neijing suwen*). On his role as the ideal student in contrast to Laozi as the cosmic teacher, see Seidel 1969, 50.

Another popular emperor who receives immortal instruction, but unfortunately is unable to amend his immoral ways in the end, is Emperor Wu of the Han. On his story, see Schipper 1965.

7. The *Xiang'er* commentary is extant in a Dunhuang manuscript (S. 6825; Ofuchi 1979, 421). An annotated edition was compiled by Rao 1956. Mugitani 1985a provides an index. A textual study in relation to the Mawangdui manuscripts was undertaken by William G. Boltz (1982).

8. For the ideas and practices of Han-dynasty *fangshi*, see Ngo 1976; De-Woskin 1983; and Yamada 1989. On the worldview of traditional Chinese medicine, see Porkert 1974; Liu 1988; Lu 1980; Sivin 1988; and Unschuld 1986. For Heshang gong's intepretation of these techniques, see Kusuyama 1966.

9. These orbs are not organs as understood in the anatomy of Western medicine. Rather, reference to any of them, e.g., the "liver," connotes the entire fabric of functional manifestations related to this orb. Consequently "liver" includes the working of the muscles and sinews, and also corresponds to the sense of vision and the eyes. See Engelhardt 1989; Ishida 1989; and Porkert 1974, 117–23.

10. On Xi Kang and his works, see Holzman 1957 and Henricks 1983. For the relation of Xiang Xiu's and Guo Xiang's works on the *Zhuangzi*, see Fukunaga 1954, 1964.

11. Certain lost passages of the *Zhuangzi* were collected by Wang Yinglin of the Song in his *Kunxue jiwen*. Their contents allow the assumption that the old *Zhuangzi* was much richer in folklore, tales of magic, instructions on rain making, dream interpretation, and so on, than it is today. See Knaul 1982.

12. For a reprint and interpretation of the postscript, see Fukunaga 1964. An English translation is found in Knaul 1982.

13. For descriptions of Guo Xiang's thought, see Fung and Bodde 1952, 2:205–36; Chan 1964, 326–35; Robinet 1983; and Knaul 1985a, 1985b. Among Japanese studies, there are especially Fukunaga 1954, 1964; Hachiya 1967; and Nakajima 1970. A translation of the first chapter of his commentary is found in Arendrup 1974.

14. Guo Xiang's subtle insight into the relation between life's realities and one's conscious or subconscious constructions of them is astounding. The thinking and acting subject shapes his world as he goes along, and the more he shapes it mentally without maintaining the experiential level the more at loss and "out of order" he will feel. See Berger and Luckmann 1966.

15. The *Zhuangzi* is cited according to the concordance edition, *Zhuangzi yinde* (Taipei: Hongdao wenhua, 1971). References indicate the page, chapter, and line number of this edition.

CHAPTER FOUR

1. For more details on shamanism, see Eliade 1964 and Lewis 1989.

2. Other scholars do not share this opinion: ". . . Shang divination appears to have involved no shamanistic flight to other realms, . . . it employed nor-

mal language, normal consciousness, and normal systems of choice . . ." (Keightley 1984, 20).

3. For a study of the love relationships between shamans and goddesses in ancient Chinese literature, see Hawkes 1974. This aspect of ancient Chinese shamanism has been carried over into Taoism and the popular beliefs of later ages. Its appearance in Tang literature has been particularly elucidated by the work of Edward H. Schafer (1973, 1978, 1978a) and Suzanne Cahill (1982, 1985).

The shaman's desolation is also a metaphor for the sadness of human lovers, just as the distant elusiveness of the god may serve to illustrate the coldness of a ruler toward his minister. Often in poetry there is no clear distinction between religious beliefs and metaphorical use. At the same time, without the actual belief, literary convention would be impossible. On the religious relevance of the early texts, see Hawkes 1974.

4. Escapists, who attain temporary access to the otherworld, relate closely to the ideal of the recluse in the Confucian tradition. Escapist poets, especially of the Six Dynasties period, were often officially labeled "recluse." Their biographies pigeonhole them as scorned and unwanted ministers, desperately waiting for reemployment.

5. For more details on immortality in the Han, see Yü 1964; Loewe 1979; and Seidel 1982.

6. See Major 1973 and 1984. Names of provinces similar to those in the *Shujing* are also found the *Zhouli* (chap. 33) and in the *Lüshi chunqiu* (chap. 13).

7. The structure of the ancient Chinese city also followed the basic understanding of cosmology. See Chang 1983, 22; Major 1984, 153; and Wheatley 1971, 411.

8. The mysterious wildernesses on the fringes are especially described in the *Shanhai jing*. Divided into eighteen chapters, the text deals with four distinct regions: the surrounding mountains, the outer seas, the central areas, and the uncultured wastelands.

The *Shanhai jing*, generally dated to the Former Han dynasty, has puzzled scholars for many years (see Ling 1970). It contains a wealth of geographical, anthropological, and mythological information. The various strange lands, peoples, and treasures it describes appear again and again in later Taoist myths and meditation manuals. For a complete translation, see Mathieu 1983.

9. The *Huainanzi* has not been translated in its entirety. Morgan's work (1935) contains chapters 1, 2, 7, 8, 12, 13, 15, and 19 with basic explanations. More recently, Benjamin Wallacker (1962) studied chapter 11; John S. Major (1973) wrote his dissertation on chapter 4; Charles LeBlanc (1978) translated chapter 6; and Claude Larre (1982) analyzed and translated chapter 7. More generally, Barbara Kandel (1973) dealt with the political history that forms the background of the work; and Charles LeBlanc (1985) subjected it to a general philosophical analysis. A monograph on the history of the text by Harold Roth is forthcoming (Phoenix: AAS Monograph, 1991).

10. These motifs play a prominent role in the *Liexian zhuan* (Kaltenmark 1953, 14) and in the *Shanhai jing* (Mathieu 1983, lxxx and civ).

11. The motif of the journey is also central to an important mystical scripture of the fifth century. In the *Xisheng jing*, Laozi sets out for the West, but in

the end ascends into heaven, to reappear later in quasi-human form to convert the barbarians with the Guardian of the Pass. See Kohn 1991.

12. On the relation between imperial and national treasures and religious symbols, see Seidel 1981, 1983. On the *Hetu* in particular, see Saso 1978.

13. The same motif occurs in the more popular story of the "Yellow Millet Dream." It narrates how the famous immortal Lü Dongbin, member of the Eight Immortals, is converted to Taoism. After flunking the imperial examinations, Lü is on his way home. On the road he meets Zhongli Quan, another of the Eight Immortals, and agrees to share overnight accommodations with him. They sit down to cook their millet. Falling into a trancelike dream, Lü lives through an entire official career, ending with his banishment to a remote border region. He wakes up. He has experienced a lifetime of joy and sorrow, but the millet is not even cooked. See Ling 1918 and Yetts 1916, 1921.

14. Both are famous immortals of the early Han dynasty. Chisongzi was a master over rain and fire in the time of Shennong, who traveled to Kunlun and visited the Queen Mother of the West (Kaltenmark 1953, 35). Wang Qiao was a specialist in music and dance, especially the crane dance (Kaltenmark 1953, 109; Despeux 1989, 239).

15. For the dating of the "Yuanyou," see Hawkes 1959, 81 and Fukunaga 1970, 108. On the development of the Han rhapsody, see Knechtges 1976.

CHAPTER FIVE

1. The most popular translation of the *Yijing* is that of Richard Wilhelm (1950). A convenient edition that also furnishes the Chinese text is Sung 1971. For interpretations of the text, see Wilhelm 1977 and Shchutskii 1979. A bibliography on *Yijing* studies is found in Cheng and Johnson 1987.

2. Sima Chengzhen's biography, including the *Daren fu*, is contained in *Shiji* 117 and was translated by Burton Watson (1968a, 2:297–342). Yves Hervouet (1964) has prepared a detailed study of Sima's life and the structure of his literary works. David Hawkes (1974, 60) notes the relation of the *Daren fu* to the shamanism of the *Chuci*. Fukunaga (1970) traces the philosophical lineage of the text.

3. The *fu* (rhapsody) is a form of recited poetry, not a song as the poetry of the *Shijing*. Also described as prose-poetry, it consists of six to seven characters per line and is distinguished by close parallelism, elaborate descriptions, dialogue, extensive cataloging, difficult language, and a general sense of grandeur. See Knechtges 1976.

4. The *Shiji* is cited according to the Jinghua edition (Beijing).

5. Chapter 28 of the *Shiji* (see Watson 1968a) describes Emperor Wu's various attempts to obtain the elixir of immortality and prolong his life. His endeavors made him a hero of Taoist exemplary fiction, especially as recorded in the *Han Wudi neizhuan* (The Inner Biography of Han Emperor Wu; DZ 292, fasc. 137; see Schipper 1965). The twin of this text, the *Han Wudi waizhuan* (Outer Biography; DZ 293, fasc. 137), records information on the numerous *fangshi* in his service. In popular fiction, the emperor later became the protagonist of entertaining and magical stories summarized as *Han Wu gushi*, "Stories on Emperor Wu of Han." Thomas E. Smith at the University of Michigan

is currently preparing a dissertation on the role of Emperor Wu in Six Dynasties literature.

6. For a detailed discussion of the similarities and discrepancies between the two texts and the different theories regarding their relationship, see Hervouet 1964, 288–302 and Fukunaga 1970, 103–4.

7. On the Seven Sages, see Holzman 1956. Ruan Ji's work is translated and discussed in Holzman 1976. The other best-known member of the group is Xi Kang. See van Gulik 1941; Holzman 1957; and Henricks 1983. Their drug-taking activities are discussed in Wagner 1973.

8. For a detailed literary analysis of how escapist poetry developed from the *Chuci*, see Mochida 1985. The author describes the development as the evolution of the poetic self from a stage at which shamans integrated themselves with nature through rituals to a point at which individuals sought a spiritual solution to their own personal terror in fantastic flights to the otherworld. She cites examples especially from the works of Cao Cao and Cao Zhi. On Cao Zhi and his immortal lyrics, see also Holzman 1988.

9. On the transformation of immortals between the Han and the Six Dynasties, see Spiro 1990.

10. Liu Ling's biography in *Jinshu* 49 tells how he tricked his wife into giving him more wine and snacks by pretending to set up a formal sacrifice for the gods. The incident is also mentioned in the *Shishuo xinyu* (A New Account of Tales of the World, 23.3; Mather 1976, 372). The same text tells of his refusal to dress properly (23.6; Mather 1976, 374). Rudolf G. Wagner links Liu Ling's nakedness to the effects of a drug commonly taken by aristocrats of the third century, known as Hanshi san or "Cold Food Powder." Stimulating the body and the mind, this drug, taken together with ample wine and meat, had an overall warming effect. Takers would strip naked and immerse themselves in cold water. See Wagner 1973.

11. The second chapter of the *Liezi* contains various related stories. Shangqiu Kai, for example, is able to perform almost miraculous feats because he has strong belief and never lets fear enter his mind. Confucius asserts that a good swimmer may reach perfection as and when he completely forgets the water and its possible perils. And Zhao Xiangzi meets a stranger in the mountains who can pass through metal and stone and walk over fire without noticing—because he does not know. See Graham 1960, 39–47.

12. The gourd is among a number of popular symbols that represent the microcosm in Chinese thought. For a detailed study, see Stein 1987. The immortal most closely associated with the gourd is Hugong, the Gourd Master, who thereby carries his very own palace around with him. See DeWoskin 1982, 77.

13. On these poets and their ideas of nature and naturalness, see Fukunaga 1958, 1958a, 1961; Nakajima 1982; Frodsham 1967; Knaul 1985; and Mather 1958, 1961, 1969.

14. The Chinese calendar places the seasons differently from the Western calendar. It centers the seasons around the equinoxes and solstices, with their beginnings and ends an equal amount of time from each. Spring, for example, begins about six weeks before the spring equinox—in early February with the New Year celebrations. See Bodde 1975.

15. Those texts are the ancient *Shizhou ji* (Record of the Ten Continents; DZ 598, fasc. 330; *Yunji qiqian* 26) and its Shangqing adaptation, the *Waiguo fang-pin qingtong neiwen* (The Green Lad's Esoteric Discussion of Outlying Lands; DZ 1373, fasc. 1041). For a detailed discussion of the *Shizhou ji*, see Li 1983. The text is translated in Smith 1990.

16. For a discussion of Shangqing Taoism as a form of Chinese mysticism, see Robinet 1988. The author shows its mythological and cosmological patterns and relates them to the inner alchemy of Song-dynasty Taoism.

17. The *Huangting jing* and the *Laozi zhongjing* describe the cosmic structure of the human body together with the deities residing therein. There is an outer and an inner *Huangting jing*, extant in various versions in the Taoist Canon, but most conveniently available in Schipper 1975. The *Laozi zhongjing* is found in *Yunji qiqian* 18–19. For its textual history, see Schipper 1979. For a discussion of the cosmology and meditation represented in these texts, see Robinet 1979 and Homann 1971.

CHAPTER SIX

1. For a detailed account on the early integration of Buddhism into Chinese culture, see Zürcher 1959; Chen 1964, 1973; and Tsukamoto and Hurvitz 1985.

2. The *Fengfa yao* has been translated in Zürcher 1959, 164–76; the translation was reprinted in Tsukamoto and Hurvitz 1985, 1011–27; for a discussion of the text, see Chen 1963. On Dao'an, compare especially the works of Arthur E. Link (1957, 1958, 1959). For Huiyuan and his stance on important issues of his time, see Liebenthal 1950, 1952, 1955 and Robinson 1967. Sengzhao's work has been translated by Liebenthal (1968) and discussed by Robinson (1959, 1967). For Daosheng, see Liebenthal 1956 and Lai 1987a.

3. For a discussion of Zhi Dun's life and thought, see Fung and Bodde 1952, 2:250; Fukunaga 1956, 86; Zürcher 1959, 116; Hurvitz 1962, 46; Chen 1964, 1973; Tsukamoto and Hurvitz 1985, 338; and Knaul 1986. Zhi Dun's biography is contained in the *Gaoseng zhuan* (Biographies of Eminent Monks; T. 2059; 50.322–424.

The Chinese *Tripitaka* is cited after the *Taishō Daizōkyō*. Citations give the number of the text, together with the volume and page numbers of that edition.

4. For first descriptions of the early Lingbao corpus, see Ofuchi 1974 and Chen Guofu 1975, 62. For a fuller treatment of the subject, including a detailed historical introduction and a descriptive catalog, see Bokenkamp 1983. On the significance of the concept of Lingbao and its relation to the talismanic tradition of Taoism, see Kaltenmark 1960.

5. The *Baopuzi* is one of the best-studied texts of religious Taoism. It is divided into an inner and an outer section: the inner chapters describe the practice of alchemy and other immortality techniques; the outer part dwells on morality and social responsibility of Taoists. The inner section of the text was translated by James R. Ware (1966), the outer by Jay Sailey (1978). Kristofer M. Schipper (1975a) compiled an index on the entire text. For an analysis of the text's concept of immortality, see Murakami 1956. For a discussion of its al-

chemy, see Needham 1976. A recent new edition was published by Wang Ming (1980).

6. On the early development of the Taoist Canon, see Ofuchi 1979a.

7. For details on Sun Chuo, see Fukunaga 1961; Mather 1961; Link and Lee 1966; and Schmidt-Glintzer 1976.

8. This text is contained in Gu Huan's biographies in *Nanshi* 75 and *Nanqi shu* 54. Gu Huan also wrote a commentary to the *Daode jing*, extant only in fragments. See Fujiwara 1962 and Horiike 1989.

9. The same kind of reasoning is found in the *Santian neijie jing* (Scripture on the Inner Explanation of the Three Heavens; DZ 1205, fasc. 876), a Taoist description of the origin and development of the world through the benign intervention of the Tao. See Schipper 1978.

10. Emperor Wu was much involved with the religions. In 574 c.e., he persecuted both Buddhism and Taoism in an effort to curb the proliferation of so-called sangha-households. These consisted of groups of lay Buddhists, who donated a certain amount of grain to sangha-officials in lieu of taxes. By the middle of the sixth century, the number of these Buddhist households had grown tremendously and the movement threatened to become an independent administrative force. After the persecution in 574, it never regained its former strength and disappeared completely during the Tang. See Lai 1987.

11. There was another set of debates under the Yuan at the Mongol court in the thirteenth century. Centering again on the question of the conversion of the barbarians, these debates led to the destruction of all Taoist materials at the time and caused great difficulties for the compilers of the Ming Canon—the one we have today. See Thiel 1961; Thompson 1985; and Boltz 1987.

12. Beyond these, texts on the debates are collected in the *Hongming ji* and the *Guang hongming ji* (T. 2102 and 2103). On the *Hongming ji*, see Schmidt-Glintzer 1976. In addition, a comprehensive summary of the debates is found in the *Fayuan zhulin* (Pearly Forest of the Dharma-Garden; T. 2122) of the year 683.

13. For an analysis and translation of the *Xisheng jing*, see Kohn 1991.

14. Chen Jingyuan's edition is contained in DZ 726, fasc. 449–50; Huizong's in DZ 666, fasc. 346–47. In addition, Fujiwara (1983) compiled a critical edition that includes the commentary of Li Rong.

15. The *Xisheng jing* is cited by numbers of sections and lines as found in Chen Jingyuan's edition. The same numbering system is also used in the translation (Kohn 1991).

CHAPTER SEVEN

1. Du Guangting (850–933) first defined Twofold Mystery as a separate trend of *Daode jing* interpretation in the introduction to his *Daode zhenjing guangsheng yi* (The Extensive Sagely Meaning of the Scripture of the Tao and the Virtue; DZ 725, fasc. 440–48). He listed its main exponents, including *Daode jing* commentators from the fifth to the eighth centuries. For a discussion of Twofold Mystery, see Robinet 1977; Sunayama 1980; Fujiwara 1980a, 1980b; and Kohn 1991.

2. Dunhuang manuscripts allowed an almost complete reconstitution of the *Benji jing*'s ten long scrolls. They are reprinted in proper order in Wu 1960 and Ofuchi 1979.

3. Cheng Xuanying's *Daode jing* commentary was reconstituted on the basis of Dunhuang manuscripts (S. 5887, P. 2517 and 2353). See Yan 1983, 239–728. Its introduction is translated in Robinet 1977, 227–60. Fujiwara Takao interprets its central concepts (1980c, 1981, 1981a, 1981b).

Cheng's work on the *Zhuangzi* is often edited together with Guo Xiang's commentary. It is found in DZ 745, fasc. 507–19.

His commentary on the *Duren jing* is contained in DZ 87, fasc. 38–39. For a discussion of this work, see Sunayama 1984 and Fujiwara 1980.

His commentary to the *Yijing* is lost today. For a general appreciation of Cheng's ideas, see Robinet 1977 and Zhao 1982.

4. Li Rong's *Daode jing* commentary is divided into two scrolls. The first is contained in DZ 722, fasc. 430; the second has survived in Dunhuang (P. 2577, 2594, 2864, 3237, 3777, and S. 2060). For a comprehensive edition of both parts, see Yan 1983, 729–1019 and Fujiwara 1986, 1987, 1988.

Li Rong's work on the *Xisheng jing* is contained in DZ 726, fasc. 449–50 and has been specially edited by Fujiwara (1983). For a discussion of both commentaries, see Fujiwara 1979 and 1985. For more details on Li Rong's life and work, see Kohn 1991.

5. For discussions of Chinese Mādhyamika, see Fung and Bodde 1952, 2:293; Chan 1964, 357; and Robinson 1967. For an analysis of Jizang's impact on Tang Taoist thought, see Kamata 1966, 84.

6. According to the *Zhenzheng lun* (52.569c), the *Haikong jing* was compiled by the two Taoists Li Yuanxing, a Chongxuan representative, and Fang Chang. The text must have been written before the later half of the seventh century. At that time, various Taoist works—such as the *Sandong zhunang*, the *Daojiao yishu*, and the *Daolei shixiang*—cite it. See Kamata 1969, 82.

7. The Heavenly Venerable of Primordial Beginning is the highest deity of Lingbao Taoism. His name goes back to the honorific title of the Buddha, "Worldly Venerable" or "World Honored One." The Heavenly Venerable is to Taoism what the *dharmakāya*, the "body of the Law," is to Mahāyāna Buddhism: the eternally existing basis of all mundane transformation, the absolute that transcends all, the body by which one can pass through the Three Worlds in an instant and be everywhere at the same time. See Kamata 1969, 83.

8. For a detailed discussion of Tao-nature and its interpretations in Tang philosophy, see Kamata 1966, also reprinted in Kamata 1969, 11–80.

9. For a comparison between different versions of the *Vimalakīrti-nideśa-sūtra* and the long passage found in scroll 9 of the *Haikong jing*, see Kamata 1969, 91–97. He also includes the entire ten chapters of the text in his volume on Buddhist materials in the Taoist Canon (Kamata 1986, 30–130).

10. The *Daojiao yishu* consists of ten scrolls and thirty-seven sections. The sixth scroll is lost today. The text is contained in DZ 1129, fasc. 762–63. An index has been compiled by Nakajima 1980. A summary is found in Yoshioka 1959, 328–50.

188 · Notes to Chapter Seven

11. On the date of the *Daojiao yishu*, see Fukui 1952, 132; Yoshioka 1959, 309; Ofuchi 1964, 217; and Kamata 1963, 202 and 1969, 173. For the question of Meng Anpai's identity, see Yoshioka 1959, 311–12.

12. For a discussion of the Taoist Canon, its divisions and development, see Liu 1973; Ofuchi 1979a; Thompson 1985; and Boltz 1987.

13. On Tang Taoist masters, see Kirkland 1986. On Sima Chengzhen's life and work, see Engelhardt 1987 and Kohn 1987. Sun Simiao's alchemical work has been studied by Nathan Sivin (1968), and his work on acupuncture was translated by Catherine Despeux (1987). On Wu Yun's life and poetry, see Schafer 1978a, 1981.

14. The best and most detailed account of Tang physical practices is found in Sima Chengzhen's *Fuqi jingyi lun*. For a detailed study and partial translation of the text, see Engelhardt 1987. For the differences between Sima Chengzhen's and Sun Simiao's approaches, see Engelhardt 1989.

Glossary

Baopuzi 抱朴子
beidou 北斗
ben 本
Benji jing 本際經
benwu 本無
Bian Shao 邊韶
Bianzheng lun 辯正論
Bozhou 亳州

Cai Zihuang 蔡子晃
chan 禪
Chen Jingyuan 陳景元
Cheng Xuanying 成玄英
Che Xuanbi 車玄弼
Chisongzi 赤松子
chongxuan 重玄
Chu 楚
Chuci 楚辭
Cui Zhuan 崔譔
Cunshen lianqi ming 存神鍊氣銘

Dahui 大慧
Dao'an 道安
Daode jing 道德經
Daode zhenjing guangsheng yi
　道德真經廣聖義
Daode zhigui 道德指歸
daojia 道家
daojiao 道教
Daojiao yishu 道教義樞
Daolei shixiang 道類事象
Daosheng 道生
Daoyin jing 導引經
daren 達人
daren 大人
Daren fu 大人賦
Daren xiansheng zhuan 大人先生傳

Dingguan jing 定觀經
Du Guangting 杜光庭
Duren jing 度人經

Erdi zhang 二諦章
Erjiao lun 二教論

fa 法
fan 反
Fang Chang 方長
fangshi 方士
Fayuan zhulin 法苑珠林
feizhi yuzhi 非指喻指
fen 分
Fengdu shan 豐都山
Fengfa yao 奉法要
Fodao lunheng 佛道論衡
fu 賦
Fu Yi 傅弈
Fuqi jingyi lun 服氣精義論

Gaoseng zhuan 高僧傳
Ge Chaofu 葛巢甫
Ge Hong 葛洪
Ge Xuan 葛玄
Gongsun Long 公孫龍
guan 觀
Guangchengzi 廣成子
Guang hongming ji 廣弘明記
Gu Huan 顧歡
Guo Xiang 郭象

Haikong zhizang jing 海空智藏經
Hanfeizi 韓非子
Hanshisan 寒食散
Hanshu 漢書
Han Wu gushi 漢武故事

Heshang gong　河上公

Hetu　河圖

Hongming ji　弘明記

Huahu jing　化胡經

Huainanzi　淮南子

Huangdi　黃帝

Huangdi neijing suwen
　黃帝內經素問

Huangting jing　黃庭經

Huang Xuanyi　黃玄頤

Huayan　華嚴

Huayangzi　華陽子

Huiyuan　慧遠

Huizong　徽宗

Hundun　渾沌

ji　跡

Jiang Bin　姜斌

jianwang　兼忘

jie　戒

jing (mental states)　境

jing (scripture)　經

Jiude song　酒德頌

Jizang　吉藏

Jurong　句容

Kunlun　崑崙

Kunxue jiwen　困學紀聞

Laolaizi　老萊子

Laozi　老子

Laozi bianhua jing　老子變化經

Laozi daode jing xujue
　老子道德經序訣

Laozi kaitian jing　老子開天經

Laozi ming　老子銘

Laozi weizhi lilue　老子微指理略

Laozi zhongjing　老子中經

Li　李

li　理

Liexian zhuan　列仙傳

Liezi　列子

Liji　禮記

Lingbao　靈寶

Li Rong　李榮

Lisao　離騷

Lishi zhenxian tidao tongjian
　歷世真仙體道通鑑

Liu An　劉安

Liu Jinxi　劉進喜

Liu Ling　劉伶

Li Yuanxing　黎元興

Lu Ao　盧敖

Lü Dongbin　呂洞賓

Luofeng shan　羅豐山

Luoshu　洛書

Lüshi chunqiu　呂氏春秋

Lu Xiujing　陸修靜

Luyi　庬邑

Lu Zhaolin　盧照鄰

Maoshan　茅山

Mawangdui　馬王堆

Meng Anpai　孟安排

Menlü　門律

ming (fate)　命

ming (light)　明

Mu Tianzi zhuan　穆天子傳

Nan Qishu　南齊書

Nanshi　南史

Nan Yangsheng lun　難養生論

Neiguan jing　內觀經

Pangu　盤古

Penglai　蓬萊

Poxie lun　破邪論

qi　氣

qian　乾

qing　情

qingtan　清談

Qingxu guan　清虛觀

Qu Yuan　屈原

Renzhenzi　任真子

Ruan Ji 阮籍

Sandong zhunang 三洞珠囊
Sanguo zhi 三國志
Sanhuang wen 三皇文
Santian neijie jing 三天內解經
sanye 三業
se 色
Sengzhao 僧肇
Shangqing 上清
Shanhai jing 山海經
shen (body) 身
shen (spirit) 神
Shengmu bei 聖母碑
Shenxian kexue lun 神仙可學論
Shenxian zhuan 神仙傳
Shiji 史記
Shijing 詩經
Shishuo xinyu 世說新語
Shizhou ji 十洲記
Shuijing zhu 水經註
Shujing 書經
Shuowen 說文
Siku quanshu zongmu tiyao
　四庫全書總目提要
Sima Biao 司馬彪
Sima Chengzhen 司馬承禎
Sima Qian 司馬遷
Sima Xiangru 司馬相如
Sun Chuo 孫卓
Sun Simiao 孫思邈
Sunü jing 素女經

Taiji 太極
Taiqing daolin shesheng lun
　太清道林攝生論
Taishang laojun 太上老君
tan 貪
Tangshu 唐書
Tan Muzui 曇漠最
Tao Hongjing 陶弘景
Tao Yuanming 陶淵明
Tiantai 天台

Tianyinzi 天隱子

Waiguo fangpin qingtong neiwen
　外國方品青童內文
Wang Bi 王弼
Wang Chou 王儔
Wang Fou 王浮
Wang Fusi 王輔嗣
Wang Qiao 王蹻
Wangwu shan 王屋山
Wang Xizhi 王羲之
Wang Yinglin 王應麟
Wei Chuxuan 韋處玄
Wei Jie 韋節
Wenxuan 文選
wu (nonbeing) 無
wu (shaman) 巫
Wupian zhenwen chishu
　五篇真文赤書
Wushang biyao 無上祕要
wushen 無身
wuwei 無爲
wuwo 無我
wuxin 無心
Wu Yun 吳筠
wuzhi 無知

xian 仙
Xiang Xiu 向秀
Xianzheng lun 顯正論
Xiaodao lun 笑道論
Xi Chao 郗超
Xie Lingyun 謝靈運
Xihua guan 西崋觀
Xi Kang 嵇康
xin 心
xing (body) 形
xing (nature) 性
Xisheng jing 西昇經
Xiwangmu 西王母
Xuandu guan 玄都觀
Xuanjing mulu 玄京目錄
Xuanxue 玄學

Xuanzang 玄奘
Xunzi 荀子

Yangsheng lun 養生論
Yangsheng yaoji 養生要集
Yang Xi 楊羲
Yang Zhu 楊朱
Yan Junping 嚴君平
Yan Zun 嚴遵
Yijing 易經
Yin Xi 尹喜
yinyang 陰陽
Yixia lun 夷夏論
Yonghuai shi 詠懷詩
Yuanshi tianzun 元始天尊
Yuanyou 遠遊
Yunji qiqian 雲笈七籤

Zhang Daoling 張道陵
Zhang Lu 張魯
Zhang Rong 張融
Zhang Zhan 張湛
Zhao Daoyi 趙道一
Zhao Jingtong 趙靜通
Zhenzheng lun 甄正論
zhi (knowledge) 知
zhi (wisdom) 智
Zhi Daolin 支道林
Zhi Dun 支遁
Zhi Qian 支謙
zhishen zhiguo 治身治國
Zhouli 周禮
Zhouyi lueli 周易略理
Zhou Yong 周顒
Zhuangzi 莊子
Zhuangzi yinde 莊子引得
Ziwei gong 紫微宮
Zou Yan 騶衍
zuowang 坐忘
Zuowang lun 坐忘論
Zuoyou ming 坐右銘
Zuozhuan 左傳

Bibliography

WORKS IN WESTERN LANGUAGES

Akahori Akira. 1989. "Drug Taking and Immortality." In *Taoist Meditation and Longevity Techniques*, ed. Livia Kohn, 71–96. Ann Arbor: University of Michigan, Center for Chinese Studies Publications.

Allinson, Robert E. 1990. *Chuang-Tzu for Spiritual Transformation*. Albany: State University of New York Press.

Almond, Philip C. 1982. *Mystical Experience and Religious Doctrine*. New York: Mouton.

Andersen, Poul. 1980. *The Method of Holding the Three Ones*. London: Curzon Press.

Arendrup, Birhte. 1974. "The First Chapter of Guo Xiang's Commentary to the *Zhuangzi*." In *Acta Orientalia* 36:311–416.

Balasz, Etiénne. 1948. "Entre revolt nihilistique et évasion mystique." In *Asiatische Studien/Etudes Asiatiques* 1.2:27–55.

———. 1964. *Chinese Civilization and Bureaucracy*. New Haven: Yale University Press.

Benn, Charles. 1987. "Religious Aspects of Emperor Hsüan-tsung's Taoist Ideology." In *Buddhist and Taoist Practice in Medieval Chinese Society*, ed. David W. Chappell, 127–45. Honolulu: University of Hawaii Press.

Berger, Peter. 1969. *The Sacred Canopy*. Garden City, N.Y.: Doubleday.

———. 1969a. *A Rumor of Angels*. Garden City, N.Y.: Doubleday.

———, and Thomas Luckmann. 1966. *The Social Construction of Reality*. Garden City, N.Y.: Doubleday.

Bergeron, Marie-Ina. 1986. *Wang Pi: Philosophie du non-avoir*. Taipei: Institut Ricci.

Berling, Judith A. 1980. *The Syncretic Religion of Lin Chao-en*. New York: Columbia University Press.

Berling, Judith. 1985. "Self and Whole in Chuang Tzu." In *Individualism and Holism: Studies in Confucian and Taoist Values*, ed. Donald J. Munro, 101–20. Ann Arbor: University of Michigan, Center for Chinese Studies Publications.

Bodde, Derk. 1975. *Festivals in Classical China*. Princeton: Princeton University Press.

Bokenkamp, Stephen. 1983. "Sources of the Ling-pao Scriptures." In *Tantric and Taoist Studies*, vol. 2, ed. Michel Strickmann, 434–86. Brussels: Institut Belge des Hautes Etudes Chinoises.

———. 1989. "Death and Ascent in Ling-pao Taoism." In *Taoist Resources* 1.2:1–20.

Boltz, Judith M. 1987. *A Survey of Taoist Literature: Tenth to Seventeenth Centuries*. China Research Monograph 32, Berkeley and Los Angeles: University of California Press.

Boltz, William G. 1982. "The Religious and Philosophical Significance of the *Hsiang-erh Lao-tzu* in the Light of the Ma-wang-tui Silk Manuscripts." In *Bulletin of the School for Oriental and African Studies* 45:95–117.

———. 1984. "Textual Criticism and the Ma-wang-tui *Lao-tzu*." In *Harvard Journal of Asiatic Studies* 44:185–224.

Bono, Joseph. 1984. "Psychological Assessment of Transcendental Meditation." In *Meditation: Classic and Contemporary Perspectives*, ed. Deane N. Shapiro and Roger N. Walsh, 209–18. New York: Aldine.

Brown, Daniel P., and Jack Engler. 1984. "A Rorschach Study of the Stages of Mindfulness Meditation." In *Meditation: Classic and Contemporary Perspectives*, ed. Deane N. Shapiro and Roger N. Walsh, 232–62. New York: Aldine.

Bucke, R. M. 1901. *Cosmic Consciousness: A Study of the Evolution of the Human Mind*. Philadelphia: Innis and Sons.

Bynner, Witter. 1944. *The Way of Life According to Lao tsu*. New York: Perigree.

Cahill, Suzanne. 1982. "*The Image of the Goddess: Hsi Wang Mu in Medieval Chinese Literature*." Ph.D. dissertation, University of California.

———. 1985. "Sex and the Supernatural in Medieval China: Cantos on the Transcendent Who Presides Over the River." In *Journal of the American Oriental Society* 105:197–220.

Chan, Alan. 1991. *Two Visions of the Way: A Study of the Wang Pi and the Ho-shang-kung Commentaries on the Laozi*. Albany: State University of New York Press.

Chan, Wing-tsit. 1964. *A Source Book in Chinese Philosophy*. Princeton: Princeton University Press.

Chang, Kuang-chih. 1983. *Art, Myth, and Ritual: The Path to Political Authority in Ancient China*. Cambridge: Harvard University Press.

Chen, Ellen Marie. 1974. "Tao as the Great Mother and the Influence of Motherly Love in the Shaping of Chinese Philosophy." In *History of Religions* 14:51–65.

Chen, Kenneth. 1964. *Buddhism in China*. Princeton: Princeton University Press.

———. 1973. *The Chinese Transformation of Buddhism*. Princeton: Princeton University Press.

Ch'en Ku-ying. 1981. *Lao-tzu: Text, Notes, and Comments*. San Francisco: Chinese Materials Center.

Cheng, Chung-ying, and Elton Johnson. 1987. "A Bibliography of the *I-ching* in Western Languages." In *Journal of Chinese Philosophy* 14.1:73–90.

Ching, Julia. 1976. *To Accumulate Wisdom: The Way of Wang Yang-Ming*. New York: Columbia University Press.

———. 1983. "The Mirror Symbol Revisited: Confucian and Taoist Mysticism." In *Mysticism and Religious Traditions*, ed. Steven T. Katz, 226–46. Oxford: Oxford University Press.

Davidson, Julian M. 1984. "The Physiology of Meditation and Mystical States of Consciousness." In *Meditation: Classic and Contemporary Perspectives*, ed. Deane N. Shapiro and Roger N. Walsh, 376–95. New York: Aldine.

Deikman, Arthur J. 1980. "Deautomatization and the Mystic Experience." In *Understanding Mysticism*, ed. Richard Woods, 240–60. New York: Image Books. Originally published in *Psychiatry* 29 (1966):324–83.

———. 1982. *The Observing Self: Mysticism and Psychotherapy*. Boston: Beacon Press.

Despeux, Catherine. 1987. *Préscriptions d'acuponcture valant mille onces d'or*. Paris: Guy Trédaniel.

———. 1989. "Gymnastics: The Ancient Tradition." In *Taoist Meditation and Longevity Techniques*, ed. Livia Kohn, 223–60. Ann Arbor: University of Michigan, Center for Chinese Studies Publications.

DeWoskin, Kenneth J. 1983. *Doctors, Diviners, and Magicians of Ancient China*. New York: Columbia University Press.

Eichhorn, Werner. 1957. "T'ai-p'ing und T'ai-p'ing Religion." In *Mitteilungen des Instituts für Orientforschung* 5:113–40.

Eliade, Mircea. 1964. *Shamanism: Archaic Techniques of Ecstasy*. Princeton: Princeton University Press, Bollingen Series 76.

Ellwood, Robert S. *Mysticism and Religion*. Englewood Cliffs, N.J.: Prentice Hall.

Engelhardt, Ute. 1987. *Die klassische Tradition der Qi-Übungen. Eine Darstellung anhand des Tang-zeitlichen Textes Fuqi jingyi lun von Sima Changzhen*. Wiesbaden: Franz Steiner.

———. 1989. "*Qi* for Life: Longevity in the Tang." In *Taoist Meditation and Longevity Techniques*, ed. Livia Kohn, 262–94. Ann Arbor: University of Michigan, Center for Chinese Studies Publications.

Erkes, Eduard. 9153. "Ssu erh pu wang." In *Asia Major* 3.2:156–61.

———. 1958. *Ho-Shang-Kung's Commentary of Lao Tse*. Ascona: Artibus Asiae.

Fisher, Roland. 1980. "A Cartography of the Ecstatic and Meditative States." In *Understanding Mysticism*, ed. Richard Woods, 286–305. New York: Image Books.

Forman, Robert K. C. 1990. *The Problem of Pure Consciousness*. Oxford: Oxford University Press.

Fracasso, Ricardo. 1988. "Holy Mothers of Ancient China." In *T'oung-pao* 74:1–46.

Frodsham, J. D. 1967. *The Murmuring Stream: The Life and Works of Hsieh Ling-yun*. 2 vols. Kuala Lumpur: University of Malaya Press.

Fukunaga Mitsuji. 1969. "'No-Mind' in *Chuang-tzu* and Ch'an Buddhism." In *Zinbun* 12:9–45.

Fung Yu-lan, and Derk Bodde. 1952. *A History of Chinese Philosophy*. 2 vols. Princeton: Princeton University Press.

Gimello, Robert M. 1978. "Mysticism and Meditation." In *Mysticism and Philosophical Analysis*, ed. Steven T. Katz, 170–99. Oxford: Oxford University Press.

———. 1983. "Mysticism in Its Contexts." In *Mysticism and Religious Traditions*, ed. Steven T. Katz, 61–88. Oxford: Oxford University Press.

Girardot, Norman. 1983. *Myth and Meaning in Early Taoism*. Berkeley and Los Angeles: University of California Press.

Goullart, Peter. 1961. *The Monastery of Jade Mountain*. London: John Murray.

Graham, A. C. 1960. *The Book of Lieh-tzu*. London: A. Murray.

———. 1961. "The Date and Compilation of the Liehtzyy." In *Asia Major*, 2d ser., 8:139–98.

———. 1969. "Chuang-tzu's Essay on 'Seeing Things As Equal.'" In *History of Religions* 9:137–59.

———. 1980. "How much of *Chuang-tzu* Did Chuang-tzu Write?" In *Studies in Classical Chinese Thought*. Journal of the American Academy of Religions Supplement 35, 459–501.

———. 1981. *Chuang-tzu: The Seven Inner Chapters and Other Writings from the Book of Chuang-tzu*. London: Allan and Unwin.

———. 1982. *Chuang-tzu: Textual Notes to a Partial Translation*. London: University of London Press.

———. 1983. "Taoist Spontaneity and the Dichotomy of 'Is' and 'Ought.'" In *Experimental Essays on Chuang-tzu*, ed. Victor H. Mair, 3–23. Honolulu: University of Hawaii Press.

———. 1989. *Disputers of the Tao: Philosophical Argument in Ancient China*. La Salle, Ill.: Open Court Publishing Company.

———. 1990. "The Origins of the Legend of Lao Tan." In *Studies in Chinese Philosophy and Philosophical Literature*, ed. A. C. Graham, 111–24. Reprint. Albany: State University of New York Press. Originally published 1981.

Granet, Marcel. 1950. *La pensée chinoise*. Paris: Albin.

Gulik, Robert H. 1941. *Hsi K'ang and His Poetical Essay on the Lute*. Tokyo: Sophia University.

Happold, F. C. 1970. *Mysticism: A Study and an Anthology*. Baltimore: Penguin.

Hawkes, David. 1959. *Ch'u Tz'u: The Songs of the South*. New York: Oxford University Press.

———. 1974. "The Quest of the Goddess." In *Studies in Chinese Literary Genres*, ed. Cyril Birch, 42–68. New York: Columbia University Press.

———. 1981. "Quanzhen Plays and Quanzhen Masters." In *Bulletin d'Ecole Française d'Extrême Orient* 69:153–70.

Henricks, Robert. 1978. "A Note on the Question of Chapter Divisions in the Ma-wang-tui Manuscripts of *Lao-tzu*." In *Early China* 4:49–57.

———. 1983. *Philosophy and Argumentation in Third-Century China: The Essays of Hsi K'ang*. Princeton: Princeton University Press.

———. 1989. *Lao-Tzu: Te-Tao ching*. New York: Ballantine.

Hervouet, Yves. 1978. *A Sung Bibliography—Bibliographie des Sung*. Hong Kong: Hong Kong University Press.

Hocking, William E. 1980. "The Meaning of Mysticism as Seen through Its Psychology." In *Understanding Mysticism*, ed. Richard Woods, 223–39. Reprint. New York: Image Books. Originally published 1912.

Holzman, Donald. 1956. "Les sept sages de la foret des bambus et la société de leur temps." In *T'oung-pao* 44:317–46.

———. 1957. *La vie et la pensée de Hi K'ang*. Leiden: E. Brill.

———. 1976. *Poetry and Politics: The Life and Works of Juan Chi (210–263)*. Cambridge: Cambridge University Press.

Holzman, Donald. 1988. "Ts'ao Chih and the Immortals." In *Asia Major* 1.1:15–58.

Homann, Rolf. 1971. *Die wichtigsten Körpergottheiten im Huang-t'ing-ching*. Göppingen: Alfred Kümmerle.

Hsu Sung-pen. 1979. *A Buddhist Leader in Ming China. The Life and Thought of Han-shan te-ch'ing*. University Park: Pennsylvania State University Press.

Hurvitz, Leon. 1962. *Chih-i (538–597)*. Brussels: Institut Belge des Hautes Etudes Chinoises.

Huxley, Aldous. 1946. *The Perennial Philosophy*. New York: Harper and Brothers.

———. 1963. *The Doors of Perception and Heaven and Hell*. New York: Vintage Books.

Ishida, Hidemi. 1989. "Body and Mind: The Chinese Perspective." In *Taoist Meditation and Longevity Techniques*, ed. Livia Kohn, 41–70. Ann Arbor: University of Michigan, Center for Chinese Studies Publications.

James, William. 1936. *The Varieties of Religious Experience*. Reprint. New York: Modern Library. Originally published 1902.

Jan Yün-hua. 1978. "The Silk Manuscripts on Taoism." In *T'oung-pao* 63:65–84.

Kaltenmark, Maxime. 1953. *Le Lie-sien tchouan*. Peking: Université de Paris Publications.

———. 1960. "Ling-pao: Note sur un terme du Taoïsme religieux." In *Mélanges publieux par l'Institut des Hautes Etudes* 2:559–88.

———. 1965. "La mystique taoïste." In *La mystique et le mystiques*, ed. A. Ravier, 649–69. Paris: Desdée de Brouwer.

———. 1969. *Lao-tzu and Taoism*. Stanford: Stanford University Press.

———. 1979. "The Ideology of the *T'ai-p'ing-ching*." In *Facets of Taoism*, ed. Holmes Welch and Anna Seidel, 19–52. New Haven: Yale University Press.

———. 1979a. "Notes sur le *Pen-tsi king*. Personnages figurant dans le sutra." In *Contributions aux études du Touen-houang*, vol. 1, ed. Michel Soymié, 91–98. Geneva: Ecole Française d'Extrême-Orient.

Kandel, Barbara. 1973. "Der Versuch einer politischen Restauration: Liu An, der König von Huai-nan." In *Nachrichten der Gesellschaft für Natur- und Völkerkunde Ostasiens* 113:58–82.

———. 1979. *Taiping jing*. Hamburg: Gesellschaft für Natur- und Völkerkunde Ostasiens.

Katz, Steven T. 1978. "Language, Epistemology, and Mysticism." In *Mysticism and Philosophical Analysis*, ed. Steven T. Katz, 22–74. Oxford: Oxford University Press.

———. 1983. "The 'Conservative' Character of Mystical Experience." In *Mysticism and Religious Traditions*, ed. Steven T. Katz, 3–60. Oxford: Oxford University Press.

———. 1988. "On Mysticism. Responses to Huston Smith and Sallie B. King." In *Journal of the American Academy of Religion* 56:751–61.

Keightley, David. 1984. "Late Shang Divination: The Magico-Religious Legacy." In *Explorations in Early Chinese Cosmology*, ed. Henry Rosemont, 11–34. Chico, Calif.: Scholars Press, American Academy of Religion.

King, Sallie B. 1988. "Two Epistemological Models for the Interpretation of Mysticism." In *Journal of the American Academy of Religion* 56:257–79.

Kirkland, J. Russell. 1986. "Taoists of the High T'ang: An Inquiry into the Perceived Significance of Eminent Taoists in Medieval Chinese Society." Ph.D. dissertation, Indiana University.

Knaul, Livia. 1982. "Lost *Chuang-tzu* Passages." In *Journal of Chinese Religions* 10:53–79.

———. 1985. "The Habit of Perfection: A Summary of Fukunaga Mitsuji's Studies on the *Chuang-tzu* Tradition." In *Cahiers d'Extrême-Asie* 1:71–85.

———. 1985a. "Kuo Hsiang and the *Chuang-tzu*." In *Journal of Chinese Philosophy* 12:429–47.

———. 1985b. "The Winged Life: Kuo Hsiang's Mystical Philosophy." In *Journal of Chinese Studies* 2.1:17–41.

———. 1986. "Chuang-tzu and the Chinese Ancestry of Ch'an Buddhism." In *Journal of Chinese Philosophy* 13:411–28.

Knechtges, David R. 1976. *The Han Rhapsody: A Study of the Fu of Yang Hsiung (53 BC–AD 18)*. Cambridge: Cambridge University Press.

Kohn, Livia. 1987. *Seven Steps to the Tao: Sima Chengzhen's Zuowanglun*. St. Augustin/Nettetal: Monumenta Serica Monograph 20.

———. 1987a. "The Teaching of T'ien-yin-tzu." In *Journal of Chinese Religions* 15:1–28.

———. 1988. "Medicine and Immortality in T'ang China." In *Journal of the American Oriental Society* 108.3:465–69.

———, ed. 1989. *Taoist Meditation and Longevity Techniques*. Ann Arbor: University of Michigan, Center for Chinese Studies Publications.

———. 1989a. "Guarding the One: Concentrative Meditation in Taoism." In *Taoist Meditation and Longevity Techniques*, ed. Livia Kohn, 123–56. Ann Arbor: University of Michigan, Center for Chinese Studies Publications.

———. 1989b. "Taoist Insight Meditation: The Tang Practice of *Neiguan*." In *Taoist Meditation and Longevity Techniques*, ed. Livia Kohn, 191–222. Ann Arbor: University of Michigan, Center for Chinese Studies Publications.

———. 1989c. "The Mother of the Tao." In *Taoist Resources* 1.2:37–113.

———. 1990. "Eternal Life in Taoist Mysticism." In *Journal of the American Oriental Society* 110.4: 623–48.

———. 1990a. "Die Emigration des Laozi. Mythologische Entwicklungen vom 2. bis 6. Jahrhundert." In *Monumenta Serica* 38:49–68.

———. 1990b. "Transcending Personality: From Ordinary to Immortal Life." In *Taoist Resources* 2.2:1–22.

———. 1991. *Taoist Mystical Philosophy. The Scripture of Western Ascension*. Albany: State University of New York Press.

———. 1991a. "Taoist Visions of the Body." In *Journal of Chinese Philosophy* 18.3: forthcoming.

Lagerwey, John. 1981. *Wu-shang pi-yao: Somme taoïste du VIe siècle*. Paris: Publications de l'Ecole Française d'Extrême-Orient.

Lai, Whalen. 1987. "The Earliest Folk Buddhist Religion in China: *T'i-wei Po-li Ching* and Its Historical Significance." In *Buddhist and Taoist Practice in Medieval Chinese Society*, ed. David W. Chappell, 11–35. Honolulu: University of Hawaii Press.

———. 1987a. "Tao-sheng's Theory of Sudden Enlightenment Re-examined." In *Sudden and Gradual: Approaches to Enlightenment in Chinese Thought*, ed. Peter N. Gregory, 169–200. Honolulu: University of Hawaii Press, Kuroda Institute Studies in East Asian Buddhism 5.

Larre, Claude. 1985. *Le traité VII du Houai-nan-tseu*. Taipei: Institut Ricci.

Lau, D. C. 1982. *Chinese Classics: Tao Te Ching*. Hong Kong: Hong Kong University Press.

LeBlanc, Charles. 1978. *Chapter Six of the Huai-nan-tzu*. Hong Kong: Hong Kong University Press.

———. 1985. *Huai-nan-tzu: Philosophical Synthesis in Early Han Thought*. Hong Kong: Hong Kong University Press.

Leeuw, Gerardus van der. 1963. *Religion in Essence and Manifestation*. New York: Harper and Row.

Legge, James. 1962. *The Sacred Books of China: The Texts of Taoism*. New York: Dover.

———. 1969. *The Chinese Classics: The Shoo King or The Book of Historical Documents*. Taipei: Jinwen.

Levy, Howard S. 1956. "Yellow Turban Rebellion at the End of the Han." In *Journal of the American Oriental Society* 76:214–24.

Lewis, I. M. 1971. *Ecstatic Religion. An Anthropological Study of Spirit Possession and Shamanism*. Baltimore: Penguin Books.

Liebenthal, Walter. 1950. "Shih Hui-yüan's Buddhism." In *Journal of the American Oriental Society* 70:243–59.

———. 1952. "The Immortality of the Soul in Chinese Thought." In *Monumenta Nipponica* 8:327–92.

———. 1955. "Chinese Buddhism During the Fourth and Fifth Centuries." In *Monumenta Nipponica* 11.1:44–83 and ibid., 11.2:64–96.

———. 1956. "Notes on the 'Vajrasamadhi.'" *T'oung-pao* 44:347–86.

———. 1968. *Chao-Lun, the Treatise of Seng-chao*. Hong Kong: Hong Kong University Press.

Lin, Paul J. 1977. *A Translation of Lao-tzu's Tao-te-ching and Wang Pi's Commentary*. Ann Arbor: University of Michigan, Center for Chinese Studies Publications.

Link, Arthur E. 1957. "Shyh Daw-an's Preface to the *Yogacarabhumi-sutra* and the Problem of Buddho-Taoist Terminology in Early Chinese Buddhism." In *Journal of the American Oriental Society* 77:1–14.

———. 1958. "The Biography of Tao-an." In *T'oung-pao* 46:1–48.

———. 1969. "The Taoist Antecedents of Tao-an's Prajñā Ontology." In *History of Religions* 9:181–216.

———, and Timothy Lee. 1966. "Sun Cho's *Yü-tao-lun*: A Clarification of the Way." In *Monumenta Serica* 25:169–96.

Liu Ts'un-yan. 1970. "Taoist Self-Cultivation in Ming Thought." In *Self and Society in Ming Thought*, ed. William Theodore DeBary, 291–331. New York: Columbia University Press.

———. 1970a. "The Penetration of Taoism in the Ming Confucian Elite." In *T'oung-pao* 52:31–103.

———. 1973. "The Compilation and Historical Value of the *Tao-tsang*." In *Essays on the Sources of Chinese History*, ed. Donald Leslie, 104–20. Canberra: Australian National University Press.

Liu, Yen-chih. 1988. *The Essential Book of Traditional Chinese Medicine*. 2 vols. New York: Columbia University Press.

Loewe, Michael. 1979. *Ways to Paradise: The Chinese Quest for Immortality*. London: George Allan and Unwin.

———. 1982. *Chinese Ideas of Life and Death*. London: George Allan and Unwin.

Loon, Piet van der. 1984. *Taoist Books in the Libraries of the Sung Period*. London: Oxford Oriental Institute.

Lu Gwei-djen. 1980. *Celestial Lancets. A History and Rationale of Acupuncture and Moxa*. Cambridge: Cambridge University Press.

Major, John S. 1973. "Topography and Cosmology in Early Han Thought: Chapter Four of the Huai-nan-tzu." Ph.D. dissertation, Harvard University.

———. 1984. "The Five Phases, Magic Squares, and Schematic Cosmography." In *Explorations in Early Chinese Cosmology*, ed. Henry Rosemont, 133–66. Chico, Calif.: Scholars Press, American Academy of Religion.

Maslow, Abraham H. 1964. *Toward a Psychology of Being*. New York: Van Nostrand Reinhold.

————. 1970. *Religions, Values, and Peak Experiences.* New York: Viking Press.

Maspero, Henri. 1924. "Legendes mythologiques dans le *Chou King.*" In *Journal Asiatique* 20:1–101.

————. 1971. *Le taoïsme et les religions chinoises.* Paris: Gallimard.

————. 1981. *Taoism and Chinese Religion.* Amherst: University of Massachusetts Press.

Mather, Richard B. 1958. "The Landscape Buddhism of the Fifth Century Poet Hsieh Ling-yün." In *Journal of Asian Studies* 18:67–81.

————. 1961. "The Mystical Ascent of the T'ien-t'ai Mountains: Sun Cho's *Yu T'ien-t'ai-shan fu.*" In *Monumenta Serica* 20:226–45.

————. 1961. "The Mystical Ascent of the T'ien-t'ai Mountains: Sun Cho's *Yu T'ien-t'ai-shan fu.*" In *Monumenta Serica* 20:226–45.

————. 1976. *A New Account of Tales of the World.* Minneapolis: University of Minnesota Press.

————. 1979. "K'ou Ch'ien-chih and the Taoist Theocracy at the Northern Wei Court 425–451." In *Facets of Taoism,* ed. Holmes Welch and Anna Seidel, 103–22. New Haven: Yale University Press.

Mathieu, Remi. 1978. *Le Mu Tianzi zhuan.* Paris Collège du France, Mémoires de l'Institute des Hautes Etudes Chinoises 9.

————. 1983. *Étude sur la mythologie et l'éthnologie de la Chine ancienne.* 2 vols. Paris: Collège du France. Mémoires de l'Institut des Hautes Etudes Chinoises.

Mochida, Fraces Lafleur. 1985. "Structuring a Second Creation: Evolution of the Self in Imaginary Landscapes." In *Expressions of Self in Chinese Literature,* ed. Robert E. Hegel, 70–122. New York: Columbia University Press.

Moore, Peter. 1978. "Mystical Experience, Mystical Doctrine, Mystical Technique." In *Mysticism and Philosophical Analysis,* ed. Steven T. Katz, 101–31. Oxford: Oxford University Press.

Morgan, Evan. 1934. *Tao, the Great Luminant.* Shanghai: Kelly and Walsh.

Needham, Joseph. 1976. *Science and Civilisation in China.* Vol. V.3: *Spagyrical Discovery and Invention: Historical Survey, from Cinnabar Elixir to Synthetic Insulin.* Cambridge: Cambridge University Press.

Ngo Van Xuyet. 1976. *Divination, Magie et Politique dans la Chine ancienne.* Paris: Presses Universitaires de France.

Ofuchi Ninji. 1974. "On Ku Ling-pao ching." In *Acta Asiatica* 27:33–56.

————. 1979a. "The Formation of the Taoist Canon." In *Facets of Taoism,* ed. Holmes Welch and Anna Seidel, 253–68. New Haven: Yale University Press.

Ornstein, Robert E. 1972. *The Psychology of Consciousness.* New York: W. H. Freeman and Co.

————. 1973. *The Nature of Human Consciousness.* San Francisco: Freeman and Co.

————. 1980. "Two Sides of the Brain." In *Understanding Mysticism,* ed. Richard Woods, 270–85. New York: Image Books.

Oshima, Harold H. 1983. "A Metaphorical Analysis of the Concept of Mind in the Chuang-tzu." In *Experimental Essays on Chuang-tzu*, ed. Victor H. Mair, 63–84. Honolulu: University of Hawaii Press.

Penelhum, Terence. 1980. "Unity and Diversity in the Interpretation of Mysticism." In *Understanding Mysticism*, ed. Richard Woods, 438–48. New York: Image Books.

Porkert, Manfred. 1974. *The Theoretical Foundations of Chinese Medicine*. Cambridge: MIT Press.

Proudfoot, Wayne. 1985. *Religious Experience*. Berkeley and Los Angeles: University of California Press.

Rand, Christopher C. 1983. "*Chuang-tzu* Text and Substance." In *Journal of Chinese Religions* 11:5–58.

Robinet, Isabelle. 1976. "Les randonées extatiques des taoïstes dans les astres." In *Monumenta Serica* 32:159–273.

———. 1977. *Les commentaires du Tao to king jusqu'au VIIe siècle*. Paris: Collège du France, Memoires de l'Institute des Hautes Etudes Chinoises 5.

———. 1979. *Méditation taoïste*. Paris: Dervy Livres.

———. 1983. "Kouo Siang ou le monde comme absulu." In *T'oung-pao* 69:87–112.

———. 1983a. *Chuang-tzu et le taoïsme religieux*." In *Journal of Chinese Religions* 11:59–109.

———. 1984. *La révélation du Shangging dans l'histoire du taoïsme*. 2 vols. Paris: Publications de l'Ecole Française d'Extrême-Orient.

———. 1988. "Taoïsme et mystique." In *Cahiers d'Etudes Chinoises* 8:66–103.

———. 1989. "Visualization and Ecstatic Flight in Shangqing Taoism." In *Taoist Meditation and Longevity Techniques*, ed. Livia Kohn, 157–90. Ann Arbor: University of Michigan, Center for Chinese Studies Publications.

———. 1989a. "Original Contributions of *Neidan* to Taoism and Chinese Thought." In *Taoist Meditation and Longevity Techniques*, ed. Livia Kohn, 295–328. Ann Arbor: University of Michigan, Center for Chinese Studies Publications.

Robinson, Richard. 1959. "Mysticism and Logic in the Thought of Seng Chao, Fifth Century Thinker." In *Philosophy East and West* 8:99–120.

———. 1967. *Early Mādhyamika in India and China*. Madison: University of Wisconsin Press.

Roth, Harold. 1990. "The Concept of *Shen* in Early Taoism: A Ghost in the Machinery?" In *Sagehood and Systematization of Thought in the Late Warring States and Early Han*, ed. Kidder Smith, 11–32. Brunswick, Me.: Bowdoin College.

———. 1991. *The Textual History of the Huai-nan-tzu*. Phoenix: AAS Monograph.

———. 1991a. "Psychology and Self-Cultivation in Early Taoistic Thought." In *Harvard Journal of Asiatic Studies* 51.2: forthcoming.

Rump, Ariane, and Wing-tsit Chan. 1979. *Commentary on the Lao-tzu by Wang Pi*. Honolulu: University of Hawaii Press.

Russell, Bertrand. 1963. *Mysticism and Logic*. Reprint. London: George Allan and Unwin. Originally published 1917.

Sailey, Jay. 1978. *The Master Who Embraces Simplicity: A Study of the Philosophy of Ko Hung (A.D. 283–343)*. San Francisco: Chinese Materials Center.

Saso, Michael. 1978a. "What is the Ho-t'u?" In *History of Religions* 17:399–416.

Schafer, Edward H. 1973. *The Divine Woman*. Berkeley and Los Angeles: University of California Press.

———. 1977. "The Restoration of the Shrine of Wei Hua-ts'un at Lin-ch'uan in the Eighth Century." In *Journal of Oriental Studies* 15:124–38.

———. 1978. "The Jade Woman of Greatest Mystery." In *History of Religions* 17:387–98.

———. 1978a. "The Capeline Cantos: Verses on the Divine Loves of Taoist Priestesses." In *Asiatische Studien/Etudes Asiatiques* 32:5–65.

———. 1981. "Wu yün's 'Cantos on Pacing the Void.'" In *Harvard Journal of Asiatic Studies* 41.2:377–415.

Schipper, Kristofer. 1965. *L'Empereur Wou des Han dans la legende taoïste*. Paris: Publications de l'Ecole Française d'Extrême-Orient 58.

———. 1975. *Concordance du Houang-t'ing king*. Paris: Publications de l'Ecole Française d'Extrême-Orient.

———. 1975b. *Concordance du Pao-p'u-tzu nei/wai-p'ien*. Paris: Publications de l'Ecole Française d'Extrême-Orient.

———. 1978. "The Taoist Body." In *History of Religions* 17:355–87.

———. 1979. "Le Calendrier de Jade: Note sur le *Laozi zhongjing*." In *Nachrichten der deutschen Gesellschaft für Natur- und Völkerkunde Ostasiens* 125:75–80.

———. 1982. *Le corps taoïste: Corps physique—corps social*. Paris: Fayard.

Schmidt-Glintzer, Helwig. 1976. *Das Hung-ming-chi und die Aufnahme des Buddhismus in China*. Wiesbaden: Franz Steiner.

Schuon, Frithjof. 1953. *The Transcendent Unity of Religions*. New York: Pantheon.

Schwartz, Benjamin. 1985. *The World of Thought in Ancient China*. Cambridge: Harvard University Press.

Seidel, Anna. 1969. *La divinisation de Lao-tseu dans le taoïsme des Han*. Paris: Publications de l'Ecole Française d'Extrême Orient.

———. 1969a. "The Image of the Perfect Ruler in Early Taoist Messianism." In *History of Religions* 9:216–47.

———. 1978. "Der Kaiser und sein Ratgeber." In *Saeculum* 29:18–50

———. 1978a. "Das neue Testament des Tao." In *Saeculum* 29:147–72.

———. 1981. "Kokuhō—Note à propos du terme 'trésor nationale' en Chine et au Japon." In *Bulletin de l'Ecole Française d'Extrême-Orient* 69:229–61.

———. 1982. "Tokens of Immortality in Han Graves." In *Numen* 29:79–122.

———. 1983. "Imperial Treasures and Taoist Sacraments: Taoist Roots in the Apocrypha." In *Tantric and Taoist Studies*, vol. 2, ed. Michel Strickmann, 291–371. Brussels: Institut Belge des Hautes Etudes Chinoises.

———. 1984. "Taoist Messianism." In *Numen* 31:161–74.

Shapiro, Deane N., and Roger N. Walsh, eds. 1984. *Meditation: Classic and Contemporary Perspectives*. New York: Aldine.

Shchutskii, Iulian. 1979. *Researches on the I-ching*. Princeton: Princeton University Press, Bollingen Series 62.

Sivin, Nathan. 1968. *Chinese Alchemy: Preliminary Studies*. Cambridge: Harvard University Press.

———. 1988. *Traditional Medicine in Contemporary China*. Ann Arbor: University of Michigan, Center for Chinese Studies Publications.

Smart, Ninian. 1977. "The Exploration of Mysticism." In *Mystics and Scholars*, ed. Harold Coward and Terence Penelhum, 63–70. Canadian Corporation for Studies in Religion.

———. 1980. "Interpretation and Mystical Experience." In *Understanding Mysticism*, ed. Richard Woods, 78–91. New York: Image Books.

Smith, Huston. 1987. "Is There a Perennial Philosophy?" In *Journal of the American Academy of Religion* 55:553–66.

Smith, Thomas E. 1990. "The Record of the Ten Continents." In *Taoist Resources* 2.2:87–119.

Soothill, William E., and Lewis Hudous. 1937. *A Dictionary of Chinese Buddhist Terms*. London: Kegan Paul.

Spiro, Audrey. 1990. "How Light and Airy: Upward Mobility in the Realm of Immortals." In *Taoist Resources* 2.2:43–69.

Staal, Frits. 1975. *Exploring Mysticism: A Methodological Essay*. Berkeley and Los Angeles: University of California Press.

Stace, W. T. 1960. *Mysticism and Philosophy*. London: Macmillan.

Stein, Rolf A. 1963. "Remarques sur les mouvements du taoïsme politico-religieux au IIe siècle ap. J.-C." In *T'oung-pao* 50:1–78.

———. 1979. "Religious Taoism and Popular Religion from the Second to Seventh Centuries." In *Facets of Taoism*, ed. Holmes Welch and Anna Seidel, 53–81. New Haven: Yale University Press.

———. 1987. *Le monde en petit*. Paris: Flammarion. English translation by Phyllis Brooks. *The World in Miniature. Container Gardens and Dwellings in Far-Eastern Religious Thought*. Stanford: Stanford University Press, 1990.

Sternberg, Leo. 1925. "Divine Election in Primitive Religion." In *Procédés du Congres International des Americanists* 21:472–512.

Strickmann, Michel. 1978. "The Mao-shan Revelations. Taoism and the Aristocracy." In *T'oung-pao* 63:1–63.

———. 1978a. "A Taoist Confirmation of Liang Wu-ti's Suppression of Taoism." In *Journal of the American Oriental Society* 98:467–74.

———. 1978b. "The Longest Taoist Scripture." In *History of Religions* 17:331–54.

———. 1979. "On the Alchemy of T'ao Hung-ching." In *Facets of Taoism*, ed. Holmes Welch and Anna Seidel, 123–92. New Haven: Yale University Press.

———. 1981. *Le taoïsme du Mao chan; chronique d'une révélation*. Paris: Collège du France. Mémoires de l'Institut des Hautes Etudes Chinoises 17.

———, ed. 1983. *Tantric and Taoist Studies*, vol. 2. Brussels: Institut Belge des Hautes Etudes Chinoises.

———, ed. 1985. *Tantric and Taoist Studies*, vol. 3. Brussels: Institut Belge des Hautes Etudes Chinoises.

Sung, Z. D. 1971. *The Text of Yi King*. Taipei: Chengwen.

Tart, Charles T., ed. 1969. *Altered States of Consciousness*. New York: Wiley.

Taylor, Rodney L. 1978. *The Cultivation of Selfhood as a Religious Goal in Neo-Confucianism*. Missoula, Mont.: Scholars Press.

Thiel, Josef. 1961. "Der Streit der Buddhisten und Taoisten zur Mongolenzeit." In *Monumenta Serica* 20:1–81.

Thompson, Laurence. 1985. "Taoism: Classic and Cannon." In *The Holy Book in Comparative Perspective*, ed. Frederick M. Denny and Rodney L. Taylor, 204–23. Columbia: University of South Carolina Press.

Tsukamoto, Senryu. 1985. *A History of Early Chinese Buddhism*. Trans. Leon Hurvitz. 2 vols. Tokyo: Kodansha.

Underhill, Evelyn. 1911. *Mysticism*. London: Methuen and Co.

———. 1966. *The Essentials of Mysticism and Other Essays*. New York: Dutton.

Unschuld, Paul. 1985. *Medicine in China: A History of Ideas*. Berkeley and Los Angeles: University of California Press.

Verellen, Franciscus. 1989. *Du Guangting (850–933). Taoïste de cour à la fin de la Chine mediévale*. Paris: Memoirs de L'Institut des Hautes Etudes Chinoises 30.

Wagner, Rudolf G. 1980. "Interlocking Parallel Style: Laozi and Wang Bi." In *Asiatische Studien/Etudes Asiatiques* 34:18–53.

———. 1986. "Wang Bi: 'The Structure of the Laozi's Pointers.'" In *T'oung-pao* 72:92–129.

Waley, Arthur. 1934. *The Way and Its Power*. London: Allen and Unwin.

———. 1955. *The Nine Songs: A Study of Shamanism in Ancient China*. London: Allen and Unwin.

Wallacker, Benjamin. 1962. *The Huai-nan-tzu, Book Eleven: Behavior, Culture, and the Cosmos*. New Haven: Yale University Press, American Oriental Series 48.

Walsh, Roger N. 1984. "An Evolutionary Model of Meditation Research." In *Meditation: Classic and Contemporary Perspective*, ed. Deane N. Shapiro and Roger N. Walsh, 24–31. New York: Aldine.

Ware, James R. 1933. "The *Wei-shu* and the *Sui-shu* on Taoism." In *Journal of the American Oriental Society* 53:215–50.

———. 1966. *Alchemy, Medicine and Religion in the China of AD 320*. Cambridge: MIT Press.

Watson, Burton. 1968. *The Complete Works of Chuang-tzu*. New York: Columbia University Press.

———. 1968a. *Records of the Grand Historian of China*. 2 vols. New York: Columbia University Press.

Welch, Holmes, and Anna Seidel, eds. 1979. *Facets of Taoism*. New Haven: Yale University Press.

Wheatley, Paul. 1971. *The Pivot of the Four Quarters: A Preliminary Enquiry into the Origins and Character of the Ancient Chinese City*. Chicago: University of Chicago Press.

Wienphal, Paul. 1977. "Feature Review Article: *Exploring Mysticism: A Methodological Essay*. By Frits Staal." In *Philosophy East and West* 27:349–63.

Wilber, Ken. 1983. *Eye to Eye. The Quest for the New Paradigm*. New York: Anchor Books.

Wilhelm, Hellmut. 1977. *Heaven, Earth and Man*. Seattle: University of Washington Press.

Wilhelm, Richard. 1950. *The I Ching or Book of Changes*. Princeton: Princeton University Press, Bollingen Series 19.

Wu chi-yu. 1960. *Pen-tsi king, Livre du terme originel: Ouvrage taoïste inédit du VII siècle*. Paris: Centre National des Recherches Scientifiques.

Yamada, Toshiaki. 1989. "Longevity Techniques and the Transmission of the *Lingbao Wufuxu*." In *Taoist Meditation and Longevity Techniques*, ed. Livia Kohn, 99–124. Ann Arbor: University of Michigan, Center for Chinese Studies Publications.

Yetts, Percifal. 1916. "The Eight Immortals." In *Journal of the Royal Asiatic Society*, 773–807.

———. 1921. "More Notes on the Eight Immortals." In *Journal of the Royal Asiatic Society*, 397–426.

Yü Ying-shih. 1964. "Life and Immortality in the Mind of Han-China." In *Harvard Journal of Asiatic Studies* 25:80–122.

Zaehner, R. C. 1961. *Mysticism Sacred and Profane*. London: Oxford University Press.

Zürcher, Erik. 1959. *The Buddhist Conquest of China*. 2 vols. Leiden: E. Brill.

———. 1980. "Buddhist Influence on Early Taoism." In *T'oung-pao* 66:84–147.

WORKS IN CHINESE AND JAPANESE

Azuma Jūji 吾妻重二. 1988. "Goshinhen no naitan shisō" 悟真篇の内丹思想. In *Chūgoku kodai yōsei shisō no sōgoteki kenkyū* 中國古代養生思想の總合的研究, ed. Sakade Yoshinobu, 600–27. Tokyo: Hirakawa.

Chen Guofu 陳國符. 1975. *Daozang yuanliu kao* 道藏源流考. Taipei: Guting.

Fujiwara Takao 藤原高男. 1962. "Ko Kan Rōshi chu kō" 顧歡老子注考. In *Kan'ibunka* 漢魏文化 3:19–29.

———. 1973. "Rōshi Kajōkōchu chōhon shūsei" 老子河上公注鈔本集成. In

Takamatsu kōsen kenkyū kiyō 高松高專研究紀要 8:213–88 and 9:70–140.

————. 1979. "Dōshi Ri Ei no Dōtokukyō chū ni tsuite" 道士李榮の道德經注について. In *Kagawa daigaku kyōiku gakubu kenkyū hōkō* 香川大學教育學部研究報告 47:1–30.

————. 1980. "Genshi muryō dojin jōhin myōkyō Shi Gen'ei chū" 元始無量度人上品妙經成玄英注. In *Kagawa daigaku kyōiku gakubu kenkyū hōkō* 香川大學教育學部研究報告 49:37–60.

————. 1980a. "Ryu Shinki, Sai Shikō, Sha Genbi no Dōtokukyō chū ni tsuite" 劉進喜,蔡子晃,車玄弼の道德經注について. In *Kagawa daigaku kyōiku gakubu kenkyū hōkō* 香川大學教育學部研究報告 49:61–77.

————. 1980b. "Rōshikai ni okeru chūgenha no kōei" 老子解に於ける重玄派の後裔. In *Ikeda Suetoshi hakase koki kinen Tōyōgaku ronshū* 池田末利博士古稀記念東洋學論集, 657–72. Tokyo: Tōhō gakkai.

————. 1980c. "Sei Gen'ei hon Dōtokukyō ni tsuite (Ten)" 成玄英本道德經について(天). In *Kagawa daigaku kyōiku gakubu kenkyū hōkō* 香川大學教育學部研究報告 50:137–72.

————. 1981. "Sei Gen'ei hon Dōtokukyō ni tsuite (Chi)" 成玄英本道德經について(地). In *Kagawa daigaku kyōiku gakubu kenkyū hōkō* 香川大學教育學部研究報告 51:1–38.

————. 1981a. "Sei Gen'ei hon Dōtokukyō ni tsuite (Jin)" 成玄英本道德經について(人). In *Kagawa daigaku kyōiku gakubu kenkyū hōkō* 香川大學教育般教育研究報告 52:1–45.

————. 1981b. "Sei Gen'ei Dōtokukyō gishu to Kajōkō chū" 成玄英道德經義疏と河上公注. In *Tōhōgaku* 東方學 61:60–72.

————. 1983. "Saishōkyō' Ri Ei chū" 西昇經李榮注. In *Kagawa daigaku ippan kyōiku kenkyū* 香川大學一般教育研究 23:117–50.

————. 1985. "Dōshi Ri Ei no Saishōkyō chū ni tsuite" 道士李榮の西昇經注について. In *Kagawa daigaku kokubun kenkyū* 香川大學國文研究 10:6–16.

————. 1986. "Ri Ei Dōtokukyō chū—ichi" 李榮道德經注(一). In *Tokushima bunri daigaku bungaku ronsō* 德島文理大學文學論叢 3:97–132.

————. 1987. "Ri Ei Dōtokukyō chū—ni" 李榮道德經注(二). In *Tokushima bunri daigaku bungaku ronsō* 德島文理大學文學論叢 4:139–77.

————. 1988. "Ri Ei Dōtokukyō chū—san" 李榮道德經注(三). In *Tokushima bunri daigaku bungaku ronsō* 德島文理大學文學論叢 5:103–39.

Fukui Fumimasa 福井文雅. 1987. "Goshinhen no kōsei ni tsuite" 悟真篇の構成について. In *Tōhōshūkyō* 東方宗教 70:22–38.

Fukui Kōjun 福井康順. 1964. *Dōkyō no kisōteki kenkyū* 道教の基礎的研究. Tokyo: Risosha.

Fukunaga Mitsuji 福永司光. 1946. "Sō Shū no yū ni tsuite" 莊周の遊について. In *Shinagaku* 支那學 12:33–73.

————. 1954. "Kaku Shō no Sōshi kaishaku" 郭象の莊子解釋. In *Tetsugaku kenkyū* 哲學研究 37:108–24 and 167–77.

————. 1956. "Shi Ton to sono shūi" 支遁とその周圍. In *Bukkyō shigaku* 佛教史學 5:86–108.

———. 1958. "Gen Seki ni okeru osore to nagusame: Gen Seki no seikatsu to shisō" 阮籍における懼れと慰め：阮籍の生活と思想. In *Tōhōgakuhō* 東方學報 28:34–50.

———. 1958a. "Sha Reiun no shisō ni tsuite" 謝靈運の思想について. In *Tōhōshūkyō* 東方宗教 13/14:25–48.

———. 1961. "Son Shaku no shisō" 孫卓の思想. In *Aichi gakugei daigaku kenkyū hōkō* 愛知學藝大學研究報告 10:33–48.

———. 1964. "Kaku Shō no Sōshi chū to Kō Shū no Sōshi chū" 郭象の莊子注と向秀の莊子注. In *Tōhōgakuhō* 東方學報 36:187–215.

———. 1970. "Daijin fu no shisōteki keifu" 大人賦の思想的系譜. In *Tōhōgakuhō* 東方學報 41:97–126.

———. 1978. *Sōshi* 莊子. 6 vols. Tokyo: Asahi. Originally published in 1956.

Hachiya Kunio 蜂屋綺夫. 1967. "Sōshi shōyōyū hen o meguru Kaku Shō to Shi Ton no kaishaku" 莊子逍遙遊篇をめぐる郭象と支遁の解釋. In *Hikaku bunka kenkyū* 比較文化研究 8:59–98.

Horiike Nobuo 堀池信夫. 1989. "Ko Kan 'Rōshichū' no shisō" 顧歡老子注の思想. In *Tōhōshūkyō* 東方宗教 74:1–19.

Kamata Shigeo 鎌田茂雄. 1963. "Dōkyō kyōri no keisei ni oyoboshita bukkyō shisō no eikyō" 道教教理の形成におよぼした佛教思想の影響. In *Tōyō bunko kenkyūjo kiyō* 東洋文化研究所紀要 31:165–240.

———. 1966. "Dōsei shisō no keisei katei" 道性思想の形成過程. In *Tōyō bunko kenkyūjo kiyō* 東洋文化研究所紀要 42:61–154.

———. 1968. "Genshuroku ni arawaretaru bukkyō shisō" 玄珠錄にあらわれたる佛教思想. In *Chūgoku gakushi* 中國學誌 5:119–44.

———. 1969. *Chūgoku bukkyō shisōshi no kenkyū* 中國佛教思想史の研究. Tokyo: Shunjusha.

———. 1986. *Dōzō nai bukkyō shisō shiryō shūsei* 道藏内佛教思想資料集成. Tokyo: Ozo shuppan.

Kobayashi Masayoshi 小林正美. 1985. "Daidōka reikai no seiritsu ni tsuite" 大道家令戒の成立について. In *Tōyō no shisō to shūkyō* 東方の思想と宗教 2:16–32.

———. 1985a. "Kajō shinjin shōku no shisō to seiritsu" 河上真人章句の思想と成立. In *Tōhōshūkyō* 東方宗教 65:20–43.

———. 1986. "Rōshi dōtokukyō joketsu no shisō to seiritsu" 老子道德經序訣の思想と成立. In *Philosophia* 73: 65–88.

Kusuyama Haruki 榀山春樹. 1966. "Rōshi kajōkō chū no shisōteki kōsatsu—toku ni ichi no kotoba o chūshin to shite" 老子河上公注の思想的考察：特に一の語を中心として. In *Tōhōshūkyō* 東方宗教 28:1–20.

———. 1972. "Rōshi kajōkō chū no shisōteki kōsatsu: Chishin chikoku no ron ni tsuite" 老子河上公注思想考察：治身治國の論について. In *Suzuki hakase koki kinen Tōyōgaku ronsō* 鈴木博士古稀記念東洋學論叢, 231–51. Tokyo.

———. 1976. "Rōkunden to sono nendai" 老君傳とその年代. In *Tōhōshūkyō*

東方宗教 47:12-30.

————. 1978. "Seiyōshi densetsu kō" 青羊肆傳説考. In *Tōhōshūkyō* 東方宗教 52:1-14.

————. 1979. *Rōshi densetsu no kenkyū* 老子傳説の研究. Tokyo: Sobunsha.

Li Fengmao 李豐楙. 1983. "Shizhou zhuanshuo di xingcheng ji qi yanbian" 十洲傳説的形成及其衍變. In *Zhongguo gudian xiaoshuo yanjiu zhuanji* 中國古典小說研究傳集 6:35-88.

Ling Chunsheng 凌純聲, ed. 1970. *Shanhai jing xinlun* 山海經新論. Taipei: Orient Cultural Service, Folklore and Folkliterature Series, vol. 142.

Miura Kunio 三浦國雄. 1983. "Shushi to kokyū" 朱子と呼吸. In *Chūgoku ni okeru ningensei no tankyū* 中國における人間性の探求, ed. Kanaya Osamu 金谷治, 499-521. Tokyo: Sōbunsha.

Mugitani Kunio 麥谷邦夫. 1985. "Rōshi sōjichū ni tsuite" 老子想爾注について. In *Tōhō gakuhō* 東方學報 57:75-109.

————. 1985a. *Rōshi sōjichū sakuin* 老子想爾注索引. Kyoto: Hōyū shoten.

————. 1989. "Dōkyō iseki sanhōki" 道教遺跡參訪記. In *Tōhōshūkyō* 東方宗教 73:63-81.

Murakami Yoshimi 村上嘉實. 1956. *Chūgoku no sennin* 中國の仙人. Kyoto: Heiraku shoten.

Nakajima Ryūzō 中島隆藏. "Kaku Shō no shisō ni tsuite" 郭象の思想について. In *Shūkan Tōyōgaku* 集刊東洋學 24:43-60.

————. 1980. *Dōkyō gishu sakuinkō* 道教義樞索引考. Kyoto: Privately published.

————. 1982. "Rikuchō kōhan yori Sui Tō shoki ni itaru dōka no shizensetsu" 六朝後半より隋唐初期に至る道家の自然説. In *Tōyō bunka* 東洋文化 62:139-74.

Ōfuchi Ninji 大淵忍爾. 1964. *Dōkyōshi no kenkyū* 道教史の研究. Okayama.

————. 1979. *Tonkō dōkei zurokuhen* 敦煌道經圖錄編. Tokyo: Kokubu shoten.

Rao Zongyi 饒宗頤. 1956. *Laozi xianger zhu jiaoqian* 老子想爾注校牋. Hong Kong: Tong Nam Printers.

Sakade Yoshinobu 坂出祥伸. 1986. "Chō Tan 'Yōsei yōshū' itsubun to sono shisō" 張湛養生要集佚文とその思想. In *Tōhōshūkyō* 東方宗教 68:1-24.

Sunayama Minoru 砂山稔. 1980. "Dōkyō chūgenha hyōi" 道教重玄派表微. In *Shūkan Tōyōgaku* 集刊東方學 43:31-44.

————. 1980a. "Sei Gen'ei no shisō ni tsuite" 成玄英の思想について. In *Nippon chūgoku gakkai hō* 日本中國學會報 32:125-39.

————. 1983. "Honsaikyō no ishō to maki kyū, maki jū no renzoku mondai ni tsuite" 本際經の異稱と卷九, 卷十の連續問題について. In *Tōhōshūkyō* 東方宗教 61:80-91.

————. 1984. "Lingbao duren jing sizhu daji" 靈寶度人經四注答記. In *Shijie zongjiao yanjiu* 世介宗教研究 2:30-48.

Wang Ming 王明. 1981a. *Baopuzi neipian jiaoshe* 抱朴子內篇校攝. Beijing: Zhonghua.

Wu Shouju 吳受璩. 1981. *Sima Chengzhen ji jijiao* 司馬承禎集輯校. Beijing.

Yan Lingfeng 嚴靈峰. 1983. *Jingzi congzhu* 經子叢書. Taipei: Xuesheng.

Yoshioka Yoshitoyo 吉岡義豐. 1959. *Dōkyō to bukkyō* 道教と佛教, vol. 1. Tokyo: Kokusho kankokai.

Zhao Zongcheng 趙宗誠. 1982. "Shilun Cheng Xuanying di chongxuan zhi dao" 試論成玄英的重玄之道. In *Zongjiao xue yanjiu* 宗教學研究, 8–15.

Index

absolute, 35–36, 37. *See also* Tao
Analects, 97, 144
Arbiter of Destiny, 111
Avatamsaka sūtra, 148

Baopuzi, 126, 185n.5
barbarians: conversion of, 127, 130; versus Chinese, 128
Being-cognition, 27–28, 177n.7. *See also* mystical experience; peak-experiences
Benji jing, 140
Berger, Peter, 17–20
Bian Shao, 43–44
Bianzheng lun, 129–30
body: in *Daojiao yishu*, 149–50, 152; deities in, 67, 110, 114, 152, 172; health of, 122, 155–57, 171; in Heshang gong, 65–69, 171; and mind, 16, 134, 157–58, 164, 169–72; as self, 65–66; seven stages of, 159–61; in Shangqing, 113–14, 115–16, 171–72; and state, 65–67; types of, 15, 149–50, 167, 170, 187n.7; as universe, 171–72; in *Xisheng jing*, 134, 136, 171; in Zhi Dun, 121
Bozhou, Laozi's birthplace. *See* Laozi
Brahma Heavens, 111
brain hemispheres, 24–25, 171n.5
breathing exercises: in Heshang gong, 68; in Li Rong, 145–46; in Tang synthesis, 156; in Zhi Dun, 122. *See also* mystical practices
Buddhism: in debates, 127–30, 149, 186nn.10 and 11; in early Chinese mysticism, 3–4, 5, 14–15, 117–38, 139, 162, 166–67, 169, 185n.2; and immortality, 117; as influenced by Taoist philosophy, 5, 60, 174; in later mysticism, 9; in Lingbao, 14, 109, 125–27, 136; in Shangqing, 111; in Tang synthesis, 139, 143, 146–49, 155; and Taoism, 124–30, 148–49; in *Xisheng jing*, 135–36

Cai Zihuang, 141
calendar, 184n.14
Cao Cao, 184n.8

Cao Zhi, 184n.8
Celestial Masters Taoism, 7, 64, 137
Chan, Alan, 62, 65
Chan Buddhism, 3, 9–10
Chang Kuang-chih, 82
chaos, 56, 123, 153
Cheng Xuanying: as Chongxuan thinker, 139; life and works of, 140–41, 187n.3; philosophy of, 142–45
Chen Jingyuan, 130
Che Xuanbi, 139
Chinese mysticism: and Buddho-Taoist debates, 127–30, 149; characteristics of, 15–16, 162–65; criticism of, 107–8; later forms of, 9–10; main traditions of, 3, 162; poles of, 80; practitioners of, 7–8; textual lineages in, 4, 9; two phases of, 5
Chisongzi, 94, 183n.14
Chuci: and ecstatic tradition, 5, 14, 99, 162, 184n.8; journey in, 84, 94–95, 99; and *Zhuangzi*, 52
Cold-Food Powder, 103, 184n.10
concentration: versus insight meditation, 30–31, 152; intense, 159; psychological studies of, 31; as purgation, 30
Confucian values: in *Daode jing*, 48; versus Great Man, 101–2; integration of, 144, 173–74; versus unknowing, 89
Confucius, 41–42, 44, 184n.11
consciousness: in *Daojiao yishu*, 151; dissolution of, 54–55; five phases of, 159–60; in Guo Xiang, 73–74, 79–80; in Tang synthesis, 157–68, 166–67; in Twofold Mystery, 142–43; versus unified mind, 29–30, 163, 167–69, 170; in *Xisheng jing*, 134; in Zhi Dun, 121; in *Zhuangzi* 57–58
cosmic self: in Guo Xiang, 75–76; as mind of the mystic, 12, 21, 27, 32, 149, 158, 164, 177n.7; in perennial philosophy; 37–38; as result of journey, 95, 98, 114; in Shangqing, 112–14
cosmology: ancient Chinese, 86–88, 171; under Buddhist influence, 139; in *Daode jing*, 46–49; in Guo Xiang, 73–74, 78;

and immortality 91, 185n.17; in Lingbao, 125–27, 186n.9; in Shangqing, 109–
12, 115–16; in *Shujing*, 86–87; stages of,
47; in *Xisheng jing*, 134
Cui Zhuan, 69
Cunshen lianqi ming, 155, 157, 159

Dahui (Mahāmati), 147
Dao'an, 117
Daode jing: body in, 158; and Buddhism, 5
18, 117; commentaries to, 15, 40, 59–69,
138, 139, 186nn. 1 and 8, 187nn. 3 and 4;
cosmology of, 46–49; in Dark Learning,
60; editions of, 59; and Guo Xiang, 75;
history of, 40; non-action in, 49–50;
overall outlook of, 40, 45; as part of
mystical tradition, 3–4, 8, 13, 45–52, 95,
162; sage in, 50–52, 66, 97–98, 106, 124,
172–73, 175–76; Tao in, 45–46, 92, 95,
165, 167–68; translations of, 179n.9;
transmission of, 41, 130–31, 180n.1; and
Twofold Mystery, 139–41; and *Xisheng
jing*, 130–31, 132, 134; and Zhi Dun,
118, 123–24; and *Zhuangzi*, 57–58
Daode zhenjing guangsheng yi, 186n.1
Daode zhigui, 59
Daojiao yishu: Buddhist influence on, 139;
compilation of, 149, 187n.10, 188n.11;
and *Haikong jing*, 147, 187n.6; Tao in,
167; teachings of, 149–54
Daolei shixiang, 187n.6
Daosheng, 117
Daoyin jing, 122
Daren fu, 98–101, 183n.2
Daren xiansheng zhuan, 101–4
Dark Learning, 4, 60, 162
deautomatization, 30. *See also* mystical
practices
Deikman, Arthur J., 177n.7
destinies, five, 152
diets: and drugs, 157, 184n.10; in Tang
synthesis, 154–56; of Wei Jie, 137
Dingguan jing, 11, 155, 159
Dipper, northern, 110, 114, 172. *See also*
stars
double forgetfulness, 74, 123, 142, 153–54.
See also oblivion; Twofold Mystery
drunkenness, 106, 184n.11. *See also* wine
dualism: in general, 15, 163, 167–69; in
perennial philosophy, 37; in Twofold

Mystery, 143; in Wang Bi, 62; in Yan
Zun, 60
Du Guangting, 140–41, 186n.1
Duren jing, 187n.3

earth: far ends of, 88, 166; journeys
through, 88–94; power over, 88; structure of, 86–87
ecstasy: in *Chuci*, 84; and control, 96, 100–
101, 115–16; and drugs, 103; in Guo
Xiang, 79–80; as journey, 86, 93, 94–95,
96, 112–14, 164, 166; as mystical form 4,
10, 14, 31, 171; in sexual encounters
with gods, 83–84, 182n.3; and shamanism, 81–82; in Shangqing, 112–16; in
Tang synthesis, 159; as temporary
union, 84; as transcendence, 159; in
Zhuangzi, 53, 56, 85. *See also* Great Man;
journey
emptiness: in Lingbao, 127; in *Xisheng
jing*, 133; in Zhi Dun, 118
"Encountering Sorrow" (*Lisao*), 95
energy (*qi*): absorption of, 113, 156–57; in
Daode jing, 52; health through, 122, 137,
146, 152, 154, 156; in Heshang gong, 67,
171; in immortality, 91; inner versus
outer, 157; in *Xisheng jing*, 134
equality of all things, 55
Erdi zhang, 143
Erjiao lun, 129
Erkes, Eduard, 62
escape: in *Chuci*, 94; as motivation for
journey, 94, 102–3; and mystical ideals,
106–7; and poetry, 4; and recluses,
182n.4

Fang Chang, 187n.6
fangshi, 67, 85, 94, 181n.8, 183n.5
"Far-off Journey" (*Yuanyou*), 84, 94–95,
96, 99–100, 106, 183n.15
fasting, 30, 114, 154. *See also* diets
fate: in Guo Xiang, 72–73, 166; in *Zhu-
angzi*, 78
Fayuan zhulin, 186n.12
Fengdu shan, 109
Fengfa yao, 117, 185n.2
Fodao lunheng, 141
Fukunaga Mitsuji, 54, 74
Fuqi jingyi lun, 154–55, 188n.14
Fu Yi, 59

mystical experience: characteristics of, 21, 171n.3; Christian versus Chinese, 10–11; cultural determination of, 36–37, 177n.6; interpretation of, 12, 20–21, 25–26, 31–32, 34–35; physiology of, 23–25, 177n.4; structure of, 25–26; universal nature of, 3 38. *See also* peak-experiences

mystical philosophy: definition of, 13, 21–22, 34–39; documents and study of, 22–23, 35–37; language in, 22, 35, 37; and perennial philosophy, 37–39; themes of, 22, 35–37

mystical practices: in *Daojiao yishu*, 152; in general, 8, 21, 30; in Guo Xiang, 74–76, 170; in Heshang gong, 68, 171; integration of, 16, 33–34, 139, 164, 169–72; in Li Rong, 146; in Tang synthesis, 154–61, 172; in Zhi Dun, 122

mystical quest, 20–21, 25, 28–34

mystical stages: in *Daojiao yishu*, 150–51; dynamic of, 21; in general, 12, 28, 172; structure of, 28, 37, 172, 178n.8; in Tang synthesis, 159–61; in Twofold Mystery, 143–44; in *Zhuangzi*, 55–56

mystical union: through ecstatic journey, 83, 90–92; in *Daojiao yishu*, 153; in Guo Xiang, 79; interpretation of, 36

mysticism: definition of, 8; as personality transformation, 12; and religion, 17, 20; study of, 22–23, 38–39, 171n.2

Nāgārjuna, 143, 169
Nan Yangsheng lun, 107
Neiguan jing, 155, 157–58
nirvāna, 6, 136, 147
no-mind, 75, 142
non-action: in *Daode jing*, 49–50, 173; in *Daojiao yishu*, 149; in Guo Xiang, 72, 174; in Heshang gong, 67, 69; and nirvāna, 136, 147, 166; in *Zhuangzi*, 57
nonbeing, 61, 71
North: direction of nothingness, 91; goal of journey, 91; in Shangqing cosmos, 109–10; in *Xisheng jing*, 135
no-self, 121, 136, 170

oblivion: and awakening, 123; in Guo Xiang, 74–75, 159; as mystical experience, 10–11, 75; in Shangqing, 115–16; in Tang synthesis, 159–60; in Twofold

Mystery, 144; in Zhi Dun, 123; in *Zhuangzi*, 56, 74, 85, 159
One, the: in Wang Bi, 61, 165; in Shangqing, 114–15, 172
ontology, 36
orbs, five, 67, 113, 156, 181n.9
order: as basis for religion, 18; as Tao, 45–46

Pangu, 171
peak-experiences: definition of, 26–27; and mystical experiences, 12, 21. *See also* mystical experience
Penglai, 85
perfections, six, 153
perennial philosophy, 37–39
philosophical Taoism, 6, 59
Pingyi, 100
play, as basis for religion, 18
poetry: and ecstatic journeys, 96, 98, 101, 103, 105; and mystical tradition 104, 107–8
Poxie lun, 129
prajnā, 118, 126, 136
Prajñāpāramitā, 146, 148
Proudfoot, Wayne, 20
Pure Land, 148, 153
Pure Talk (qingtan), 60
purgation, 29–31

Qi Bo, 181n.6
Queen Mother of the West, 43, 93, 100, 111, 183n.14
Qu Yuan, 52

Rain God, 100
religious Taoism: and Lao-Zhuang tradition, 7
return: in Wang Bi, 61–62; in *Xisheng jing*, 134–35
rhapsody, 95, 183n.3
River God, 100
Robinet, Isabelle, 61, 112
Ruan Ji, 101–4

sage: in *Daode jing*, 50–52, 65, 173; as Great Man, 16, 146, 175; in Guo Xiang, 72, 76–77, 123–24, 173–74; mind of, 76, 173; as mystic, 29; powers of, 77, 134, 145–46, 152, 175–76; as ruler, 49, 65, 145, 172–76; social role of, 76–77, 172–76; in Twofold